MEETINGS WITH REMARKABLE MEN AND WOMEN

ALSO FROM EAST WEST HEALTH BOOKS:

Natural Childcare

Cooking with Japanese Foods

Sweet & Natural Desserts

Fighting Radiation with Foods,
Herbs, and Vitamins

MEETINGS WITH REMARKABLE MEN AND WOMEN

*Interviews with Leading
Thinkers on Health, Medicine, Ecology,
Culture, Society, and Spirit*

FROM THE EDITORS OF

EAST WEST
THE JOURNAL OF NATURAL HEALTH & LIVING

Introduction by Tom Monte

EAST WEST HEALTH BOOKS
1989

EAST WEST HEALTH BOOKS
17 Station Street
Brookline, Massachusetts 02146

ISBN 0-936184-08-6

Published in the United States of America

First Edition

135798642

Distributed to the natural food trade by
East West Health Books, 17 Station Street, Brookline, MA 02146
and to the book trade by
The Talman Company, 150 Fifth Avenue, New York, NY 10011

Cover and Text Designed by Betsy Woldman

Design electronically implemented and typeset using software
from AT&T and Textware International

*This book is dedicated to all remarkable
men and women whose courage and vision contribute
to a brighter future for all of us.*

CONTENTS

ACKNOWLEDGMENTS

East West began in 1971 as a magazine to foster cultural exchange between the Orient and the Occident. The magazine felt that the traditional values of the East were relevant for modern Western society, and that through rediscovering those values there would be increased hope for the future. Thus was born the curiosity that led to meetings with many remarkable men and women.

For the past two decades *East West* has interviewed over two hundred men and women who have contributed to the collective wisdom and knowledge of the last quarter of the twentieth century. The excerpts contained in this book from the best of these meetings represent ideas that are as vital today as when they were first printed in the pages of *East West*. We hope this thought-provoking collection will encourage your further exploration of these universally important issues.

We are deeply grateful to the men and women who shared their insights with us and so have made this book possible. Their selfless dedication and creative vision are lighting the path to a healthier, saner society. Our gratitude goes, too, to the writers and editors, themselves remarkable people, who contributed many hours of their time to the original interviews.

We want to thank Mary Colson for her hours of typing that transformed hundreds of pages of back issues of *East West* magazine into a book manuscript. And finally we thank *East West* associate editor Linda Elliot, who honed the extensive interviews into a readable and lively book.

If you would like to keep current with the issues discussed here, and meet the remarkable men and women who will define the coming decade, contact *East West* at its offices in Brookline, Massachusetts for information about subscriptions. If you would like information about other East West Health Books, such as *Natural Childcare*, *Cooking with Japanese Foods*, *Sweet & Natural Desserts*, and *Fighting Radiation with Foods, Herbs, and Vitamins*, contact our Brookline office.

INTRODUCTION

There are points in your life when you encounter something that wakes you up, or, perhaps more accurately, causes you to remember. Whatever that magical stimulus might be, the feeling that results is often one of such exhilaration and intense desire for adventure that you hardly know what to do with yourself. It may take you years before you can translate your emotional and intuitive excitement into action, but whatever you do from then on is somehow inspired by that moment of epiphany when you touched something deep within. That was the feeling I had in 1976 when I first laid eyes on the *East West Journal*.

East West, then only five years old, was still in its tabloid format, having graduated from its original incarnation as a full-size newspaper a couple of years before. I forget now the range of articles in that early edition, but the overall tone and message of that issue, and the ones that would follow, will never leave me. *East West* represented nothing less than a monthly image of a better world, a world that was indeed more kind and gentle than anything I'd encountered before.

Each month, the pages of *East West* were alive with the spirit, the good sense, and the practical ideas needed to found a peaceful revolution.

For those who started the magazine in 1971, that revolution began with the establishment of health and judgment through the application of a universal philosophy and sound dietary principles. Thus appeared in the pages of *East West* every important thinker or contributor to the goal of personal health or world peace. Topics covering everything from physics to farming, medicine to music, ecology to economics were explored. The prevailing methods were critiqued and alternatives offered.

In addition, the magazine provided hard-hitting investigative reporting on the National Cancer Institute and American Cancer Society; articles about Findhorn, natural healing, diet and health, childbirth, solar energy, spirituality, the human potential movement, the ancient world, and the visionary ideas that would shape the future.

While the subject matter was diverse, all the ideas presented in *East West* were based on the fundamental notion that beneath the infinity of details that make up the material world, beneath the violence and materialism, the egotistical drives, and the competition for survival, lies a truth that is at once orderly and benevolent and that can be used to guide humankind toward a peaceful world.

That truth is beautifully represented in the book you have in your hands,

Meetings with Remarkable Men and Women. This collection of interviews is a sampling of the hundreds that have appeared in the pages of *East West*. The people gathered here are among the most fascinating and important of our century. There are eighty-seven all-stars here, eighty-seven men and women who have dedicated their lives toward making this planet a better place to live.

Given today's media coverage of various dietary and environmental problems, it may be hard to appreciate the vision of these people, or that of the editors at *East West*, but ten or fifteen years ago the problems that are obvious today were not so readily apparent. Even into the late 1970s, the American Medical Association and American Cancer Society were saying that there was no link between diet and health, especially between diet and cancer, and that the American diet was the best in the world. Most people, even those in national leadership, considered the problems of the environment unimportant. The depletion of the ozone layer, the destruction of the rain forest, the erosion of topsoil, the problems of pesticides—these were regarded by many as mere claptrap from kooks. Even more dubious—according to the cynics—were the calls of the spirit from the gurus, swamis, spiritual teachers, and sages who regularly turned up in the pages of *East West*.

Now, Michio Kushi's warnings that diet caused disease; or David Brower's concerns for the environment; or Rolling Thunder's warnings of a crisis in the human spirit appear as prophecies come true. In fact, *Meetings with Remarkable Men and Women* is a collection of eighty-seven prophets sharing their vision for a better world.

But it is much more. For these people not only still sound a warning, but they also provide solutions.

These men and women are applying their ideas to real life problems. Their results are not only positive and important; at times they seem miraculous. People like Wes Jackson, Wendell Berry, Harlan Lundberg, and Masanobu Fukuoka are growing food in abundance according to organic, natural agricultural methods. They are demonstrating that agriculture needn't rely on petrochemicals, nor destroy the soil. The ideas of other thinkers in the book remain equally viable and inspirational.

When I first encountered *East West*, I was struck by the consistency of its message: that our ideals and practicality are not mutually exclusive, but complementary, each one needing the other in order to bring forth the most successful approach possible.

No subject *East West* covered better illustrated this point than its reporting on diet and health matters.

In the coming century, scholars will look back and see with terrible clarity the suffering wrought by perhaps the single most devastating blindspot of the twentieth century: the importance of daily food. We have corrupted our food and the land that gives rise to it, and with it have poisoned the foundation of our lives.

This would indeed be a bitter truth if there wasn't so much hope of recovery. Each month, *East West* hammered home the message of health through better nutrition. It reported the science and philosophy of diet; the dietary traditions of virtually every native culture; and the anecdotes of people who used diet to overcome serious illnesses. It reported the work of Michio Kushi, Louise Hay, and Nathan Pritikin, all of whom were demonstrating that you could successfully treat the most serious illnesses using the regenerative methods of diet, exercise, and the powers of the spirit. Meanwhile, Robert Mendelsohn, Marian Tompson, Rudolph Ballentine, Christiane Northrup, and others offered alternatives to impersonal, high-tech hospital births, inappropriate Cesarean sections, labor-inducing drugs, and formula feeding.

As for matters of the spirit, *East West* excelled as few other magazines or newspapers ever hoped. The people written about and interviewed by *East West* represented as broad a cross section of spiritual backgrounds, disciplines, and understanding as could be imagined. There were historians and academics; gurus and senseis; the leaders of the human potential movement; American Indian sages and those who drew their inspiration from Native Americans. There were also a wide assortment of artists, musicians, writers, and outlaws.

No matter from which background these people emerged, the orientation among most of them was decidedly holistic and ecological. They shared the view that no matter where you looked—at the atomic level, the workings of the human body, the environment of the planet, or the cosmos itself—close examination revealed an interdependent relationship among all the parts that made up the whole. This provided a sense of unity to the magazine's approach, but it also reflected the growing consciousness that was just beginning to spread throughout the United States and the Western world. This orientation has been the basis of all Eastern religions, as well as the underlying philosophy of the American Indian. Remarkably, quantum theory has begun to prove the validity of such philosophies and has shown them to be a most accurate way of describing the universe.

As physicist Fritjof Capra puts it: "The new world view is a view where the universe appears as a web of relationships rather than separate objects as in a machine. There is a second important aspect of the holistic world view and that is the notion that the universe is intrinsically dynamic.... What we call things are really patterns in an overall cosmic process. We have found that everything is connected to everything else and that everything is always changing, always in motion, in transformation.... Mystics also have this organic view that things and phenomena are profoundly interrelated, dynamic, and that the web of events includes the human observer and his or her consciousness in a very essential way."

Indian mystic Swami Satchidananda puts it succinctly: "There is only one consciousness."

To a young idealistic writer searching for a voice and a way to contribute something to the world, the parade of people who graced the pages of *East West* each month was an answered prayer. When I graduated from college in 1977, I took a job writing for a daily newspaper in Trenton, New Jersey. After a year of reporting local politics and school board elections, I wrote a piece about a college professor who claimed to have cured himself of pancreatic cancer by changing his diet. My editors at the newspaper refused to print the story.

Consequently, I quit my job and moved, with my wife Toby, to Washington, D.C., where I began writing for *East West* about the explosion of scientific information then coming from the federal government linking diet to health.

In 1980 I wrote another piece about a "miraculous" cancer cure, this one about a medical doctor, Anthony Sattilaro, who had used the macrobiotic diet to cure himself of prostate cancer. *East West* published that piece in March 1980. *The Saturday Evening Post* published the same article six months later. Soon after, I wrote a book about Sattilaro entitled *Recalled By Life: The Story of My Recovery from Cancer* (Houghton Mifflin, 1982). I've been writing about health and environmental issues ever since.

What is in this book, at bottom, is the revelation of the spirit moving in all matter. It is about the spirit in the musical "vibrations" that heal, which are described by Yoko Ono; in the "true nature" spoken of by Masanobu Fukuoka; in the "Order of the Universe" described by Michio Kushi; in the "sacred architecture" perceived by Keith Critchlow. It is the reflections of eighty-seven people searching for God in everyday life.

Consequently, you will find much practical information that you can use daily to improve your own health, assist in pregnancy and child rearing, enhance the healthfulness of your home, or improve your sense of spiritual well-being. You will also find the guidance of those who have journeyed the lonely and dangerous trail to the inner self—that vault of riches where all real answers lie.

But, on top of everything else, you'll also find this book to be thoroughly entertaining. For sheer wit, entertainment, and wisdom, I especially recommend the interviews with Alan Watts, Salvador Dali, and Dick Gregory. Dali, ever the surrealist, contemplates such weighty matters as DNA, Sigmund Freud, why he paints, and the spiral of the "thirty-five or thirty-six wrinkles" of the anus which contracts at the speed of light! Dick Gregory waxes eloquent on the political and social influence of diet, never failing to keep his comedic sense close at hand: "It's easier to make a political statement than it is to change your diet.... I never *believed* segregation was right, or racism was right.... But I thought I *needed* that ham sandwich to survive...."

This book, inspired in part by Gurdjieff's *Meetings with Remarkable Men*, would surely have included the Russian mystic himself had he still been alive to be interviewed by *East West*. For no magazine then or now has provided a forum for a more diverse and radical group of thinkers, entrepreneurs, artists, and activists than *East West*.

For me, 1976 and those early issues of *East West* seem like another lifetime, but in rereading the interviews in this collection, I realize that these are not the ideas of the past, but the ones that will shape the future.

TOM MONTE
Amherst, Massachusetts
March 1989

HOME

Paul Bierman-Lytle

Debra Lynn Dadd

Murray Bookchin

KEITH CRITCHLOW

In Search of Sacred Architecture
March 1987

For those who find much modern architecture deplorable, Keith Critchlow, author (Orders in Space) *and Fellow at the Royal College of Art in London, lectures about and designs structures based on the ancient principles of sacred architecture. He stresses harmonic proportion in buildings, and wholeness, or integrity, in their design and construction, as provided by a numerical ratio, "the Golden Mean."*

East West *contributing editor Rebecca Theurer Wood interviewed Critchlow during his annual two-week workshop at the Lindisfarne Mountain Retreat in Crestone, Colorado.*

EAST WEST: What do you mean by "sacred architecture"?

KEITH CRITCHLOW: We used to use the term "sacred architecture" because it most immediately describes what we're concerned with. However, for people who do not have a proper sense of the sacred, the term is easily ridiculed. They say, "Oh, you're a sacred architect, are you? Hah!" So I say, "I am not a sacred architect—I am an architect of the sacred."

We're probably going to use the term "integral architecture" in the future, but that doesn't mean we're neglecting "sacred." The function of integral architecture is to integrate, on all levels, the people who experience it.

The foundation of all of humanity's major spiritual philosophies is that the quality of being human is characterized by a fourfold nature of reality—physical, emotional, intellectual, and spiritual. The acceptance of the reality of these four worlds of existence is fundamental to integrate the range of dimensions in which humanity must operate in order to be fully human.

It is the responsibility of humanity's architects, who share stewardship of this planet, to interpret and present these sacred principles within the context of an architectural expression. As a reflection or "model" of the nature of the universe, each sacred edifice demonstrates how the laws of formation and manifestation operate in the four worlds of existence.

EW: Is sacred architecture based on number?

KC: If certain numbers appear throughout nature as a measure of growth, it indicates that harmony exists. If we create a space based on these same numbers, we're going to create a space that is harmonious with nature and with our own natures.

Numbers confer no blessings or sacredness. The awareness, however, of the significance of these things in relation to a traditional teaching—such as the Eightfold Path or the Ten Commandments—can do so. The value lies in the awakening quality that number and spatial intervals can have in helping the experiencer recall the underlying structure of the world and our relationship to it. There is no doubt that these number intervals or proportional periodicities work at subliminal levels as well as an awakened level, for otherwise they would not be able to *re*-mind or wake up the experiencer.

EW: So the intent of sacred or integral architecture is to awaken the experiencer?

KC: One of its purposes is to help people change their perceptions, or to move beyond their everyday perceptions—to see the world freshly and to rediscover the wonder.

EW: Through your independent studies in geometry you rediscovered basic principles and have studied their application in traditional structures?

KC: That's right. Particularly, one just has to observe nature. What is the Golden Mean? Every fir cone [he picks one up] is giving you the eye to see the Golden Mean. I have to call anything in the natural realm an expression of intelligence. Study the intelligences inherent in natural form and see how this intelligence got interpreted into sacred buildings.

By going to nature and the sacred buildings and extracting their principles you then have pure objective principles. You can then say, "OK, let's see how we can use this to satisfy certain conditions." Now, the conditions for building the Lindisfarne Chapel include the land, which is desert; the shape that Bill Thompson [see William Irwin Thompson, page 180] wanted; and the materials that were available.

Thompson had the vision, coming from Dante, of the multi-foliate rose where all the petals were all the different peoples and all the different faiths. The Chapel is designed very much to his requirements.

We also needed to make spiritual contact with the land here. And so our first task was to be in touch with those who traditionally worshipped here. It's important, and I don't want to sound sentimental or condescending at all. A sweat lodge was arranged with a medicine man, Red Ute, from nearby Ignacio, Colorado. Without his blessing it would have been very hard to do this project.

EW: Did you help with the construction of the Chapel?

KC: Yes. The Lindisfarne Chapel was built in the traditional way with the architect, builders, and students all working together. The word edifice means self-edification, to build yourself as you're building a building. So it was hands-on. And this is the way you understand yourself. You also get a terrific lift from a collective accomplishment. It's a much greater satisfaction when "we have done something," rather than "I have done something."

PETER DAVID GILBERT

Architect of Sacred Design
March 1987

Giving practical impetus to Keith Critchlow's (see previous interview) ideas of contemporary application of sacred architecture is Peter David Gilbert, a talented American architect who designed buildings with Critchlow following the principles of harmony.

Interviewer Wood spoke with Gilbert while he was assisting with the workshop at Lindisfarne.

EAST WEST: How might the principles of sacred architecture be applied to my home?

PETER DAVID GILBERT: In any architectural project there's a trinity of things to consider—earth, human, and spirit. So, to attune ourselves to the earth we would first need to spend a lot of time on the site.

EW: What's a lot of time?

PG: We like to spend a week on the site to get a sense of the area, to look at the vegetation, to see what's happening with the alignment, to look at the stars in the heavens, and to look for orientations. We might also do an invocation and a meditation on the site. We allow the earth to speak to us personally and we attune to its subtle energies.

We would obviously also spend a lot of time with you. What, for example, are your symbols, your inspirations, your practicalities? We would want to know the "level of metaphor" on which you live. We can use things like your astrological chart. On a very mundane level we might actually use the physical measurement of your body.

By taking into account the earth, the human, and the spirit we're led to what we would call "the soul of the building" and the symbolic language which is being asked to be presented on that site now. From this we would develop a geometric brief. We would go from there. You'd probably get a nice design out of it.

EW: How would I find a builder who could interpret this design and build in the spirit of the design?

PG: Obviously it would be best to find someone who would bring conscious care and attention to the project. Our construction drawings take different things into consideration than do conventional drawings, but they're still construction designs and any builder can use them.

EW: I understand that electricity disturbs the electromagnetic energies. How do you deal with this?

PG: In terms of the wiring and the plumbing, we hope we are able to design for as little interference with the electromagnetic energies as possible. We wouldn't, for instance, run wiring or pipes underneath the bedroom or meditation area. We're operating with certain functional requirements. We have to make a distinction between a sacred building, one that is specifically for meditation, and one that is a domestic building.

EW: Is it correct that the use of the Golden Mean doesn't arbitrarily provide an architect a design?

PG: Right. Proportion and geometry do not give us the design. They merely act as a kind of rudder, or a tail that guides the wings of the idea. You can have the best idea in the world and proportion it and it will be a beautiful building. But if you start out with a bad idea and proportion it, you still have a bad idea. When it's right, the proportions and geometry complement the functional and structural requirements. It's a completely different attitude from traditional architecture. If I were to say this in a conventional architecture office they would probably fire me, or suggest I seek therapy.

EW: When you were a conventional architect were you using these geometries unintentionally?

PG: I wasn't using them. When doing a design I would specifically address the function or requirements. I would base my room sizes on how much space I needed to fit in furniture, or what structural span I could accommodate.

Now my initial impulse is to understand what is the inherent geometry that is required for this particular site, the energies of the site, and the particular meaning and purpose for the structure. In proportioning a room, one of the initial considerations would be the harmonics and the tones that are being generated by the relationships between dimensions. That's not ignoring the functional or structural, but it's acknowledging that there is also a subtle kind of inaudible level of each room creating a tone or vibration that needs to be considered. Each part of that is somehow related to the whole building. Like a symphony, you're creating pieces within the design that need to harmonize with the whole.

PAUL BIERMAN-LYTLE

Blueprint for the Nontoxic Home
March 1987

Connecticut craftsman and architect Paul Bierman-Lytle is one of only a handful of builders and architects in the U.S. who has adopted a whole-house approach to working with the problems associated with toxic substances used in home construction. A practicing architect with a master's degree from Yale University, Bierman-Lytle has been designing and building homes for over ten years, and within the past few years he has decided to build only natural and nontoxic homes. He has lectured on building and design at Yale, UCLA, and a number of universities in Europe, and his projects and philosophies have recently been the focus of stories that have appeared in Architectural Digest, Builder, The Atlantic Monthly, The New York Times, *and various other publications.*

East West editor Mark Mayell caught up with Bierman-Lytle at the New Canaan, Conn. offices of his company, Masters Corporation.

EAST WEST: How did you become interested in the concept of natural and nontoxic building?

PAUL BIERMAN-LYTLE: We began as a small firm of architects and craftsmen in 1976. We modeled ourselves after the master builders of the Renaissance, who both designed a building and physically built it. The elements we were concerned with included good architectural design from the aesthetic standpoint, such as harmonious proportions, well-craftedness—that is, how the building is put together—energy conservation and avoiding the use of fossil fuels, and safety, both for the inhabitants as well as for the construction people.

By three years ago we had developed our skills to the point that we felt we had perfected the quality home with all those concerns involved. Then one day one of our carpenters approached me and said he was feeling ill due to some of the products he was using, primarily plywood. It dawned on me that we were missing one of the primary considerations, which was health. So we immediately began researching what was in the products we were using.

People in this country tend to assume that everything is safe, that the

7

government will watch out for consumers. We discovered that although there is well-documented evidence that indoor air pollution may be one of the greatest threats to our health in the coming decade, much of this information was not readily available to the public. We had to do a lot of aggressive phone calling, talking to people in universities and laboratories, to find out about the products we used in building. We identified about 1,500 hazardous products in the home that are commonly used.

The next step was to determine safe levels for all these toxins in the home. Government agencies and manufacturers try to establish standards of acceptance for hazardous products, how many parts per million of formaldehyde, for instance, are acceptable in the home. We quickly got disillusioned with that approach. We decided instead to find quality alternative products that are completely void of toxins. Why have *any* parts per million of a toxic substance in the house if there's a good alternative product available?

In addition to being toxin-free, these alternative products had to stand other tests. They had to be durable, and to pass the other criteria we have. We began to find these nontoxic and natural products and use them.

Our overall strategy is to remove as many known toxic products as we can from our buildings. This keeps us researching on a daily basis. We're constantly looking at the products that are being put into a home. We have to call up the manufacturers and chemists to try to find out what's being put into the product, and even find out what the chemical composition is. Unfortunately, most of the alternatives that we've found are not made in this country, but in Europe. The U.S. is slow to develop alternatives because, I think, building product manufacturers are so heavily capitalized into their existing system, and currently there is no public outcry about their products, so why change?

EW: Is it enough for you to substitute natural materials for the synthetic ones, or is that just the first step?

PB: I think that one of the beautiful things about a healthier home is that it doesn't necessarily affect architecture. It's simply a matter of substituting products. However, I think that although the general public doesn't recognize them, there are ways that architecture affects your health. Also, I think that the placement of a building can affect health, and we do take precautions to locate the buildings properly on a building site.

EW: What extra costs are incurred by substituting nontoxic building materials?

PB: If you're building from scratch, and you're taking all precautions (no plywood, for instance, and using all the alternatives that we would use on a full scale), then you're looking at probably 25 percent more cost than the conventional home. If you're just decorating or making an interior renovation, it's probably 10 to 15 percent. That's mostly because the nontoxic products in this country are all imported.

EW: What's it going to take to get these products made here?

PB: The place where the greatest change has to occur in this country is the ethical standpoint of manufacturers. Manufacturers have to consider more than merely whether a product is going to be viable economically. There's a big uphill climb before that will happen, but I think this country will be the one to lead it.

There's so much to be done that is healthy for human society and there are lots of businesses that could be created that are also economically viable. If people are alive and feel good then they're going to buy a product; if they find out that they're dying from it, or sick, then you've got a bad product. That's got to be the main change.

EW: Have you built a nontoxic house for yourself?

PB: No. It's like the shoemaker who never has shoes for his family. Building a home is very time consuming. I would have to take a leave of absence.

EW: So you can't really say what the experience of living in a nontoxic home is?

PB: I know as a designer and craftsman working in them, I feel good and I'm not immediately irritated by toxic conventional products. Few homeowners do these toxic building procedures themselves, and there's good reason why they hire someone else. You walk into your house and a guy's polyurethaning your floor and he's wearing a mask—it should tell you something. When he leaves, the fumes are still there.

Of course, some people can be allergic even to natural products. These products are not a cure-all. We simply know that they are ecologically balanced, they smell good, you don't have to wear masks to use them, the clean-up and waste management are easy, there are no known toxic offgasses.

EW: What's next on the agenda for your company?

PB: What we're doing now is not only looking at the new materials and tools, but also reviving some of the past traditions like plastering. Plastering is a lost art in this country, but many shaped areas can be more easily surfaced with plaster than with sheetrock. Good sheetrockers are few and far between and there is indeed a true art to doing it properly, but it is not a good surface. Sheetrock was obviously developed to speed up the building process, to make things cheaper for people.

What we're seeing is a trend of homeowners who are looking for craft again. They're willing to pay a premium for a building they can call their home, rather than a building in which "What's the resale value going to be?" is the main question.

Homing is coming back. We don't like the word housing at all, it's not in our vocabulary. You don't house people, you house objects. That's why housing projects look the way they do, because they are not for humans. It could just be terminology, but if people start thinking of where they live as homes again, I think you'll see a change.

DEBRA LYNN DADD

Nontoxic & Natural
April 1985

While others are investigating environmental pollution in streams, lakes, and soil,
Debra Lynn Dadd is looking into the livingrooms, bathrooms, bedrooms, and kitchens
of America. Dadd's interest in toxic household substances stems from the discovery of
her own sensitivity to them. She self-published a book, A Consumer Guide for the
Chemically Sensitive, *which catalogued the possible dangers in the most common*
household items. Nontoxic & Natural *followed, and she has since authored* The Nontoxic Home *and co-authored* Healthful Houses! *with architect Clint Good. Dadd*
continues to write, lecture, consult, and research in the area of nontoxic consumer prod-
ucts, as well as edit the monthly Everything Natural.

East West publisher Leonard Jacobs interviewed Dadd at her home in San Fran-
cisco.

EAST WEST: If you could develop a scale for the factors that were causing your
health problems, how would you rate things like food, cosmetics, furniture,
and clothing?

DEBRA LYNN DADD: I don't think I would be able to rate what made me sick, but I
think I can rate what things in the environment are more toxic than others.

Number one of course is to not smoke. The second thing I would say is
that if you have any gas appliances in your house, turn them off. Gas appliances give off all kinds of combustible byproducts like sulfur dioxide and formaldehyde.

Number three would be carpeting. I've seen people change every single
thing but their carpeting, and then find that the carpet was really the cause of it
all. The fourth thing would be cleaning products. Window cleaners, scouring
soaps, laundry cleaners. Next would be cosmetics. (We haven't gotten to food
yet.) Then water.

I think the natural foods industry has it all backwards, because food is probably the least toxic of all the things you'll run into on an everyday basis.
Although there are certainly a lot of toxic components in it, if you look at

what is in all these other products, there's a lot more toxic things in them, and people just don't pay any attention to these at all.

EW: You say in *Nontoxic & Natural* that the more information people have, the more likely they will affect the manufacturers to change their formulations. Do you know of any instances where this has happened?

DD: I get asked this question often. Are the manufacturers really bad guys? Are they trying to provide harmful things? I feel that the answer is no. I think that at some point in the past twenty years, they quite innocently started formulating their products. Now they're discovering that natural foods and nontoxic products are starting to emerge as a new market is being identified. As more consumers support these new companies and buy these products, and recognize the quality that they are providing, gradually the sales of other manufacturers will fall off. I think that as consumers we have lots and lots of power. Each one of us takes responsibility for a better environment by our purchase choices.

MURRAY BOOKCHIN

Homeward Bound
July 1984

Murray Bookchin, "human ecologist" and "anarchist," is director emeritus of the Institute of Social Ecology in Plainfield, Vermont. Bookchin grew up in the Bronx, where he became a vegetarian at the age of six and a member of the Communist Party at fourteen (which he left three years later). He has been both factory laborer and college professor, and has authored The Limits of the City *and* Post-Scarcity Anarchism, *which incorporate the principles of ecology into a new utopian vision.*

Bookchin's most recent work, The Ecology of Freedom, *deals with the emergence of hierarchy in society and its devastating effect on the natural world. His thinking is spirited, penetrating, and impassioned, and crosses boundaries of thought and philosophy that normally do not intersect. His criticism of Marxism (that it fails to take into account the exploitation of nature) is founded on a world view that also rejects environmentalism for its assumption of humanity's dominance. And it is probable that few former Marxists have stressed the importance of organic gardening.*

East West *associate editor Meg Seaker and editor Mark Mayell discussed "the problem of housing today" with Bookchin at his home in Vermont.*

EAST WEST: In *Post-Scarcity Anarchism*, you wrote that having free time is a condition of freedom, and yet it seems that almost all of us are compelled to work constantly just to pay our rent.

MURRAY BOOKCHIN: Yes. We used to speak of spending 25, at the most 30 percent of our income on housing. Now people spend 50 or 60 percent and some are obliged to spend even more than that, and they have to earn more. This puts us all in a pressure cooker. You have to earn so that you can earn. It's a strange tautology: You have to work hard to live in a place where hard work is necessary to live.

And it affects your personality. Many people have to hold down two jobs. One job literally pays for the housing. So what happens to them? They move into the city, or they are born into the city, which is supposed to provide them with cosmopolitan culture—concerts, fine musicians, good plays, cinema—and a presumably richer social life. But when they have to work twelve hours a day partly to pay for the exorbitant rent, the cultural side of the city, which is supposed to enrich their lives, is inconsequential owing to the fact that they don't have the time to enjoy it. They become disempowered. And when you feel less powerful as a personality—I don't mean trying to dominate people, but just that you have control over your life—the more passive you become and the more neurotic.

This profoundly affects middle class people as well as ethnic minorities. We should think about it. We should look at our housing and ask, how much of my earning time am I giving to my home? How much of it is really my home? Am I sharing it, do I really own it? Do I feel secure in living with it, will I be able to meet my next rent hike, will I be dispossessed, will my mortgage or interest payments go up?

EW: What besides social policy contributes to housing problems?

MB: We all agree that housing should be solarized, winterized, made of renewable materials, that plastic should not be the most essential ingredient of the house. But aside from these issues, let's not forget that the house is also the embodiment of tradition. It should not only be organic, it should not only have such things as skylights, but it should be where tradition can be fostered, just as the farmstead was handed down generation after generation.

Houses should be built with the flexibility, charm, warmth, and uniqueness that mark a particular tradition, which another generation can inherit and incorporate into its newly found lifeways until finally, in a house, there is a history. The house without a history is the house that Orwell most feared in *1984*. It is of the eternal now, which has no past and no future, it's just located on that one day in that one moment of now, or what we snappily call the "now generation."

But if you don't have a past, you can't have a future. Because you've taken the moment in which you live, or the time in which you live, and you've pulled it out of history. You've removed it from process. And the flow which is the essence of life as growth, decline, and finally death, is interrupted. I'll venture to say that people fear death more today who live without a sense of the past than people who, living on farmsteads, or living in neighborhoods that have a history, feel in their death that they blend back into the environment, they don't disappear.

We do not have houses anymore that have histories. Architecturally they do not incorporate a different time so that we can live not only in our own time but share a past one. They are not cumulative structures which bring past eras into our lives. And without the contrast that different architectural styles which reflect different periods create in your mind and thinking, you have no way of comparing and offsetting your own time and personality with those of past years. We have no sense of contrast by which we can compare whether our lives are improving or degenerating; nor a sense of direction, drawn partly from the past into the present, so that we know which way the future is going.

And so we lose the sense of hope, because hope depends upon the belief that new things can evolve without destroying old things. We lose the everyday utopianness of our daydreams, which become contrived to the linear geometry of the high-rise building. If you're always in an institution, you're always institutionalized. And that's what most housing, and most building, is today.

In the past there was an attempt—it was often quite vulgar but at least it was an effort—to bring in the Roman or Greek facade. We still see this in old banks, which have Doric or Corinthian columns; we still have the Romantic houses that hang around, with spires and gables, but they become curiosities; we turn them into historical museums, and charge money to visit them. We have to treasure houses that are old, not replace them. But we have to make them *lived* treasures, not museum pieces.

We have to look at housing as an expression of our lives. We have to see it not only in the social dimension and try, not so much to decontrol it in terms of rents, but in terms of the idea that housing is really a way of making money; because a house is *not* merely a way of making money. It profoundly affects every aspect of life—from the way in which you spend your days working and the number of jobs you have, to the extent to which you're free to enjoy the amenities of a community, be it city, town, or village.

EW: What can we do as social beings or as a community to create this kind of economy? Is rent control then a symptomatic treatment?

MB: Well, we must, everywhere along the way, try to preserve. That means that we have to get together as groups and create alternative institutions to the ones that exist right now. And we have to do that on the local level. If we can't cope with our own neighborhoods, we're not going to be able to cope with our own country, our own state, not to speak of the United States as a nation. The need to develop ecology-oriented groups, tied in with neighborhoods and localities, which will create ways in which ordinary people can express their will, is vital right now.

The first thing we have to do is start getting people active in their neighborhoods. One of the elements of neighborhood activity is to make sure that there's good housing. The housing is often there. If the community can get together to reclaim shells of buildings, for instance, and take them away from the gentrifiers, there is some hope.

More important than rent control is literally housing control in the sense that I've been discussing it. Rent control presupposes that somebody else owns the building, or controls the building, but by virtue of law is obliged not to charge too much. And rent control is in a state of debris right now anyway; it's evaporating in every part of the country where it exists, because of the enormous power of realtors and landlords, especially under the present administration.

A second thing that has to be done is to bring gardening into communities. It's terribly important, for two reasons: first, so that people feel there's a direct connection, not only between housing and their everyday lives, but also between food and their everyday lives. The connection from the ground up yields a sensibility of place, not only of house. The rate at which we are devouring extremely fertile farmland, some of the richest in the world, irreparably ruining it with housing developments, shopping centers, and often whole cities which spring up, is occurring at an appalling rate today. The problem now is to arrest that development. Drastically. That means trying to make our city dwellers realize that every true city—not an urban belt, which is not a city at all—every true city historically was always self-contained; it had a wall around it, not only for protective reasons but to define it. That was city space, and then the countryside unfolded. It is not enough to get legislation passed, which I think is monumentally important. It is also important to change sensibility. Because as long as urban dwellers think only in terms of streets and concrete, they will have no sensitivity to the problem. In many ways they wouldn't even perceive it.

Ultimately these are what I would call defensive actions, however creative, against the tendency to uproot people from locales, to shuffle them around, to build monstrous high-rise dwellings or to re-gentrify old, traditional neighborhoods. But when you do these things, you begin to feel that you're doing *something*. And it has an effect that's visible and tangible, like filling out the shell of a house, or gardening, or sharing and communizing. People who have a sense of power can move on to change larger institutions.

I am heavily committed to political localism. When people can begin to form a neighborhood out of the rich material of growing things, restoring buildings, and sharing skills, then the next thing they can do is start going for control of their community. And hopefully, the institutions they create, such as town-type meetings or neighborhood assemblies or councils, or even block committees, can lead to the next level, the municipal level, then to the country-wide level, and who knows where you stop.

I wouldn't venture any further opinions because our goals and our strategies will obviously change as we move along. I have no blueprint. A blueprint is dangerous, like a dogma—you have to stick by it. But I do know that on a local level we can do such marvelous things once we put ourselves to it and recognize the importance of what we're striving for, mainly to rescue our very identities in an age of homogenization.

FAMILY

Marian Tompson

Rudolph Ballentine

Alexander Leaf

Aveline Kushi

Christiane Northrup

17

ROBERT MENDELSOHN, M.D.

In Praise of Large Families
April 1980

Robert S. Mendelsohn, M.D., for many years an outspoken critic of conventional modern medicine, served on the Health Advisory Board of East West. *He was a popular author* (MalePractice: How Doctors Manipulate Women, Confessions of a Medical Heretic, *and* How To Raise a Healthy Child in Spite of Your Doctor), *lecturer, newsletter editor* (The People's Doctor), *newspaper columnist, and radio personality whose views put him in constant conflict with established medical authorities. Until his death in April 1988, Mendelsohn had been a practicing pediatrician for nearly thirty years, as well as holding teaching and administrative posts at such institutions as Northwestern University Medical School and Project Head Start.*

In East West's *tribute to Mendelsohn after his death, freelance writer Carolyn Reuben said, "Mendelsohn describes the old time family doctor as 'a friendly, sensitive, unpretentious, reassuring, compassionate figure in our lives.' This was how many characterized Mendelsohn himself."*

In the original interview, East West's *Sherman Goldman and Leonard Jacobs spoke with Mendelsohn about families—a subject close to his heart.*

EAST WEST: Can you briefly sketch the advantages of having large families, both individually and also for society?

ROBERT MENDELSOHN: On the individual level, there are plenty of medical studies that show that large families have a lower incidence of chronic diseases like asthma, atherosclerotic heart disease, coronary disease, and hypertension, as compared to small families. So the large family is likely to be healthier.

If you then want to go to the socio-political level, the societies that have survived have all been characterized by large, strong families and comparatively weak institutions. For example, our country in its early days had very few doctors, social workers, and agencies, but lots of large, strong families, which is exactly the opposite of the situation today. Society can be seen as a see-saw, with the institutions on one side and families on the other. The two have a reciprocal relationship.

EW: What about the economic problem of raising a large family? That's usually the first objection that people voice when defending Zero Population Growth (ZPG).

RM: At the present time, since our society is so anti-family, we have made it almost impossible for anybody to maintain a reasonable standard of living and still have a large family. Therefore, most people if they want to have large families now will have to accept poverty for the sake of having them. As far as I am concerned that is an obscene trade-off. La Leche League has taken up this issue, particularly now, when mothers have already demonstrated that they want to breastfeed and therefore they have to stay home: their breastfeeding has become a political issue. It's always been a political issue, of course, but now it is a visible one. We could turn the whole thing around right now, but what we have decided to do in this country is to make it work the other way.

All social and political legislative acts and economic policies are directed either toward encouraging or discouraging families. For example, we can create a model in which 80 million people have to work, so that both husband and wife have to work, or we can create a society where only 40 million people work, but where they earn twice as much. We can create a tax policy that gives a $500 deduction for each child or a $5,000 deduction for each child. We can create tax policies either to encourage or discourage families.

EW: Some middle-aged women now seem to feel bitter that they did not have what they see as the advantage of modern women's liberation.

RM: The things many feminists complain about distract from the real issue. It seems to me they should start with a complaint about having been deprived of the childbirth experience and the nursing and child-raising experience. They should be complaining about their obstetricians and their pediatricians and their doctors, who encouraged them to have surgery and take drugs.

In La Leche League you find that there are people who are not only in favor of home births and breastfeeding but who also have a lot of other related characteristics: they tend to have larger families, they tend to take care of their older people at home, they tend to be self-empowered, they have a very low divorce rate. I think America would do very well to recognize that the ultimate in the women's movement, the classic example, is La Leche League.

EW: How much of the future do you see being created through legislation?

RM: My general impression is that legislation follows and does not lead, so I don't think we have to worry about legislation. I think that will happen, because I believe these issues are going to become political. I think we are going to ask our candidates a few key questions: "What is your position on breastfeeding, what is your position on home births, what is your position on large families?" I think these ought to be political issues; why should the main political issues for women be ERA and abortion?

I'm very hopeful. I think the 1980s are going to be a great decade, at least for me, because I see everything turning around now. In the first place, people are in the process of destroying their idols; confidence in modern medicine has been seriously eroded. People don't trust their doctors, their hospitals, or health educators, and I think that's excellent. Therefore I encourage all those forms of iconoclasm. On the other hand, I see all around me signs that both young people and old people are now going in the right direction. I see home births increasing much faster than ever before; I see now that breastfeeding is practiced again by sixty percent of mothers, or is it even higher? I see old folks throwing away their medicines. I see people taking an increased interest in nutrition. As far as I am concerned, there is plenty of room for optimism.

CHRISTIANE NORTHRUP, M.D.

A Dynamic Approach to Women's Health & Pregnancy
December 1981

A 1975 graduate of Dartmouth Medical School, Dr. Christiane Northrup did her residency training at Tufts New England Medical Center, St. Margaret's Hospital, and Cambridge Hospital in the Boston metropolitan area. She worked for several years in a six-person private practice center in Portland, Me. specializing in obstetrics and gynecology, and has served as the president of the American Holistic Medical Association. Currently, Dr. Northrup is on the staff of Women to Women Health Services in Yarmouth, Me. and is on East West's *Health Advisory Board.*

    East West *associate editor Tom Monte and publisher Leonard Jacobs spoke with Dr. Northrup about pregnancy, birth, and women in medicine.*

EAST WEST: What are your general recommendations for pregnant women?

CHRISTIANE NORTHRUP: First of all, I like to see a woman and her husband before she's pregnant. And more and more women are coming in to discuss preconception nutrition and health. In general, I tell them that sperm is being produced continuously, but you have all the eggs you're ever going to have at birth. Also, the quality of the sperm can be changed much more easily, so I will often counsel a change in diet with a decrease of processed food. I sometimes encourage someone who is not necessarily predisposed to good diet to take nutritional supplements, because if someone is not going to change their diet then a good multivitamin is of some value. There's a study published in Alaska in 1980 that shows that the pre-pregnancy supplementation of the diet with a certain amount of nutrients decreased the level of neural tube defects. The kind of defect I'm talking about is when the spinal cord is open and the sac is coming right out the back, or hydrocephalis, "waterhead babies." This is an astounding study.

EW: So the first step is to help the person before she becomes pregnant to improve her health through better diet?

CN: That's right. And I often counsel to stop smoking because of the devastating effects upon reproduction, and to reduce or eliminate coffee or caffeine consumption.

EW: Once the pregnancy takes place, what do you recommend?

CN: I recommend that the woman continue doing what she's doing but include exercises such as prenatal yoga. There are a lot of women who jog. But there are some days when jogging more than two or three miles can be harmful to the baby because it increases body heat, and there's no way to dissipate that heat. Pregnant women should really be advised not to use hot tubs. I also advise them to avoid adverse environmental stimuli; for instance, not to read books that are on tragic subjects or very frightening subjects; to keep the quality of their thoughts high.

EW: Is there any data to support the recommendation that pregnant women should avoid horror movies, for example?

CN: Yes, scientists have found that a frightening movie will cause the fetus to react—totally independently of the mother. Even if the mother is calm and not scared by the film, the baby will nevertheless react. We also know that the baby will move in rhythm with the mother's voice at birth; language is already there, somewhere in the baby's brain, so the baby is extremely sensitive to the mother during pregnancy and is sensitive to what the mother does and says. I think we are finding more and more that there is an individual personality in utero who must be treated as a person who is a passenger but also as an integral part of your body. The mother has a direct effect.

EW: Besides protein, what other nutrients do you encourage women to be aware of?

CN: Calcium. A woman can get plenty of calcium by eating green, leafy vegetables like kale and collard greens and eating sesame seeds and sea vegetables. I will also sometimes recommend dolomite.

If a woman is not in the mental shape to change her diet, I will recommend milk, though I will say that cow's milk is not the best food in the world for you. Also, I will stress that if they are going to drink milk, they should try to get raw milk from a farm, and in Maine that is still possible to some extent. I try to encourage women—if they are going to eat dairy products during pregnancy—to seek the very best quality.

EW: What other kinds of advice do you give parents?

CN: I just tell them to be in the best health possible and to listen to their bodies. I give them my little talk on circumcision, which I think is an early form of child abuse. The doctor straps the baby down and cuts off the foreskin with no anesthesia. To me it's definitely abuse of a helpless child. I feel a need to educate parents against this practice. The doctor will tell you that the child doesn't feel it, but any person off the street can see that the child can feel it. I try to stress the sensitivity of the child; many women believe the baby can't see, can't hear. Even Darwin, who observed his own newborn, felt that they were sort of subhuman and that their nervous systems were so poorly developed that they couldn't feel the circumcision. So there's a lot of educating that's necessary to make parents recognize the sensitivity of their child.

EW: Do you recommend natural childbirth?

CN: Yes, absolutely. You see, the more drugs in the body the more they affect the child during birth. When you use drugs during delivery, the child's suckling reflexes decrease; also the mother is not in a state to appreciate the child, and the maternal/infant bonding is hampered. This is a very important thing. Right after the birth of the baby, a period called critical state, the mother is optimally suited to become attached to her newborn. And all the things that a baby does at first to enhance this are dulled by the anesthetics. Sometimes an anesthetic is needed, and it doesn't mean a woman can't bond with her child or the father can't bond with the child, but it's definitely decreased. Babies should nurse right after birth; their suckling instinct and reflexes are very strong, and this enhances breastfeeding. Studies have shown that the incidence of child abuse is low among mothers who breastfeed and have a good experience the first hour after birth.

One of my big campaigns is to get mothers and babies together in the hospital. Studies have shown that when a mother goat is separated from her kid during the first five minutes after birth, the goat will not accept the kid back. Maternal behavior is distorted. She may not even accept it at all. Each species has a specific critical period. Cesarean section mothers have a ten times higher incidence of child abuse than non-Cesarean section mothers.

For humans, this critical period is the hour after birth, because the baby is in a quiet, alert state. The first hour after birth, babies won't cry. They'll be very quiet. They open their eyes immediately if the room is darkened, and they look all around, and they look very old and very wise. They're very awake. They sleep and start to hybernate a few days after delivery, but on that first day, and certainly in that first hour, they're ready to interact with their mother and father.

The problem today is that hospitals are not equipped for this kind of delivery. Most hospitals are set up according to the needs of the forties, not the 1980s. Babies are tucked away in fortresses. Human beings are the only species on earth that routinely and systematically separate the newborn from its mother at birth. And that's another reason why people are afraid of hospitals, because they have just given birth and they're feeling vulnerable; women are in a very emotional state after delivery, and they really can't fight the whole institution, which feels that the baby should be observed for a couple of hours somewhere else in the building.

EW: Would you feel comfortable issuing a caution to women who have their births in the hospital?

CN: Yes. I just orchestrated a meeting of nurses and physicians in southern Maine on the subject of giving birth in a hospital, and there was a tremendous show of concern over the issues. The problems involve logistics, because the hospitals were built in the forties and now can't meet the needs of the present. But there is a real commitment among many people who work in hospitals to improve the birth experience. At present, I tell my patients about the bonding needs and about breastfeeding. And I also point out that their baby has been in the womb for nine months and ask if it makes sense that suddenly the baby should be put in a room with forty other screaming babies under fluorescent lights in a sterile environment. This is a very shocking environment to say the least. Once you tell people this, many of them want to control their birth experiences. What hospitals need today are birthing centers where the facilities are present to keep the mother and child together.

EW: When do you recommend starting to introduce solid foods?

CN: It's usually about six months, when the baby is beginning to show an interest. I strongly urge mothers to nurse their babies for a minimum of six months. If a mother can nurse her child for a year or even two years, it's really great for the child. Of course, we're assuming now that everyone knows that breastfeeding is far superior in every category to formula feeding. It is far superior nutritionally, and it strengthens the bonding between mother and child. Breast milk is the baby's source of calcium and antibodies; it protects against childhood illnesses, strengthens the immune system, and is living tissue. There's no way formula can duplicate it.

The first food I recommend that the mother introduce is a little brown rice cereal. Mothers should make their own baby food. You can make it yourself in one of those food grinders. It's nutritionally superior to the commercial baby food and much cheaper. Breastfeeding a baby saves you over a thousand dollars a year.

EW: Do you see yourself as an advocate for a more intuitive understanding?

CN: Yes, I see women in medicine promoting this. There's a wonderful book called *Woman and Nature: The Roaring Inside Her* by Susan Griffin, which talks about women in healing. And women have always brought this intuitive, mothering understanding to medicine, unless the woman has become so male-identified in the medical school or in the male-dominated medical profession that she loses that female instinct. And when that happens, she is like a traitor; you feel betrayed. You go to a female physician for certain reasons. You think you're going to get some different approaches. The woman can provide more of the right brain, intuitive, holistic approach, and I think that as women we need to trust this. And this is what's happening to women in medicine. Women in medicine will be instrumental in bringing about a more holistic and intuitive healing approach. Also, it's okay if a woman physician wants to hug her patient or show more emotion than what is normally demonstrated. Men are becoming more this way as well. And I see that as good. A lot of medical school students are coming through and are remaining very sensitive. So in the future it will be less of a male/female thing. This is the direction I'm heading in and the direction I see medicine going in, too.

DR. YESHE DONDEN

Tibetan Practices to Ease Childbirth
July 1976

Most people are now aware of certain aspects of Tibetan culture, such as meditation and iconography; but few are aware of its medical system, a system as rich and sophisticated as Tibet's other traditions. One of the most impressive treatments found in the system, especially in contrast to our own, is that given to mothers during childbirth. It is on this treatment that the interview by Glenn H. Mullin with Dr. Yeshe Donden, chief physician to H. H. the Dalai Lama, centered. Donden currently directs the Tibetan Medical Center in Dharamsala, India.

EAST WEST: The medicines administered in the early phases of labor [two sets of five pills, given at approximately ten-minute intervals], the main element in the Tibetan childbirth technique, seem tremendously effective. How do these medicines shorten the labor time?

YESHE DONDEN: They have two main functions: The first is to cool all physical and mental tensions that the mother has; the second is to prevent the mother or child from developing any infections during or after the birth. These two tensions are the greatest obstacles to childbirth; so relaxing them accelerates the process. Certain herbs in the medicines also strengthen the muscles that push out the baby.

EW: In the Western system, a mother is usually kept on her back during labor and is covered with only a single sheet or a light blanket. In the Tibetan, she is kneeling and is kept perspiringly hot by being covered with several thick woolen blankets. Is there any significance in these differences?

YD: If she is maintained in the "on knees" position, the weight of the baby works for the birth; in the "on back" position its weight works against the birth. Also, if the mother is in the former position, her "pushing" muscles can develop more pressure, speeding the delivery.

As for the bedcovers, we believe that keeping the mother very warm helps the vital energies to flow and her muscular system to unwind. Both of these actions aid childbirth. The only possible benefit that I can see in using only one covering is that the inconvenience of dirtying a larger number of them is avoided and there is less work for the aides involved.

EW: What sort of advice do you give to women on how to take care of themselves during pregnancy and after having given birth?

YD: In general, she should be careful always to move gently and to avoid jarring her abdominal area; she should avoid exposing herself, especially her abdominal area, to extremes of temperature. For example, she should not take baths that are overly hot or cold, nor should she eat foods that are excessively hot or cold. Extremes disrupt the balance of the vital energy flows and lay the foundations of complications for delivery; as well, they cause unnecessary pain to the unborn child. Obviously, she should avoid alcohol and strong spices, which, again, disturb the vital energies. Her diet must be rich, for she will lose quite a lot of blood after the baby comes out; vegetables eaten should preferably be local and seasonal, for this enhances harmony of the energies.

All that is really required (for a home birth) is a few blankets, something clean to wrap the baby in, a few pieces of cloth with which to clean up, and a piece of sterilized string and a pair of sharp scissors with which to tie off and cut the umbilical cord. One need not worry about the umbilical cord after this; it is only necessary to put a couple of drops of oil on its base each day. It will turn black within a few days and drop off after a week or so. If the mother has taken the Tibetan childbirth medicine, there is almost no chance of it becoming infected. The baby should, if at all possible, be given nothing but the mother's breast milk for the first month, after which it is permissible to give it a couple of spoonfuls of cereal daily as supplement. The mother should stay in bed for at least a week after giving birth, to give her abdominal organs and muscles a chance to readjust themselves after the trauma of labor.

EW: What do you consider to be the greater advantages of the Tibetan childbirth medicine? Do you think there is any hope of it becoming widely available in the Western world?

YD: In terms of time ratio, the length of labor is reduced to one-quarter: births that would normally take eight hours are reduced to two. It cuts the pain of labor by about half, without abrogating consciousness, and substantially reduces the percentage of postdelivery infections in both mother and baby. Also, by relaxing the mother's muscles it greatly diminishes the possibility of tearing and reduces the chances of internal hemorrhage.

As for its availability in Western countries, the Tibetan form of Buddhadharma is now spreading throughout the West at an astounding pace, and medicine is one of its integral aspects. How can it be overlooked?

MARIAN TOMPSON

The Revival of Breastfeeding
February 1978

Marian Tompson is a mother of seven, and one of the seven founders of La Leche League. This organization offers extensive personal attention to women worldwide, and disseminates a wide variety of information about breastfeeding through its publications and classes. East West's Barbara Jacobs spoke with Tompson about the importance of mother's milk and breastfeeding in general, prenatal care and childbirth, childcare, nutrition, and psychological aspects of breastfeeding.

Like the other six original founders of La Leche League, Tompson is still active in the group's affairs.

EAST WEST: Why do you think women stopped nursing their children? Is it just an American or European phenomenon, or is it worldwide?

MARIAN TOMPSON: It seems to be happening all over the world, little by little, but probably began here. I think the cause is really a combination of things. One is that through pasteurization, milk feeding became safer for infants. Then, when women started taking jobs, they could leave their babies with someone else. But I think the biggest impetus came during World War II when childbirth was moved to the hospital, where women were routinely anesthetized and separated from their babies. Also, by that time the formula companies had come into the picture.

EW: Do you have any statistics on how breastfeeding has changed over the past twenty years?

MT: We have statistics from different kinds of studies. I don't know that you can compare one kind with another, but there was a study done every ten years in the U.S. on the number of new mothers leaving hospitals who were breastfeeding. The point at which fewest women were breastfeeding, according to this study, was in 1966 when only eighteen percent of new mothers leaving the hospital were breastfeeding. Last year, one of the formula companies who does regular market research surveys said that thirty-eight percent were breastfeeding their babies, which means that in ten years it has more than doubled. A recent study [of the readers] of *American Baby* magazine indicated that more than fifty percent of the mothers responding had nursed at least one child.

EW: Are you familiar with any studies on the nutritional value of mother's milk versus cow's milk or formula?

MT: Well, they're basing the formulas on the composition of breast milk; they are trying to approximate breast milk. The problem is that our chemistry isn't sophisticated enough to really analyze and isolate all the components of breast milk at this point. So, as they find things out, they add them to cow's milk. If you really understand chemistry, you realize that the problem is that things work synergistically; you might find through a new chemical analysis that one component of breast milk is vitamin B6. So you can put that vitamin in, but there are other things that work with it to make it effective.

EW: That's why they put vitamin D in.

MT: Right, and now we find we don't even need that vitamin D. You see, when we're depending on science to give us the answers, we have to wait until it gets sophisticated enough to give us the answers we need.

It would make sense that human milk has everything needed for a human baby because for millions of years it's been adapted and worked out for human beings. For years it was said, using chemical analysis, that there wasn't enough vitamin D in human milk. Doctors said that this is one thing you have to give the baby. It was usually given in the form of drops, though some more naturally oriented doctors would say to put the baby in the sun. But in the past few months they've said that the reason they thought there wasn't enough vitamin D was that they thought vitamin D was only fat soluble, so they were measuring the amount in the fat portion of the milk, which was only about four percent of the milk. Now they've discovered that there's another kind of, and much more vitamin D in the water portion of the milk than in the fat portion. So breastfed babies are getting much more vitamin D than was ever suspected. When you try to analyze something like this you will run into problems until you can analyze it correctly.

EW: What is the difference between a breastfed and a bottle fed baby?

MT: I think it makes a lot of difference to the mother and to the baby. I've also heard this from mothers who have bottle fed and then breastfed. They've said, "You never told me how much I would enjoy being a mother." Now, it's important that if you have a job you should enjoy it; your whole attitude toward your work will be different if you enjoy it rather than if you are doing something just because it's a duty, or because you have to earn money, or whatever. So, I think there's an interaction that goes on between a nursing mother and her baby that makes motherhood more enjoyable. The nursing mother secretes a hormone called prolactin, which makes her feel more motherly, so even though it's a hard job and involves a lot of time, she doesn't really feel tied down or like a martyr. Even though people may look at a woman carrying a baby and think, "Oh, that poor girl, she can't put that baby down," actually it's a different thing for that mother. She wouldn't want someone else to take that baby and go off someplace; she'd feel only half there. So, it's something that almost has to be experienced to be appreciated or to know what the difference really is.

EW: What about the father's role?

MT: Good fathering is extremely important. Many mothers couldn't succeed at breastfeeding if they didn't have a husband who was interested in being a good father. Initially, the father's role is not to feed the baby, or even to diaper it, but to provide stability and support for the mother so she can concentrate on taking care of the baby. He does this by financially supporting them if he can, so the mother doesn't have to go out and work. Another thing he can do is fend off the people who might make the mother start questioning what she's doing. He can encourage her by saying that she's doing a good job, and that it's wonderful to see the baby growing on her milk. With this kind of support, she's going to relax, her milk's going to let down, and her baby will be happy. Thus the father will be contributing in a very important way to the health of that baby.

EW: What do you think of the people who say that if a baby is bottle fed the father can play an equal part?

MT: I think mainly that they have a misunderstanding of the father's role. The father is not a substitute mother. He really has a very special role to play, that no one else can duplicate.

EW: What do you recommend about weaning?

MT: This is a very individual matter. Women are so used to bottle feeding that they think of breastfeeding simply in terms of nutrition. But breastfeeding is more than that, it's a very special kind of close relationship between two people. Everybody has different needs, and you could no more tell a woman how much or how long to nurse her baby than you could tell a husband and wife how many times a day they could kiss.

For some babies, this cuddling and closeness and the sucking that goes along with it is needed for a longer period of time than for other babies. I think it's unusual for a baby to wean itself totally by one year of age. For some babies the nursing will go on for several years. In the Bible they talk about two years as the minimum weaning age. But our society is so hung up with the sexual use of breasts that people get very nervous about a toddler nursing. I remember a story my mother told me of how, in Italy, a little child would bring a stool to his mother working in the fields so she could sit down and nurse him, and I thought, "Oh, is that weird!" until I nursed a three-year-old and didn't think it was weird at all. So it just depends on your point of view. But from the child's, it's perfectly natural.

EW: What do you see as the trend in breastfeeding over the next twenty years?

MT: I think there will be an increase because people are intelligent and will be more appreciative of how important breast milk is. I think we will be seeing that the effects of breastfeeding are long-term in the areas of physical as well as psychological health. As women see how much other mothers enjoy nursing, they will be inspired to try it themselves. It just can't help but grow.

AVELINE KUSHI

The Motherly Art of Macrobiotics
January 1977

Aveline Kushi, mother of five and author of several books on natural lifestyle and cooking, has been teaching macrobiotics throughout the world for over twenty-five years. Barbara Jacobs spoke with her about a macrobiotic approach to childcare.

EAST WEST: Can you give us some specific examples of the effects of food on your children or the way you treated any sickness they had?

AVELINE KUSHI: When you are breastfeeding or when you are pregnant, it is easy to control the food the child receives, but after you separate, it is more difficult. In my own case I never had any problems with my children until they began to eat solid food.

I have five children: one daughter, the eldest, and four boys. The girl was a really strong baby, and she had a great appetite. But looking at the total view, I think that since she was a girl I should have given her more sweet foods, like fruit, as she was growing up. She was the first, and I was most strict with her diet.

Also, no one was talking about natural foods or macrobiotics almost twenty-three years ago. I had just come from Japan, and I didn't know this country very well. I was only able to get Long River brown rice and that was it—maybe some oatmeal in the supermarket, also some buckwheat groats and some pumpernickel bread. Also, in some Japanese food stores I could get seaweed and buckwheat noodles. Those things were available, but nothing else. We could not even get good sea salt. As for tamari and miso, they were unheard of in America then. And, of course, vegetables were not organic at that time. We had only city water.

It was under those conditions that we were raising children. But my first child was very easy to raise; she didn't have any difficulties. When she was in the first or second grade, I started to experiment with making yeasted breads, and I also started to teach macrobiotic cooking. I didn't have any previous experience with making bread, and I thought you had to use yeast. I didn't know about natural unleavened breads. My daughter was eating these breads and I am sure I used a little too much yeast. I also think my cooking was too salty at that time. Japanese macrobiotic cooking uses almost ten times more salt than American macrobiotic cooking. It was very salty, and naturally, I think, too salty for her. Around that time I found out that she was near-sighted. I was so sorry; it was completely my fault.

EW: That condition was due to too much salt?

AK: I think so. Too much salt creates a great appetite and desire for sweets. Too much salt and sweets puts a strain on the liver, and eye troubles are a sign of liver problems. With macrobiotic children (girls, especially) I think you can give more yin food, less salt than I did, and give them a little more variety of yin, especially grain sugar. You can make them natural desserts without refined sugar.

When my children got sick, it was not from yin but from too much yang. When the cooking is very salty and strong—if it's cooked with much fire and for a long time—boys at about ten years old might tend to have some trouble. Muscles get a little too tense. With two of my sons these things came at about that age.

EW: Do you think you should learn to trust your own intuition, and theirs, in raising your children?

AK: Of course. One of the most important things to watch is your children's attraction to certain foods. When you put a meal on the table, one takes greens, another wants an apple, another rice—they are all different. I don't have a lot of knowledge about how to treat many kinds of children's sicknesses, just what I learned from George Ohsawa's [Japanese philosopher and macrobiotic educator, died 1966] books and teachings—very simple methods.

EW: How do you make sure that your children are not attracted to sweets and junk foods?

AK: If you can show them the relationship between certain foods they eat and the effects those foods have on them, then they can see for themselves what happens. Explain to them and tell them just to be careful.

EW: Do you have any advice about weaning?

AK: Macrobiotic mothers sometimes chew their babies' food for a time after the baby is weaned. I think this practice is good in moderation, especially for hard beans and the like, but the mother's saliva is very strong for the baby, so this shouldn't be done too much or for too long. If you do this all the time, the baby becomes too yang. That is why I suggest that food to be given to a baby should be well mashed but there shouldn't be so much pre-chewing of everything.

Once something is written in a book, the practice seems to become rigid. That is why people have to read with a flexible mind; otherwise mistakes arise. No one writer can explain in written form the one hundred thousand ways of doing things.

For instance, George Ohsawa once wrote, "Do not pick up your baby." He was writing to a Japanese audience, where the family is very close and someone will pick up a baby as soon as it starts to cry. He felt this was not so good. In America on the other hand, many mothers just give the baby a bottle; the baby sleeps in a fancy room, separated from her; often the parents don't even take care of the child, it is raised by a nurse. In those kinds of situations, it is better to tell the parents to touch the baby, to hold it next to their skin for healing and to develop a warm, peaceful type of person. That shows how you must always read written advice with a flexible mind. That is why it is important to be very careful about trying out remedies that you just read about in a book.

MICHIO KUSHI

Watching Our Children Grow
July 1977

Michio Kushi is one of the world's foremost teachers of macrobiotic philosophy and lifestyle. His interpretation of macrobiotics has been the subject of numerous books, and he continues to lecture worldwide while keeping to a full schedule at the Kushi Institute in Brookline and Becket, Mass. Barbara Jacobs and Kushi discussed early childhood development and education.

EAST WEST: Do you have any particular method that you recommend for helping a child learn to talk?

MICHIO KUSHI: The important things to keep in mind when teaching children to speak, understand words, and read is always to consider the children's brain wavelengths and proceed slowly. Even many children who have been designated mentally retarded are actually not mentally retarded but have just been taught at the wrong tempo and with letters and numbers that are too small for them to understand completely. They have been taught at adult speed and with adult sizes of letters and objects, and therefore they cannot understand. If we use the method of proceeding slowly and using larger sizes of letters and objects, even by the age of five years the children can have a command of many adult expressions.

Of course, at the same time as this mental development takes place, children are developing physically. Physical development always precedes mental development. So the child should be active in both play and learning. The adults should not interfere in the child's physical development. For example, if parents are overprotective, or pick up a child too much who is just learning to crawl or walk, the child's physical and therefore mental development will be impaired.

Crawling is very important to a baby, because it is through crawling that the muscles and joints are developed and strengthened. Through that kind of activity children are also developing their brains and judgment properly. When they become proficient at one stage, they can proceed normally to the next stage of physical and mental development. That is why it is very important for the child to be active and develop at his or her own pace and not be interrupted by an overprotective parent.

EW: Many of our readers object to immunization. What advice do you have regarding inoculation?

MK: The idea behind immunization is to create a sickness artificially so that the body will create a natural resistance to a second and stronger appearance of the same sickness. But why are some people more susceptible than others to the same illness? Because their daily way of life, their daily way of eating, is unhealthy. If their daily way of life is healthy, they will not get such sickness.

There is no reason to make someone artificially sick. When this is done there is a resistance created to that disease as a natural result, but at the same time, some other aspect of natural growth is lost. This is because the growing and developing abilities are being used for resisting, for battling that sickness. So for that reason we should avoid vaccinations as much as possible.

The idea of using vaccinations is based on somewhat of a misconception of the natural order: Modern people think that some kind of bacteria or virus is the cause—so they plan a counterattack through artificial immunizations. But that is not actually the cause—it is only an agent. The real cause is unhealthy quality of blood, due to an unhealthy way of eating. The artificial treatment is an attempt to compensate for poor quality of blood. This represents a misconception of natural order. If we are eating badly, there is definitely a need for these medications—that is natural, to become sick. If the family cannot nourish children properly with good food, then they may be afraid and get vaccinations. However, that vaccination may be the distant cause of some future physical or mental problems. The whole point is that we should eat properly and live according to the laws of nature.

EW: Before we talk about school as it exists, I'd like to hear your views on the ideal school. What is the purpose of education?

MK: The purpose of education, at the present time, is to make the child develop as a useful social person. But that "useful" means someone who will contribute to the progress and prosperity of society by making money, working in organizations, pursuing intellectual careers. Certainly these fields have some merit, but that is only partial progress.

The primary purpose of education is to help children become healthy, happy, and strong as whole human beings, not only as social persons. For that, we need to establish their understanding of why they came here, why they were born, what their goals are, and how to keep their health and happiness on this earth. That is understanding number one, common sense. The most important thing is to develop common sense and intuition. Second come the technical problems of how to maintain good health, how to develop judgment, how to behave, and how to interact with people. After that comes social relations. At this point some part of modern education can be helpful for the problem of what kind of technical service can be done in the future. But modern education alone is not enough. Before that kind of education, we must have a broad basic education of human beings.

In grammar school all children should learn how to take care of themselves. This includes how to take care of their health and how to select and prepare their daily food. They should also know how to make dwellings, how to grow food, and have an understanding of the relationships within the natural world, including that of earth to the stars. All these matters of basic common sense should be established in grammar school.

In high school this basic commonsense education should be continued, but other things are introduced, such as human relations—in the sense of learning and giving respect to elders, being loving to younger people, and relating to people in society. High school students should then study history, geography, social and natural sciences, and other intellectual directions.

Modern studies are completely fragmented. The reason for this is that there is no principle that works in all areas. From grammar school through all of high school, children should be learning the universal principle. This principle is what we express as balance, or yin and yang. This principle should be a part of all aspects of their education, and it should be used in learning physics, chemistry, health problems, cooking, social science, and so on. Throughout their education, that principle should always be there. Then they could finish their college-level studies by the age of seventeen or eighteen. After that they can do whatever they want, in social education or social experience. They can begin any kind of research work, or adventures, or experiments. As far as college is concerned, that part should be using the universal principle of yin and yang in original creation. Students should write, they should discover or invent something; university education should be their own creative experience or discovery.

EW: How would you suggest that parents who are not totally in agreement with the public schools' way of teaching cope with the differences between the school ideology and their family life?

MK: If we don't have our own school, it's fine for the children to go to public school or private school. But then home education becomes even more important. Let the children encounter any kind of chance or opportunity to learn outside of school about life and living, including making clothing, cooking, or other practical things. Parents should also be explaining to the children the order of nature, in terms of yin and yang, and letting them develop, through their own observations, a way of seeing relationships in nature and between people.

EW: Modern education seems to emphasize competitiveness. I remember how important grades were. How do you see the natural differences in people, the personal abilities that are sometimes overlooked in a school situation or even at home?

MK: When children are evaluated, it is done with a narrow scope. Some children have an excellent school record, but that is only one small part of the whole person. The standard of present-day evaluations is very conceptual and one-sided. If children have a good mechanical memory, then they will be high scorers. But this kind of memory is only a very small part. More important are children's insights, their broad understanding and clear judgment. Those things do not appear on school records. Even more important is their physical, mental, and spiritual health. That, again, doesn't appear on school records.

Children need guidance and encouragement from their parents. The parents should encourage the children to do whatever they like to do in the future. "Do your best in school, in society, in whatever you like to do, and don't worry about competition. When you do your best in what you really want to do, that is the best." Some children go to school and get a D, others may get an A. The most important thing is which group was putting forth its best effort. The child's ability is most important, and the marks received are only of secondary importance.

Many great world leaders had very bad school records. Parents should give guidance in these matters, because the school doesn't make provisions for it. So you can totally erase any idea of competition. Just encourage children to do their best, whether in school or in their responsibilities at home. When they put forth their best effort, it doesn't matter whether their marks in school are the best or the worst—they have done wonderfully.

RUDOLPH BALLENTINE, M.D.

Better Family Health
December 1985

Dr. Rudolph Ballentine is a family doctor and psychiatrist who practices mainly at the Himalayan Institute (of which he is president) in Honesdale, Penn. Ballentine came to the Institute in 1973 after getting his M.D. from Duke University, studying psychology at the University of Paris (Sorbonne), and serving as assistant clinical professor of psychiatry at Louisiana State University in New Orleans. In India, Ballentine studied yoga, homeopathy, and the traditional Indian system of medicine known as ayurveda, all of which he uses in his practice at the Institute. Ballentine is probably most well known as the author of Diet and Nutrition: A Holistic Approach *and* Transition to Vegetarianism.*

Mark Mayell and Leonard Jacobs focused their questions on the topic of how best to keep a family healthy and happy.

EAST WEST: Do you try to be home for meals?

RUDOLPH BALLENTINE: Generally, yes. Most days I manage to be home for lunch, and sometimes my family comes here. But we try to have that main meal together. Usually we have supper and breakfast together, too, which are lighter meals.

EW: What are the problems most people have in terms of trying to arrange that?

RB: Of course, everybody these days has so many things going on. But if you're going to have a family then I think that has to be your priority.

I think we should try to see that the time that we have with children is really relatively short, and the time we have to be a family is ten or fifteen years. It's a sixth or a fifth of the years you may expect to live. The one-pointedness of many disciplines such as yoga teaches us to focus with full attention, so that when you leave something, you can go on to the next thing and focus on that with full attention. Well, this also applies to the phases of your life. If you're a family person and all your attention is on what you're going to do once you get rid of the family, then you're not going to benefit from the family experience. I think that it really behooves parents to realize that they

have a relatively short time to raise a family, although it may seem at times bur-
densome or all-consuming.

So, we try to organize our life around the family unit and the children, and
the input which is so critical for the children's development while they're
young. If you're distracted during the time that you're raising small children, I
think you're more likely to have to put a lot of time and effort into coping
with adolescent crises. An important part of an intact home is at least one meal
a day together.

EW: Are there special considerations in the West, where the extended family is an
exception?

RB: Some of my perspective does come from having lived and worked for awhile in
India, where the situation is quite different. The family unit is still, aside from
the very urban areas, very much intact, and life still revolves around family
organization. Because of that, I think, many of the principles of healthful, sane,
coherent living have continued to be propagated through the family setting,
primarily through the mother, who is the bearer of all those traditions. And
what I find is that so many of the things that we in alternative medicine are
struggling to educate the public to do, people from such a setting as the Indian
family do automatically. I do feel that a lot of what we see in a doctor's office
today is the result of not passing on to our children the simplest, most obvious,
commonsense habits and practices for their health and sanity.

EW: How can you establish that type of tradition when the family is more fragmented?

RB: People come to me in my office in New York and say, "I understand what
you're suggesting about my diet and so forth but I never have a regular time
that I can eat lunch. I'm rarely at home in the evening, and there is no way I
can eat the way you're suggesting. What should I do?" And the answer is
obvious: "I advise you to reorganize your life so that you can do these things."
People think this is outrageous. I say it's a matter of priorities. You have to
decide what makes sense. If you completely undermine your health and your
sense of tranquillity and judgment by living a chaotic life, then whatever goals
you thought were important enough to justify that need to be re-examined.

The same thing is true for families today. If parents are busy going off in
different directions, how can they provide the context in which to educate and
train their children?

EW: Do you think it's important for the woman to be doing the cooking or just
however the family arranges it to be done?

RB: I happen to love to cook and I cook every time I get a chance. On the other
hand, I think that there are many reasons why it is often more practical for the
wife to do the majority of the cooking. Number one, she's more at home,
especially when the children are young, and the children need her to be. Also,
the woman has the role of nourisher. She is biologically and psychologically
suited to nourishing. It's something that goes deep into a woman's soul to
want to nourish. And thank God for that. The continuity of the species relies
on that. On the other hand, I think that it's very appropriate for a man to
learn to cook and for him to do it when he can. I think it's good to relieve the

woman of the responsibility sometimes.

Cooking shouldn't be a burden. It should be a joy and that's why it's helpful for people to share it. How many things can you do in life where you have no question that they are necessary, important, and will have an impact on other people's lives? Where else can you have that confidence?

EW: Is eating out as a family unit the same as eating at home?

RB: It's a sad comment for parents to say to children, "We think you should be fed but we can't feed you ourselves. We have to take you to someone we don't know, whom we've never seen, cooking in a kitchen we know nothing about, preparing food that we don't know where it came from, to feed you." What a horrible message to offer children. Is it really necessary or are you doing it because of something else that seems important, but on examination isn't important enough to justify this?

EW: You don't think it can suffice as a type of entertainment?

RB: Oh sure. As an adventure, it's something different and fun. What you're saying is, "Look kids, we are doing this because we want you to have the opportunity to go with us and this is the only way we can do it. We brought along one meal but then we're going to be there for two days so we'll eat tomorrow at that place and this is part of our adventure together." Then I think you can justify it. But that wouldn't be something you'd do every day. Adventures cease to be adventures when they happen daily. Then they become confusion and chaos.

EW: How do you cope with children's cravings?

RB: I think that the more people eat separately the more different they become and then the harder it becomes to get them back to eating the same thing on the same schedule. I think the more we do eat together, the more our tastes and nutritional demands become congruent.

EW: Why is eating together so important?

RB: Many different purposes are served, biologically and psychologically. When somebody who just ate meat and sugar and somebody who just ate beans and vegetables sit down and try to talk, they have a hard time. They're vibrating at different wavelengths and they have trouble finding a point of contact. I'm sure that applies to the family, too.

I don't know if we understand all the effects of the experience of taking nourishment together. In many traditions people would not eat together unless they wanted to establish some kind of friendship. Enemies would never take food together. There is something unifying about taking nourishment from the same source.

We need a little welding, because the family is falling apart. I don't think anyone would pretend it's an accident that the disintegration and dissolution of the American family is happening at the same time that eating habits are changing. Some people would say one is the cause, the other effect, and some people would reverse that, but they're definitely bound together.

EW: What lessons do single people have to learn from the lessons of family nutrition?

RB: We're all family people because we've all been children in a family. The only difference between being parents and being non-parents is that as parents we're now having the chance to play the other role. So there's a certain potential here for re-addressing or reaching a resolution to some of the problems that were left over from our childhood experiences.

Whether you're a parent or a single person, many of us are part of a transitional generation—we are the ones who grew up with certain practices and values, and we are having to re-examine those. And that's hard. But we should do it. We shouldn't push it off onto the kids. We should resolve it and let the children grow up in a new generation, not in a transitional generation. So, basically, parents and single people aren't all that different. We're struggling with the same issues.

ALEXANDER LEAF, M.D.

New Views on the Very Old
September 1984

Perhaps no single person is as responsible for the explosion of interest in extreme longevity that began in the early 1970s as is Alexander Leaf, M.D. In 1973, articles by Dr. Leaf that appeared in National Geographic, Scientific American, *and the professional journals* Hospital Practice *and* Nutrition Today *focused worldwide attention on three areas where living to be 100 seemed almost commonplace: the village of Vilcabamba in Ecuador, the land of Hunza in the Pakistani Himalayas, and Abkhazia, a republic in the Caucasus Mountains of southern U.S.S.R.*

Leaf is a professor at Harvard Medical School and Chairman of the Department of Preventive Medicine and Clinical Epidemiology at Massachusetts General Hospital in Boston, where East West *publisher Leonard Jacobs and editor Mark Mayell interviewed him.*

EAST WEST: In the process of setting up this interview, you mentioned briefly that you had changed your views on longevity considerably since the early 1970s when you visited Vilcabamba, the land of Hunza, and Soviet Georgia. How have your ideas changed?

ALEXANDER LEAF: I'm much more skeptical now of the claims for extreme age. In Vilcabamba, the one place where we could check objectively what the ages were, they turned out to be entirely false. I suspect that in the other two places ages are much exaggerated also. Particularly in Russia the age claims are quite outlandish.

EW: What makes you think that?

AL: Well, for instance, the authorities there have been promoting Shirali Mislimov as the oldest person in the Soviet Union. He died at the age of 168, they said, and they put out a commemorative stamp. And then a few years later there was a picture of him with his great-great grandson, but now Shirali Mislimov is 172. If you resurrect him that way I guess you can get to almost any age you want.

The documentation shows that the biological limit of humans is probably somewhere around eighty-five, plus or minus ten years, and the outer limit is somewhere around 100. That's been the case throughout the centuries. What we've been seeing happening, as nutrition, housing, and public health measures get better, is that more people at birth are attaining ages close to the maximum.

EW: These figures are for an average Western population?

AL: Yes. If you look back, and one can do this at least in the records of the royal families of England, the maximum age centuries ago was still out to about 100, as it is now, but more people at birth now are getting through to their seventies and eighties.

EW: But most of the claims for ages over 100 or so are probably exaggerated?

AL: I think so. If you take this as one person at 115 or 118, out of a population of the earth of four and a half billion people, the probability of any one person getting to that age is very remote. It's a normal distribution curve, with the mean probably around eighty-five or ninety. Therefore, as we get older and older there are fewer and fewer people of that age.

EW: In the *National Geographic* story, you said that there are a large number of very vigorous elderly persons that you encountered that really impressed you, regardless of their true ages. In other words, even if they weren't 110, but were between eighty-five and 100, they seemed to be much more healthy and vigorous than an average elderly population in industrialized countries. Do you still feel that way?

AL: There's no question that that's the impression, but there are no statistics to support that. I discussed this with Dr. Zhores Medvedev, the Russian biologist now exiled in London, and that was his impression also. The figures that the Census Bureau sent me in the literature indicated that if you actually look at the health status of our elderly in the seventy-five to eighty-five group, the figures aren't very different from what researchers have found among the peasants of the Caucasus. It may be that the latter are more evident because they're outside, it's a farming community, and you see them, whereas in our society you don't encounter them so often.

But one does have the impression that there are a lot of vigorous, healthy elderly people there. Some of the individuals that I saw were quite remarkable. We had been hearing stories of an elderly man alleged to be 116 who followed the local custom of taking his goats to the high alpine area for three or four summer months. When I got up there, I estimated he was probably closer to ninety. Even so, I have some pictures of the hillside where the goats were, and it would take one of us a while to get into condition to chase goats around those steep slopes.

EW: Is the physical activity associated with living in a very steep area an important factor that kept them very healthy?

AL: Yes, I think there's fairly good evidence that physical activity is good for the heart and blood vessels. A study in New Mexico looked at the coronary artery disease mortality of people at different thousand-foot levels and found that for males there was the lowest incidence in people living at ten thousand feet or above. The researcher attributed that to the physical activity of going up and down the mountainside.

EW: What conclusions do you have from your studies on longevity?

AL: Some very definite ones. First, the major cause of death in our society is coronary artery disease, which now accounts for about 49 percent of the mortality in the U.S. (fifteen years ago it was about 54 percent). They don't have that in these areas, so that's very significant. Epidemiologic evidence shows that atherosclerosis is not a necessary accompaniment of aging, it's a consequence of our culture, the way we live, what we eat, smoking, our lack of exercise, and so forth.

These people eat a diet that is mostly vegetarian, and engage in a lot of physical activity. If we could implement those two things in our society and get away from saturated fats, we could at least reduce the major cause of death and morbidity in our society.

EW: In addition to lifestyle and dietary changes, what part would you say positive outlook plays in establishing someone's health and longevity?

AL: I think it plays a large part. There are actually studies that show very clearly that individuals who are withdrawn and disconnected from any social network don't live as long as those who have a positive relationship with others. And it was very interesting in these travels that these are all agrarian cultures, where people live in an extended family. As they got older the chores that they did were diminished in physical requirement but everybody knew that they were doing things that contributed to the economy and social life in that society, which is in marked contrast to retiring people, putting them on a shelf, and indicating very clearly to them that they are not needed. It's terribly important that people get caught up in interests and activities that they enjoy, whether it's something socially useful or not. You should be able to get up in the morning and say, 'Hooray, another day to enjoy.'

FOOD

Helen Nearing

Dick Gregory

Frances Moore Lappé

Edward Espe Brown

Harvey & Marilyn Diamond

DICK GREGORY

Up From Soul Food
July 1981

According to East West *contributing editor Peter Barry Chowka, who interviewed Gregory in Boston, "It is a challenge to list the myriad activities and involvements of Dick Gregory. Although often referred to as a comedian, he is in reality a unique, complex phenomenon, traveling non-stop around the country and to other continents, speaking, demonstrating, researching, and networking—as his biography notes, 'making people laugh, making people listen, and ultimately helping them understand one another.' "*

Gregory's name is synonymous with progressive social and political causes. His participation in the civil rights movement of the '60s, his legendary fasts, his efforts for world peace, hunger, and rights of Native Americans, are all indicative of his ongoing struggle on behalf of human dignity. Almost two decades ago Gregory began to experiment, principally using diet, with his own health and spiritual development, which led to his involvement in researching nutritional solutions to world and domestic hunger. One of his current projects includes calling attention to the problems of obese individuals, many of whom he works with personally. Gregory is the author of nine books, including Dick Gregory's Natural Diet for Folks Who Eat *and his autobiography,* Nigger.

As Chowka notes, Dick Gregory is "that rare combination of activist and healer, one whose own life illustrates how real change first must come from within."

EAST WEST: Many of your activities are overtly political, including the use of fasting for political ends. Can you make a political statement, as well, by detaching yourself from the modern American diet, by becoming a vegetarian?

DICK GREGORY: Yes, but it's much easier to make a political statement than it is to change your diet. I never *believed* segregation was right, or racism was right; I always heard my grandmother and grandfather say it was wrong, and the people I was born to and raised around say it was wrong. But I thought you *needed* a ham sandwich to survive—if you didn't eat it you would die. I have never, ever underestimated the power of misinformation, particularly on poor folks and oppressed folks. To jump up and say, "Hey, man, stop eating that way"—first you got to understand that my *church* never told me that the way I eat was wrong, OK? My *school* never told me I was eating wrong.

EW: Doctors never told you that you were eating wrong.

DG: We never had doctors.

EW: You may have been lucky then.

DG: You're not lucky when you think you need them. As long as I think I need one, as long as I've got an ear problem, and by the time I get ten dollars to go to a doctor my whole face is infected, then that ain't luck. That's like telling me I'm lucky 'cause I can't eat in that bad white restaurant. Now once I get in there and have the right to eat in there, I can tell you, "Wow, that food is bad!" But it's always good as long as I'm outside and can't get in. Consequently, the fact that nobody who *loved* me had ever told me something was wrong with a porkchop, or a Pepsi Cola, or sugar, or candy—hey, man, my mama gave me candy as a *reward*. Now are you gonna tell me she's killing me?

To counteract all that I decided I would run from Chicago to Washington, D.C. taking only fruit juice and a little food formula I had put together. For the Bicentennial, I wanted to dramatize world hunger and health and talk about this bad diet we eat and hunger in America. So I ran from Los Angeles to New York, averaging fifty miles a day for seventy-two days. Now when I sit down on television to discuss my health book, and the dudes who believe that nutritionist from Harvard ask me, "Hey, Dick Gregory, what about so and so and so and so?" I can say, "*Wait a minute.* I just *ran* fifty miles a day for seventy-two days. I don't even want to *hear* it, OK?" That's one reason I ran, so I can say, "I don't debate health, health ain't debatable. It's like debating 'Is the sun hot?' Y'all debate it if you want to, but not me—I'm not gonna dignify it."

And so, knowing how people are locked in—remember how we talk about a drug addict and an alcoholic? People didn't start taking drugs on day one. People didn't start taking alcohol on day one. But bad food—people start drinking cow's milk and sugar water the first day they're born. So when you talk about changing your diet, to me it's like taking drugs and alcohol and multiplying them by a trillion. Remember that fathers felt that a meal wasn't complete without meat, and that the more you ate, the more of a status symbol it was. You have to have compassion and know how scary, how horrible it is— Grandma saying "God, son, you got to *eat*"; your kinfolk slipping cookies to your children, and looking at you as a bad, evil man. They're not doing that because they want to hurt them. On Thanksgiving Day, a day that should be for fasting and praying and giving thanks, we eat more food than we eat on normal days.

People are into an eating thing, and to go against that takes a long time. That's why I walked out of nightclubs. In 1973 I said, "How can you talk about health and work nightclubs? How can you say drugs and alcohol are bad on you and then say, 'Come on to my nightclub and have a taste and catch my act'?"

EW: Could you summarize what the change in nutritional consciousness has meant for your political and other awareness?

DG: Oh, I couldn't even say political awareness. I'd say spiritual.

EW: You don't think it's made you clearer, though, in your political focus on—

DG: No, once you get clear spiritually, it's gonna clear up everything you're gonna do. You shoot dice better. You play cards better. You see color better. Your reasoning gets better. Once you get clear, it clears up the whole thing. And then a lot of old petty things that you normally get hung up with, you don't. That's the first step. The second step is flushing out the mind. Eating right will not put that negative stuff in, but it ain't gonna dump it out. I mean, your petty hangups, your fears, your hatreds—you have to recognize that they exist and then throw 'em out.

One of the fantastic things about eating right is the way you feel physically. To go to bed every night and know you're gonna wake up the next day feeling good—that's what changes.

EW: Do you feel that your audiences are responsive to this information, that there is an enhanced awareness that what we eat is very important?

DG: Let me just say this: I run so fast that the burden of what I do ain't got nothing to do with them. It's got something to do with me. It's like I run and drop you $10,000. Now, if you starve to death, it wasn't because you didn't have no money. Now, I didn't say back there, "Did he get it? Is he gonna buy some food with it?" All I did is, I dropped it.

EW: But you must have a sense of whether or not people are responding, because you continue to mention food so prominently.

DG: I don't. Oh, I hear people say, "Hey, man, I *did* it." I see people coming back. Today a woman came to me and said, "My son heard you the other day and sent me a letter; he said nothing has ever touched him like this, and 'Mom, if you ever get the chance to hear....' " You hear this every now and then, but I don't even deal in it. I don't hear it because it's insignificant to me. I'm responsible for my part of doing the research, of making the schedule, of getting there, of dropping it, *boom, boom, boom*, and keep running. It's there for you if you want it; and I assume people do.

When you're dealing in universal order, there's a time for planting and a time for harvesting. Long ago I expected to do something and get results. Now I realize that you just go on planting the seeds, and be honest and ethical and regardless of what anybody thinks, there's gonna be harvest time.

EW: Now the issues of food and hunger are coming to the fore. In Reagan's budget cutting, about ten percent of the cuts have come from food assistance programs like school lunches, food stamps, aid to women, infants, and children—

DG: First you have to understand that poor folks didn't have nothing to do with all of the things here. Poor folks didn't demand school lunches. Poor folks didn't demand food stamps. That's the A&P. That's Safeway. That's General Mills. All those programs were put together for the big business rip-off. Anybody ever march for food stamps, anybody ever march for school lunch programs? Hey, man, you ever use food stamps?

EW: Once.

DG: OK. Did they tell you you couldn't buy shoestrings with it? Did they tell you you couldn't buy soap? Man, you can buy most anything you want to buy. The stores don't care. You buy beer, you buy cigarettes. See, what we always needed was a *nutrition* stamp, that says all you can get with this is something that's gonna put nutrition in your body.

EW: People must wonder how they can make a difference, what they can really accomplish up against this system that appears so entrenched.

DG: I tell them to change their diet, to look into themselves. That's where the difference is....

Now other people come up to me and I tell them if you go to the health food store and don't touch nothing but the health food, and don't touch the books, then you're doing yourself a disservice.

EW: Self-education as a process—

DG: Not as much for them as for the folks that's around them; and not out of fear, but out of love for them. Nobody's telling you to eat bad because they want you to eat bad. They tell you to eat bad because they genuinely feel that way. This cat say, "Look here, man, Dick Gregory told me to go on a four-day fast." His friend, or his folks, say, "You check with your doctor?" Well, I say, "You started drinking, you started snorting that cocaine, nobody ever asked you to check with a doctor." That's the built-in self-destruct mechanism that we're born with in our subconscious minds, and, knowing that, I try to get people to read as much as they can and explain it to other folks.

Look, I'm an entertainer. What I'm doing is like a one-act play. And here today, at this suburban white school, I've got to be very careful talking about food because people are locked into their mothers and dads; so how do you tell a high school child, "Hey, man, meat's no good." All right, they go home and say that, and they get run out of the house. But you *can* say drugs are bad, and alcohol's bad. As to how you get out of this other craziness—to the people who come to me I say, "Those of you that believe in God and believe in prayer, hey, I don't want to tamper with anybody who don't! I'm a firm believer that you make a difference, and you *do* make a difference. And you can make a better difference if your diet is together." If the nutrition thing is right, you lose some basic fears. It's a helluva thing, man, to know that you cannot die from cancer because of the way you eat.

FRANCES MOORE LAPPÉ

Beyond Diet for a Small Planet
February 1982

An activist against world hunger and economic injustice, Frances Moore Lappé is co-founder and trustee of the San Francisco-based Institute for Food and Development Policy, for which she accepted a 1987 Right Livelihood Award from the Swedish Parliament. Since writing Diet for a Small Planet *(in 1971) she has become a power in international food and agriculture policy, her name virtually synonymous with a grain-and-vegetable-centered diet and the concept of eating low on the food chain. Author of the highly acclaimed and influential* Food First *and* World Hunger: Twelve Myths, *Lappé's most recent work is* Rediscovering America's Values.

Frankie, as she likes to be called, was interviewed by Alex Jack.

EAST WEST: Looking back over the last ten years, how would you evaluate the food changes that have taken place in our country and how do you feel about your role in contributing to that change?

FRANCES MOORE LAPPÉ: I guess that the biggest change, of course, is simply the increased awareness of food. To give you some sense of what I thought the level of awareness was in 1970 when I first worked on *Diet for a Small Planet*, I thought that it might appeal to five hundred people in the greater Berkeley area. I intended to publish the book myself because I was sure that it didn't have any commercial promise. As it happened, several million people read the book. So to go from that perception to where we are today is just one representation of the change in interest and understanding.

I don't want to be the one to say what role *Diet for a Small Planet* has played relative to others, but I think that many things have come together over the last decade, including the book. For example, about the same time I started writing I was very much affected by the ecology movement that developed in the late '60s and early '70s. The idea of the limits to growth which the small-planet image brought about was part of that growing consciousness on many levels. Every aspect of our lives is, in a sense, a vote for the kind of world we want to live in. Food is just one of those votes, but an important one and one that has special appeal because it is so personal and yet universal.

EW: In the first editions of your book you originally emphasized protein as the standard. You popularized the idea of complementary proteins, warning that vegetarians must balance the right proportions of grains and beans, seeds, or nuts at every meal in order to obtain the equivalent complete protein found in meat, eggs, or dairy food. How has your own understanding of nutrition changed over the last decade, and have you made any major changes in dietary recommendations in the tenth anniversary edition?

FL: Basically, the new book says that while protein complementarity is a real phenomenon, for the vast majority of people it is irrelevant, and certainly so for people eating in a country like ours where we have so much abundance. As I said in my first editions, it is true that we do get more protein if we combine grains and beans, for example, rice and lentils, and eat them together rather than if we eat them separately. But over the years I've come to the conclusion that if we eat a very balanced diet, there is absolutely no danger of not getting enough protein.

EW: What you're now saying is that you don't have to sit down at every meal and work out your protein needs on a hand calculator?

FL: Exactly. I hope that the new book will be much easier for people. I've tried to make it as convincing as possible by putting in actual menus and showing how many kinds of protein you get without any problem. I've showed that even with no accounting for complementarity and having no animal food in your diet—meat, fish, eggs, dairy—you can still get all the protein if you eat a healthy grain and vegetable diet.

You see, when I first wrote *Diet for a Small Planet*, the idea that you didn't need to eat meat was earth-shaking, at least in my perception. It was a revelation to realize that you could combine proteins from different plant sources and obtain equivalent nutrition so that it never really occurred to me or many other people to ask the more fundamental question: Why even try to get more useful protein? Do we need that much protein to begin with? Thus the paradigm shifted. It took several years—in my case, the whole decade—to really be able to see that the focus on complementarity just contributed to this overemphasis on protein. I know that there are many people who have been saying this for a long time, but I think that in terms of public awareness we had to go in stages. The first revelation was that we didn't need meat to get our protein. The second is that we don't need all the protein that we think we do.

However, there are exceptions. I think that complementarity is important for lactating women and for pregnant women. Also there are certain people, a small percentage of the population, who have a very high protein need. So I've retained my charts in the appendix to the book. Individual needs must be considered, and I really stress this in the new book. There is much more individuality in variations among us than most of us realize.

EW: How do you reconcile your vision of the future with the demands of daily life, and what is the guiding image or metaphor by which you live your life?

FL: My mother is the only one who asks me questions like this, but I will try to respond.

If we attempt to be totally consistent, eschewing all links between ourselves and the exploitive aspects of our culture, we drive ourselves—and those close to us—nuts. If the solution, for example, to needless hunger lies in the redistribution of decision-making power, we must become part of that redistribution. This means taking ourselves seriously and really exploring questions such as what do we eat, where do we shop, what do we study in school, how do we try to learn about the world, where do we work, and how do we choose our friends?

Few people can change alone. We must choose friends and colleagues who will push us to what we thought we could not do as well as catch us when we push ourselves too far. We must learn to associate risk with joy as well as with pain.

At the age of thirty-seven my view of the good life is different. I've discovered that a life without risk is missing *the* main ingredient—joy. If we never risk being afraid, failing, being lonely, we will never experience the joy that comes only from learning that we can change ourselves. To this end we can draw inspiration from ordinary people around the world whose lives entail risks much greater than ours. And last, we must develop a perspective longer than our lifetimes.

MICHAEL JACOBSON

The Eater's Ally
May 1987

Since founding his watchdog Center for Science in the Public Interest in 1971, Michael Jacobson has become perhaps the nation's most effective consumer activist. He has concentrated on forcing the federal government to recognize its responsibility to protect the health of its citizens—pressing Congress and federal regulatory agencies to initiate such reforms as the banning of chemical additives such as red dye number 40 and sodium nitrite; halting deceptive food advertising and ads for sugary snacks aimed at children; and warning pregnant women of the dangers of caffeine. CSPI has been instrumental in awakening people to the dangers of fast foods, revealing astonishingly high fat levels in such items as McDonald's Chicken McNuggets and Filet-o-Fish, and has been the principal proponent of better food labeling, especially for salt and sugar content.

Jacobson is regularly solicited for articles or used as a source for nutrition information by the print media and has been interviewed on leading television and radio programs such as "Donahue," "The McNeil-Lehrer Report," and National Public Radio. His most recent initiatives have been to lobby Congress to force fast-food producers to label their products and to ban alcoholic beverage ads from television, and to organize Americans for Safe Food, a CSPI campaign for contaminant-free food.

Michael Jacobson was interviewed by East West *contributing editor Tom Monte.*

EAST WEST: In the past two years, you've devoted a great deal of effort to stopping deceptive ads. Why is that?

MICHAEL JACOBSON: The American diet has been changing, in some cases fairly rapidly, in other cases slowly. But the direction of the change is in line with the dietary guidelines issued by the federal government. People are eating fewer eggs, somewhat less meat and milk, and switching from whole milk to skim milk. Some of the changes have been very good, but some of the industries see the market as just disappearing under their feet. Per capita sales of eggs have gone down by at least a third in the last thirty years. The egg industry is fighting back. Overall, coffee consumption has declined by 40 percent, and among young people it's down by two-thirds in the last thirty years. That's a remarkable change, and the coffee industry is fighting back. Meat has a bad name, because meat is generally high in fat and contributes to heart disease and probably cancer. The meat industry is fighting back. The dairy industry is concerned about its sales and so they're fighting back with a major advertising campaign. Most of these ad campaigns have been deceptive. The coffee industry told us that coffee picks you up and calms you down. Coffee does not calm anybody down. We managed to get those ads stopped. The beef industry had a major ad campaign, "beef gives strength," that was totally deceptive. Beef gives heart disease. We worked with the New York State Attorney General, who forced the beef industry council to make some changes in the ads. Ultimately, the ads were killed completely.

EW: What do you think of the new dairy ads?

MJ: They're deceptive in that they make you think that all dairy foods are good. One ad says that whole milk is low in fat, but fifty percent of milk's calories come from fat. Americans get about one-third of their saturated fat from dairy foods, and should be eating less of many dairy foods.

We've tried to get the Federal Trade Commission to crack down on deceptive advertising. They refuse. They would almost like to close down the FTC's advertising division, it would appear. I don't think we're going to change that particular tiger's stripes. We haven't given up hope, but considering that Reagan will be in office for two more years, it's going to be difficult to get a change there. But we can still expose the companies and try to get state and other agencies to stop the ads.

EW: Do you put national policy changes above public education?

MJ: The two really go together. Our uniqueness is trying to get policy changes. And rather than tell people what the latest study on vitamin B6 happens to be, though we do some of that too, our real emphasis is to find out where the government policies are not consistent with scientific knowledge. In the case of a dangerous food additive, we may need only one good study before we demand changes in policies. In the case of dietary fiber, fat, or cholesterol, we needed many, many studies. In the case of vitamin A and prevention of cancer, I think the critical studies are being done now.

EW: Between the slow mule of nutritional science on the one hand and the Reagan administration and his industry cronies on the other, how can far-reaching programs for changing the American diet really have a chance?

MJ: I think there have been major victories in terms of nutrition policies, but further improvements at the government level will be very slow. We'd like to come up with some ways of disseminating good solid nutrition information much more broadly than it is now. We'd also like to be able to give individual consumers personalized advice, but we're going to concentrate on the components of diet that we focused on in the past. We're not going to get into a lot of controversial areas where there's very little scientific evidence and it's usually mixed, anecdotal, or uncontrolled. That's just not our forte. Our basic message to people is to eat more fresh fruits and vegetables, low-fat dairy foods, low-fat poultry products, whole grains and beans. These are foods that make up a diet high in fiber, vitamins, and minerals, and low in fat, cholesterol, sodium, and refined sugars. That, in a nutshell, is our nutrition message, and I think that's an important message for the public to get. It's very simple—not something that people need huge books to understand.

EW: Do you agree that the consumer movement in general seems to be moribund these days?

MJ: I think there has been less interest in public interest advocacy among people of college or law school level, because of the tight economy. It's harder to get a job now than it was ten years ago, so many people are going to business school. I think there is an awful lot of propaganda to portray people in business as heroes. A lot of it has to do with computers. There's such a proliferation of hype, of great fortunes made and lost. Young people are being brought up on a diet of articles about the entrepreneurs, not social activists. The pendulum swings. Social concern is not dead, it's just not chic.

EW: Is the government doing enough?

MJ: I think there's certainly enough evidence for the government to come out with much stronger dietary information. Not only stronger, but to make it available everywhere. Why don't we see government public service announcements urging people to eat whole grains? Why don't grain producers promote their products?

EW: Do nutrition scientists have a social responsibility?

MJ: Nutrition scientists are a benighted group. Their interest, in general, has not been in improving health, but in publishing papers, in getting the next research grant. I have found it very interesting to begin working in the alcohol area, where there are tremendous numbers of former government officials and researchers who are extremely concerned about not just doing research, but about applying the research and reducing the rate of alcohol problems. It's not like that in nutrition. There are occasional people—William Castelli, Jean Mayer, Mark Hegsted—but they are certainly the rare exceptions. Most nutrition researchers are concerned about what the knowledge says, but not about applying it or speaking out. They haven't exerted that leadership role. And groups like the American Society for Clinical Nutrition, the American Institute of Nutrition, the Nutrition Foundation, have all been either pro-industry or neutralized into worthlessness. I think the real leadership role in nutrition has to come from citizens groups and government. The government, even under Reagan, is doing a much better job than fifteen years ago when nutrition wasn't even a consideration. It's not a lot, but maybe it's a seed that will grow.

If I were in charge of nutrition policies or nutrition education in the government, there would be some vast changes. I would love to see either community-wide or national health education campaigns that would bring together medical communities, supermarkets, restaurants, natural foods stores, school systems, radio and TV stations, to really have a national influence on the importance of changing diet.

EW: Do you feel that CSPI is as vital as it was, let's say, five years ago?

MJ: I think the world has caught up with us in certain areas, and now there are other engines of change, especially in the food industry. We used to complain that everything advertised on television was junk, that all processed foods were junk, and that people just had to eat basic plain foods. The situation has really changed. There are supermarkets and natural foods stores that provide nutritious foods, not loaded with additives, some even grown organically. But in terms of keeping an eye on the government and trying to keep advertisers honest, of identifying dangerous food additives, I think we are as necessary as we ever were.

BILL SHURTLEFF

Charles Atlas Versus the Bodhisattva
January 1977

Bill Shurtleff and his wife Akiko Aoyagi are the co-founders and directors of the Soyfoods Center in Lafayette, Calif. They are the authors of fifteen books that have been instrumental in the burgeoning interest in soyfoods, the most influential of which they feel are The Book of Miso, The Book of Tofu, The Book of Tempeh, *and* Soyfoods Industry and Market *(a market study), and their* SoyaScan Computerized Database.

Shurtleff was interviewed by East West's *Sherman Goldman.*

EAST WEST: Would you explain the specific links between a return to the use of miso, tofu, and other traditional foods, and the solution of the world food crisis?

BILL SHURTLEFF: We are working with three factors: The first is the world food crisis; the second is the protein crisis, which is actually at the center of the food crisis; and the third is soybeans.

United Nations statistics estimate that somewhere between 15,000 and 60,000 people are dying of starvation every day now. An additional 400 million children—twice the population of the United States—have such protein deficiencies that their physical and mental growth is permanently impaired. And an estimated one quarter of all the people on the planet experience severe hunger at some point every year.

Now, as people become more affluent, they want a larger and larger percentage of their foods to be animal products. The primary offender is meat, followed by poultry, milk, eggs, cheese, and yogurt. The system that we have for producing these foods is the feedlot system, which was developed during the 1950s, when America had great agricultural excesses. We presently feed an astonishing 78 percent of all our grains in this country to livestock, and 50 percent of all the land used to grow crops is used to grow crops that are fed to animals. This tendency is becoming worse and worse. It has to be turned around, because it is now becoming a major cause of the world food crisis.

Therefore, experts studying the crisis have agreed almost unanimously that the simplest thing that individual human beings can do to relate to the world food crisis is to move in the direction of meatless and vegetarian diets, and work for the elimination of this terribly wasteful feedlot system.

The key problem in developing countries is to find enough protein—which traditionally is the highest-cost, least available source of nutrients. Experts studying the crisis are now in unanimous agreement that soybeans, consumed in the traditional forms of miso, tofu, and other soy products, are going to be the protein source of the future on planet Earth.

There are three good reasons, I think, for this prediction: First, if you had an acre of land and you wanted to grow as much usable protein on that one acre as possible, you would plant the land in soybeans. Soybeans will provide somewhere between 33 and 250 percent more usable protein per acre of land than any other farm crop. (Interestingly, brown rice is the second-best protein producer.) Second, if you had one dollar and you wanted to buy as much usable protein as possible, you would buy that in the form of soy protein. Third, for over two thousand years roughly one quarter of mankind has used soybeans as the protein backbone of their diet. The people of East Asia have been involved in an ongoing experiment to find the best ways of using soybeans as basic foods, and the results of that experiment are now manifest in terms of their daily usage. The number one most popular way of using soybeans is in the form of tofu. Roughly 50 percent of all soybeans in Asia are used as tofu, and in Japan today there are 38,000 tofu shops which make tofu daily. That's kind of like gas stations in the United States—they are everywhere. Second is miso, and third is shoyu, natural soy sauce. In addition, there is tempeh in Indonesia and a wide variety of other delicious soy products throughout East Asia.

Therefore, we feel that these traditional ways of using soybeans to produce basic foods are the most relevant to the great majority of mankind who will be using middle-level, "intermediate," technology to produce foods locally at low cost.

Many Americans are surprised to learn that their country is the largest soybean producer in the world. We produce about two-thirds of the planet's total output. These people are also surprised to learn that 95 percent of our domestic crop—after the oil has been extracted in large factories—is fed to livestock. This represents enough protein to provide all the needs of every American for three and a half years and to provide 25 percent of the needs of every person on earth, which is just about the difference between what people are getting and what they need.

It is ironic that we in the United States have taken so long to realize the tremendous value of our soybean crop. When President Nixon was in office, in one of his unguarded moments during a press conference he asked if someone could bring him one of those soybeans which were then making headlines. A Japanese news reporter who was present picked up the comment, and it was splashed all over the front pages in Japan: "Nixon's never seen a soybean." The thing that amazed the Japanese was that the president of the largest soybean-producing nation in the world didn't know what soybeans are. This is, in fact, typical. Many Americans are just now beginning to realize what soybeans are—to realize that they are, in fact, our second-largest farm crop, ahead of wheat and led only by corn. Historically, we are at a crucial juncture where we are about to realize that there is gold in the fields.

EW: Would you compare dairy food and soybeans?

BS: Even the most ecologically efficient animal products, milk and eggs, require an input of 100 pounds of grain protein in order to produce 25 pounds of eggs or milk protein; therefore, they are extremely wasteful.

The basic inefficiency in that process is now predicted to lead to the phasing out of dairy products on the planet as a whole. We were talking with people who work with one of America's largest producers of cheese, and they said that the president of the company had told them that within ten to twenty years they expect dairy milk to play a very minor role in the production of cheese and other dairy products in this country and that all of their research is going into soy proteins. The development of high-quality soymilk and soy cheese— which can be sold for a fraction of the cost of the increasingly expensive dairy cheeses and other products—will certainly be one of the major trends in the future.

Soybeans can produce high-quality protein at very low cost and still create the entire range of flavors and textures available from dairy products. The problems with digestibility of dairy foods for many non-Western peoples disappear, and therefore these foods have become highly relevant to people throughout the world.

After World War II, a man by the name of K. S. Low watched the way Pepsi-Cola and Coca-Cola were coming in and adversely affecting the health of children, so he decided to develop a soymilk product sold in Coca-Cola-type bottles. He did excellent nutritional publicity, and two years ago the sales of his product, VitaSoy, reached 150 million bottles a year—past Coca-Cola—to become Hong Kong's number one selling drink. In response to that, Coca-Cola opened its own soymilk factories. The United Nations now has a $1 million soymilk factory in Indonesia, and soymilk is well on its way to becoming one of the key sources of protein in developing countries.

Anyone can prepare their own soymilk at home for 15 cents a gallon, versus about $1.40 a gallon for dairy milk, or produce their own tofu at home in less than forty minutes for 10 cents a pound. In fact, there are many communities throughout the United States that now have a tofu maker. This person gets up in the morning, makes 10 pounds of tofu at a total cost of $1 for the entire community, which revolutionizes their food budget. The tofu is served in creamy dressings, salads, casseroles, deep-fried, or sautéed with vegetables and served in a wide variety of dishes throughout the day. Tofu is really becoming a discovery.

EDWARD ESPE BROWN

The Heart of Tassajara Cooking
April 1986

Edward Espe Brown is a Zen priest, a poet, and the author of five cookbooks: The Tassajara Bread Book, Tassajara Cooking, The Tassajara Recipe Book, Favorites of the Guest Season, *and most recently,* The Greens Cookbook, *with co-author Deborah Madison. At the time of this interview by* East West *contributing editor Barbara Stacy, Brown was head resident teacher at Green Gulch Farm, a Zen center near Mill Valley, Calif. Now "retired" from Green Gulch, he teaches cooking and leads meditation retreats.*

EAST WEST: How has your cooking been influenced by your religious practice?

EDWARD ESPE BROWN: Perhaps a good way to speak of this is to discuss some of the advice Zen master Dogen gives to cooks. One important point, he says, is to treat the food as if it were your eyesight—as though you were handling your eyes. With that kind of carefulness. Valuing each ingredient. He says that a good cook can prepare a soup with wild grasses as well as with butter. We tend to think that if we're going to make something good, we need cream and butter, some of this or that. Rather than thinking, "I have these simple ingredients and I'll make something good with these things—see what I can do with what I have." Don't treat different greens differently, don't be overjoyed with different quality ingredients, don't be discouraged with poor ingredients. A good cook will make good use of the ingredients he or she has. This not only refers to cooking—it's a good general analogy.

Dogen also said, "Don't cook with ordinary mind and don't cook with ordinary eyes."

EW: How do you interpret that?

EB: As a poetic way of saying what I've been saying. Ordinary mind and ordinary eyes say, "This is good and this isn't good. I want to use this and I don't want to use that." It's not so ordinary to find some virtue in something you might not otherwise feel deserves respect or value. The ordinary way is to have some idea of what you want to do, and everything is supposed to conform to that idea. The not-so-ordinary approach is to examine the ingredients and to let them inspire you. Then the ingredients don't have to fit into your idea of what would be good. The ingredients have their own boundless virtue—which is your virtue too. That's something I emphasize. That is the Zen spirit, so to speak.

EW: That's a good point. When we cook for guests, we tend to rush out and buy special things.

EB: A year ago I had dinner with someone who grew up in Ghana. He said that when he was growing up, they would never have thought of eating anonymous food—that is, when they didn't know who grew it or where it came from. And I was very struck by that, by how much we are willing to eat food that is anonymously grown, prepared, and packaged. It leaves out so much about what food is. Food is not just a commodity. It has something to do with the people who grew it, the people who prepared it.

I don't mean that I'm such a fanatic that I will eat a carrot only when I know where it was grown. I'm willing to eat anonymous food, but at the same time I notice that I feel less satisfied, less sustained with this food. When I have a relationship to the people at a restaurant, for instance, I feel sustained with that food much more than in another restaurant, where perhaps things may be more delicious by some standards.

I also notice the difference when I eat food from the gardens at Green Gulch or at a friend's house, where we go out and pick our vegetables. Something comes out of that—a different relationship. It's our usual way to think that food is somehow interchangeable—that one carrot is interchangeable with another, that one bunch of spinach is interchangeable with another. When things are interchangeable they lose their value. We lose our value. So with this attitude about things being interchangeable, we can't experience the bountifulness of the earth and our own generosity of spirit. I'd like to encourage people to have small gardens—or even big ones.

EW: Do you think of food nutritionally, as providing fuel for a healthy body?

EB: No, I've always found that to be a bizarre idea—"fueling," as though the body were a machine. It seems to me that there are several qualities in food, and that nutrition is only one aspect of what we're doing when we eat. There is also a spirituality and an aesthetic aspect. If you enjoy eating, you are more nourished by the food.

Then there are associations with food psychologically, like what you ate when you were growing up—you eat that kind of food and it feels reassuring. People have likes and dislikes. I don't have any problem with that. When one thinks about food strictly in terms of the right food or nutrition, it ignores people, humanness. It's like saying you're wrong to have some feeling for when you were growing up. It feels critical. I don't mean just to cater to what kind of food people like or don't like, but to relate thoroughly to who you are or who the other person is.

There are so many different ideas about the "right" diet. So if you're doing it by an intellectual approach and you're overlooking your feelings, at some point the food loses its poetic or spiritual or wider kind of sustenance.

I heard Ivan Illich [see Society, page 196] talk at Berkeley awhile back about water. He looks at things in a rather fresh way. He pointed out that people, especially in cities, no longer experience the water of dreams and imagery. We don't see water as streams and ponds, we see it as tap water, so water loses its poetry or mythology, its dream quality. Tap water is a commodity, and the same things have happened with food. When you get vegetables from a grocery, you get a plastic-wrapped package that you can't associate with sunshine and rain and earth and insects and birds and seabreeze and fog. So a lot of the food we get has lost its poetry and imagery—and the understanding of what's really included. How much the whole universe is there. We control our environment, but we don't have that universal, magical experience any more.

EW: What would you consider reasonable, basic attitudes about food in terms of your own experience and in terms of Zen teaching?

EB: When we eat, I feel very much the idea of having some appreciation and gratitude for the work that went into the food, rather than some assessing of the characteristics in scientific or nutritional or macrobiotic terms. The food as a kind of offering of various creatures, plants, or animals, and all the people's efforts that went into it. The transportation of the food, the growing of the crops. It's easy to criticize someone's effort as not being perfect enough—the farmer who is using too many pesticides, for instance—and overlook the efforts that people do make to provide and make a livelihood. For myself, all these years of living in a community and having been a cook, I can appreciate how much work goes into it once the food gets to the kitchen—the washing, the cutting, the preparing. So I feel as if I am receiving an offering, and I don't feel particularly critical or fussy. Of course, maybe I'm spoiled in that I live in a community where people are fairly careful and have certain standards.

I think that Zen emphasizes doing something with sincerity—this is how I interpret it—and with wholeheartedness, rather than the food itself being valued highly in its own context. Don't forget that the earliest Buddhist monks begged their food, so they ate whatever people offered them. That is one basic form of practice—receiving what you have been offered rather than thinking, "I'm going to take this and I'm not going to take that. And I'm going to arrange everything so that I never have to put up with things that I don't want." At the same time, if one ignores completely where the food comes from, that's a kind of carelessness, too.

EW: What do you think makes for a good cook? Do you think that some people innately have a sure sense of taste, in the sense that artists are strongly visual and musicians are strongly sound-conscious?

EB: Yes, I think someone makes a good cook who is aware of taste, and can combine that with some kind of visual awareness and awareness of textures. And again I think that there's some aesthetic sense of romance or poetry—the food's quality and vitality reflects the cook. Good cooks are people for whom food is not just a physical phenomenon.

It's not something that I can explain, but I think that the cook and the food become very much identified. I mean, I feel like after I've cooked the food, it literally has become my body—in the same way that the food is also the sunlight and the rain and the earth, and so on. It's my body and my being, and people can tell in the food.

You can change the consciousness of the person who eats what you make. It's not just the food itself, but also the kind of effort that goes into preparing it. The kind of effort that respects the food, the bountifulness of nature, and the work that's gone into it. If the cook honors all that, then someone who eats that food also feels appreciated and respected. And that's real nourishment, not just physical nourishment. Dogen says that a good cook should arouse the delight of the monks. I don't mean to belittle cooks who are more utilitarian and more tradition-conscious in providing for their family or friends—people who are making a sincere effort.

EW: In *The Tassajara Recipe Book* you have a meal chant that I like very much: "We venerate all the great teachers and give thanks for this food, the work of many people and the suffering of other forms of life." I assume that you might say that before eating—a Zen form of grace?

EB: That is a *gattha*, a verse to promote awareness. It provides a kind of concern that is as important as what you eat. Sometimes in terms of health there is perhaps too much emphasis on what you eat, rather than the spirit with which you eat.

EW: *How* you eat, you mean?

EB: How you eat. When I talk about how you eat, I don't mean to neglect *what* you eat. Because how you eat can be a way to lead you to change what you eat. The more mindful you are, the more likely you are to change your eating patterns—through awareness rather than through scientific or nutritional advice or other objective data.

At Green Gulch during a retreat week with Thich Naht Hanh, a Vietnamese Zen monk who is active in peace work, we practiced a series of verses which went throughout the meal. We did all these verses silently. I like these particular verses so much I want to share them with you.

With an empty plate we said, "Now I have this empty plate in front of me, and I am fortunate that it will soon be filled with food for today's dinner." And when the plate was filled we said, "Now that my plate is filled with food, I see the entire universe reflected here and how it contributes to my existence."

We were serving ourselves, buffet or cafeteria style, and when we sat down there was another verse: "Sitting here is like us sitting under the Bodhi tree, the body of mindfulness is upright and I am unassailed by confusions." Of course the Bodhi tree is the tree Buddha sat under when he attained enlightenment.

We looked at the food on our plates, and we said, "I see this food on my plate. I am aware that all living beings struggle for life and I hope that all living beings have enough food to eat today. I wish that they all have enough food to eat today."

Before eating we said, "I am aware that each morsel of food is the result of many labors on the part of those who produce it and bring it to our table." And when we started to eat we said with the first mouthful, "With this first bite I promise to practice love and kindness. With the second bite I promise to relieve the suffering of others. With the third bite I promise to experience the joy of others as my own. With the fourth bite I promise to live even-mindedly."

There was a verse afterward: "Now that I have finished eating and my plate is empty, I feel satisfied and content. Grateful to my parents, teachers, friends, and all beings. I vow to keep their spirit alive."

If you practice like this, it's not so easy to overeat or eat forgetfully, and I think that over a period of time, practicing these *gatthas*, someone's diet may change quite a bit. With these *gatthas*, we eat our food in a different way. With different spirit.

LAUREL ROBERTSON

Inside Laurel's Kitchen
January 1986

In this interview by East West *contributing editor Thom Leonard, natural foods cookbook author* (Laurel's Kitchen *and* The Laurel's Kitchen Bread Book *with co-authors Carol Flinders and Bronwyn Godfrey, and* The New Laurel's Kitchen *with Carol Flinders and Brian Ruppenthal) Laurel Robertson divulged her magic ingredient: "packing up love." Currently, Robertson's and her associates' principal work is the publication of the teachings of their spiritual guide, Eknath Easwaran, through their own publishing company, Nilgiri Press.*

EAST WEST: How do you see someone in the kitchen helping to end war and hunger?

LAUREL ROBERTSON: In a recent interview, Liv Ullman said you have all this love and the important thing is that you channel it. Some people can go out and move the world and some people stay at home and care for their families. That was so wise to me, because you look around and you see the drug and the teen suicide problems, and you see people who honestly thought they could have a career, go out and work, and raise their kids with one hand. We now know you can't. You can't raise your kids with one hand. You have to give it your whole self.

I think that when you're a mother—and some of the best mothers I know are fathers—there's nothing more important that you can do than make sure that your kids grow up strong and courageous and secure and sensitive to the people around them. Then you've made a contribution to the future that can't be matched by any other contribution. That's the kind of miracle that no one can work who's not a parent, though even those without children can play a part in that.

When you give that same kind of love and support to people, you're sending them off in shining armor even when you send them off with just a wonderful lunch. Because you know that by the time they get to the middle of the day when they're worn down and probably frazzled, they open up that lunch and say, "Gosh, this is great!" It's a way of packing up love and sending it off. I think it's been very much underplayed. I think the support group is just as important as the people who are out there on the front lines.

EW: How do you make an effort to eat in a way that supports local, sustainable agriculture?

LR: Just to become a vegetarian is taking a step forward. And then to start trying not to use the things that are really inappropriate. As you learn about them, to find substitutes and to keep exploring and keep trying new foods. Step by step. Things are changing. When we wrote *Laurel's Kitchen*, it was really hard to find some whole food items. It's much easier now.

EW: You say that just being a vegetarian is a big step, the first step that many people could make. Does that imply that those who choose to include some meat in their diets aren't making the first step? Can't one choose to include some meat in the diet and yet support most of these other issues we've been talking about?

LR: For myself, I think it's important to realize that other creatures love life also. To choose not to take another's life just for your own pleasure is a very positive step. I think if people were to live closer to animals it would make a difference. I don't want anyone to feel that I'm putting them down for their choices. It's such a personal decision. People are doing phenomenal work in so many areas. Everybody has to decide for themselves.

EW: A lot of people when faced with the possibility of life without meat wonder what they could possibly find to replace it.

LR: The thing that we discovered, when we first became vegetarians, was that there's a whole lot of interesting food that's non-animal. The way that we eat now is a hundred times more nutritious and is not at the expense of other creatures. We try not to buy imported produce—that's so important. Because of our choices, I think a lot of energy was freed in some way, because all of us became much better cooks. The food that we eat now is much more delicious and interesting and varied, even though we have these limitations. When you limit, you make choices that increase other things. It draws out resources from within you to make do within these limitations.

The Buddha said if you can't do something to alleviate suffering, at least do nothing to add to it. In looking around us, we see so much suffering that's unnecessary, that's constant, because people just do not know. We don't have to suffer so much, and the animals don't have to suffer from our greed if we know how to eat in a way that doesn't include them.

HELEN NEARING

The Irrepressible Helen Nearing
November 1986

Helen Nearing is perhaps best known as co-author, with her late husband Scott, of Living the Good Life, *and for her homestead, Forest Farm, which has been a pilgrimage site for alternative lifestyle seekers. Freelance writer Costas Christ interviewed Nearing at Forest Farm, near Harborside, Maine.*

EAST WEST: You and Scott often spoke of the virtues of fasting. What were your reasons for it?

HELEN NEARING: We felt that along with eating good food, it is also good to go without food occasionally. Every spring and every fall we have gone on a ten-day water fast. We did it because we thought it was an excellent rest for the body. On holidays we also fasted. When other people were overeating on Thanksgiving, Christmas, New Year's, Easter, and July 4th, we would deliberately undereat. We were conscientious objectors to overeating. People should not overeat when there are others in the world starving. What food there is should be shared. Our contribution was to eat less, when others were eating more.

EW: On several occasions you have voiced criticism of natural foods advocates for being preoccupied with their bodies. Is it possible to pay too much attention to what we eat?

HN: Basically, one should have enough to eat, and one should have the right kinds of foods, but from then on your whole life begins. Food is a basic part of life, but it should not be all-important. Beyond it lies creative expression through one's interests and activities.

EW: From the exploration of Eastern mysticism with Krishnamurti, you went on to join and eventually marry Scott Nearing, one of the most outspoken radicals in America. You have also co-authored several books on socialism. How have you been able to bring together the spiritual and political dimensions of your life?

HN: I think it's a whole process of wanting to live as fully as possible, to contribute as much as possible. It can be on the physical plane or the spiritual plane. I look at life as a great opportunity, as a day in school, with the possibility of learning and contributing. One can do this in many ways—physically, by growing great food, by cultivating a good garden—and also by one's political activities, making sure that everyone has the opportunity that is the most for their growth. From there it goes on to spiritual things. It is all a part of the branches of a tree reaching up and reaching out. I don't feel that my socialism in any way goes against my spiritual ideas.

EW: You are best known today as a teacher of "the good life," a title taken from your books. What is the essence of your good life philosophy?

HN: To grow, to learn, to experience, to contribute, to share, to be intensely in the moment in which you are living, to get the most out of everything that happens to you and to realize that we are all here to contribute and to share. It is all a part of a unity.

KIM CHERNIN

The Hungry Self
January 1987

In The Obsession: Reflections on the Tyranny of Slenderness *and her subsequent book,* The Hungry Self: Women, Eating & Identity, *Kim Chernin shows that anorexia, bulimia, and obsessions with weight are actually symbolic masking systems hiding a more profound distress of confused or estranged female identity in a male-dominated culture. Chernin's analysis of the roots of eating disorders led her through a series of revealing psycho-analytical forays. She examined the complexities of early infancy and childhood, emotional relations between mother and daughter, the lack of developmental models for girls and women at important life-turning points, the pressures of male culture for women to conform to aesthetic ideals, and how all this results in obsessive preoccupations with food, dieting, calories, weight control, and tacit self-destruction that presently grip many modern women.*

Kim Chernin was interviewed by East West *senior writer Richard Leviton.*

EAST WEST: What is an eating disorder or food obsession?

KIM CHERNIN: It's a preoccupation with food, dieting, body size and weight, and control of the appetite that gradually takes over many of one's other interests. Or it becomes the focus for such an enormous distress, as in anorexia or bulimia, that one has to say, "Help me, somebody, I can't live with this." Obviously there are minor degrees of that, but when you use a word like "disorder" you're speaking about a life that has come to be disordered, that can't go on as before. The presenting of that symptom of distress among most women today is as an eating disorder, rather than, for example, as alcoholism or an obsession with the male body. Men often will be obsessed with the female body but they too are dealing with serious issues they can't express differently. But oddly enough in our time the typical way these issues show up for a woman is with a food obsession.

EW: In *The Obsession* you note, "An eating disorder is a profoundly political act." What did you mean by this?

KC: If a group of suppressed women cannot become conscious of what is happening to them, they will find a disguising symbolic system through which to express their unhappiness, their discontent, their outrage, their refusal. In spite of women's liberation, which was a very important social phenomenon, many women have not articulated their discontent at being women. And as a culture—even including women's liberation—we have failed to articulate this through the entire scope of the problem. Basically, as women we have no sense of what it means to be a woman. We know what we've been *told* women are, yet we have a sense that we can't possibly be that, that there's more to us. When we start to liberate ourselves, the impulse is to take on power through an imitation of men. But this leaves the whole female problem unarticulated, and this inarticulate distress comes up with an overwhelming concern with how the body looks, this body that has in fact never been invited to enter culture.

When a woman goes into a new job, returns to the university, becomes a professor, she thinks she needs to be tailored and slender, which is to say, having her body become much more like that of a man. Although we don't admit this, because many of us are feminists and outspokenly in favor of female development, through our bodies we express our compliance. Every time we try to be thin and more like a man in the body, we are saying, "We don't quite have the right or courage or the daring to be women in the sense that we would define ourselves."

EW: Were you addressing this male repressive attitude when you wrote that an eating disorder "is an effort to control or eliminate the passionate aspects of the self in order to gain the approval and prerogatives of masculine culture"?

KC: Yes, it's an effort to eliminate the passionate aspects and everything that is reminiscent of the mother's power from the point of view of a helpless, dependent child. Everything that has to do with nature and the uncontrollability of natural cycles. Ultimately I see this as a struggle between body and mind, mind representing an effort to be in control, body representing something that cannot be controlled. This long-standing cultural problem, which we date back to the beginnings of patriarchal civilization, has been dumped in the woman's lap and has reappeared as eating disorders. That's why I call it a very dense symbolic system, one that in fact contains all the old cultural concerns, but in such a disguised form that we can't recognize them. As a result, we trivialize the problem.

EW: Throughout your books you often refer to the new or "future woman." You say there is a "sleeping giant in the female psyche," a "female soul which is not starving itself to death" and in which "there must be hiding all that the dominant culture has driven away from itself." What is this woman like?

KC: We don't know at all. We cannot even begin to imagine what this woman would be like because, first, we're presently stripping down the negatives that have always been said about women, and second, we must undo the effort we make to imitate men in order to have a self or social power. These two are such enormously preoccupying labors that we haven't had the opportunity yet to dream up, create, or even fantasize this future woman. I definitely stop myself in this leap ahead to imagine the future woman because it's a leap of bad faith until I have finished the work of exploring all the obstacles that presently exist to creating that woman. I'm still involved in the work of trying to figure out why we immediately try to imitate men, why we so dislike ourselves, and to state for ourselves how fundamentally *empty* we as women are, how we don't have a clue what we're really about. I've only taken the step of fully acknowledging this fact, that if I'm not this negative female creature I've been called for several thousand years of patriarchal culture, and if I'm not this pseudo-man, somebody attempting to have a self and power by imitating men, then I'm nothing. So I've reached the stage of being willing to confront the nothingness of myself as a woman, but I dare not yet step beyond that. I mean a real absence of any authentic qualities as a being.

EW: In this case what is food?

KC: Food is precisely the effort to fill that existential howling, to give yourself as a woman something, desperately and urgently, that will make your terrible hunger for your Self go away.

EW: This symbolic hunger can sometimes lead to actual obesity?

KC: Definitely. The desire for food typically arises in the psyche when you split off part of your potential for development. In the case of women, since we have split off our entire potential for development in order to adapt to a patriarchal setting, we come of age howling with hunger. Since we don't know how to name the hunger existentially, and we don't know how to fill it developmentally, we fill it with food. It's not as if this is unique to women. Men often fill it with women, alcohol, or cigarettes. But the urgency of our coming into social power now for the first time and finding out that social power is not the answer to this serious soul crisis—this I feel is worth articulating.

EW: Do you feel it is enough to develop a new identity for women, or do you have to change the men as well?

KC: You have to change everything, but if you start out changing the women, you'll end up changing everything else. If a woman authentically comes to the awareness of what these thousands of years of patriarchal culture have meant, and what it really means to step out and say, "I'm now going to create a woman, for the first time ever"—because woman is certainly not what men have told us we are—therefore every woman alive today has this amazing task of creating the new woman.

EW: With women knocking on the closed door of American culture and the dominant male values denying them authentic entry, isn't what is at play a complete denial of what you call the Mother or the Feminine, both in society and in the individual males? Is there among men a widespread non-acceptance of the other half of their wholeness which is then projected outwards into a rejection of living women?

KC: Yes, when we raise the issue of an eating disorder, we're talking about a split. The first split is the mind/body/spirit split. Then there is the culture/nature split, a male/female split. Ultimately the problem is a question of human wholeness, though it's a difficult one to raise because of our gender-training. We are so taught that certain qualities belong to a certain gender, that it is difficult to entertain the idea that any one human being might contain *both* the qualities assigned to either gender, and that the fundamental human task is precisely to contain and develop these qualities in oneself. But these splits and our lack of wholeness come up in eating disorders simply because of the way men view a large body in women and the way women come to view this large body in themselves. The body is the carrier of these disowned qualities.

EW: So the whole eating obsession aspect of your work is really a doorway to another level of awareness?

KC: Yes. The eating disorder is like a Band-Aid placed over this enormous spiritual yearning. What we're talking about is an overwhelming yearning for a Self, a place in culture, and a spiritual tradition of our own. Believe it or not, we are trying to handle this yearning by giving ourselves food to eat, or transforming our bodies into what we think they should be. But what's raging and roaring inside women is this hunger for an authentic female spiritual and cultural tradition.

The point at which a woman is dealing with an eating disorder, trying to move on to the fundamental spiritual quest, is a point where crisis means both danger and opportunity. It is overwhelmingly dangerous until you become conscious of what you're struggling with. You could actually manage to starve yourself to death because you cannot awaken to the fact that your hunger is a spiritual hunger. You could starve to death from not knowing what you're starving for.

EW: You write that "weight belongs to us by nature" and it is not, according to new research, medically dangerous for a woman to be overweight, and that we should "let women grow large, become mature, and carry in pride the natural wonder of the human body in all its abundance." Is this a kind of alternative aesthetic bodily ideal?

KC: No. It means that she should have a body that tells her how it wants to be, rather than a body she's constantly trying to prune and pare back and reduce to match a cultural ideal. Some women end up slender, some end up larger than they would have imagined they'd like to be, and some end up in the middle. Very few women in any case are going to conform to a cultural ideal that is right for a thirteen-year-old, and very few women past thirteen or even at thirteen are going to have the kind of body which is currently fashionable—adolescent, slender, and underdeveloped.

EW: Do you ever recommend specific dietary programs?

KC: Right now I'm in a profound crisis of disbelief about systems. There must be some intuitive knowledge about what every person needs. I gave up the effort to have a diet that matches any one system, because it's like saying, how many hours of sleep is correct, how much pleasure, how much air?

HARVEY AND MARILYN DIAMOND

Fit for Life
February 1987

"We're the only species in the world that, when finished eating, must medicate itself to move the food out of our guts," say Harvey and Marilyn Diamond, authors of the immensely popular and controversial "natural hygiene" books, Fit for Life *and* Fit for Life II. *The Fit for Life program includes eating a primarily raw, whole foods, vegetarian diet, regularly exposing oneself to fresh air and sunshine, staying physically active, and developing a spiritual outlook. Although detractors within nutrition and health research fields criticize it, the Diamonds' program continues to gain proponents and generate interest among many who see a personal need for a change to a cleaner lifestyle.*

East West *editor Mark Mayell interviewed the Diamonds at their home near Los Angeles.*

EAST WEST: Were you surprised at the sales for *Fit for Life?*

HARVEY DIAMOND: We always knew it had the potential, but we have to say we were surprised. Nobody thought that it would become the biggest-selling health book in the history of publishing.

MARILYN DIAMOND: I had told Harvey when we started it that we would sell three million copies in hardcover, and we probably will in the long run. We've already sold almost two million.

EW: What do you think was the main reason behind what can only be described as the phenomenal popularity of *Fit for Life?*

HD: Number one, it is extraordinarily simple, so any person can pick up and understand it without a medical dictionary. Number two, and I think most important, it was instantly verifiable. We made this point over and over—don't take our word for this, just do it for one week. And the fact is that one week of doing it *will* prove it. It has subsequently proved itself in the marketplace because people did it. The only way to sell two million copies is by word of mouth. There's no publicity on earth that can get that kind of sales. And word of mouth happens when people use it and it works, and then they share it out of enthusiasm.

EW: In addition to the very good word of mouth, you also received much criticism from doctors and nutritionists.

MD: We received criticism at the same time that we received congratulations. The criticism got the press. Not everyone in the medical profession was stacked up negatively against our book. There was a small, noisy group of offended people, but there was an equally powerful group that expressed their delight about being able to present to the people that they were treating a common-sense, natural, well-balanced program of eating that not only helped people lose weight, but that also remarkably reduced their symptoms of degenerative disease.

The only thing that affected us in that period of time when there was a considerable amount of negativity was the rudeness of it. People were being dishonest. They were quoting us out of context. They were attacking us when it was obvious they hadn't read our material. It became obvious to us that this was a group of people speaking out for the interests that they were trying to protect, like the sugar, dairy, and livestock industries.

HD: There's been a tremendous backlash from that. Now that the book's been out for over a year and a half, the results are starting to come in. So a lot of these detractors have shut up because there's nothing to talk about. You can't stand around saying something doesn't work if hundreds of thousands of people say, "Hey, this is great." You start to look like an idiot. Time has been our best ally.

EW: How do you respond to charges that the scientific evidence isn't there to back up your claims?

HD: That's hardly worth discussing. I'll tell you honestly, the science is there. If people say it's not there it's like saying the moon's made of green cheese.

EW: Or that the studies are old?

MD: The fact that the studies are old only substantiates that this has been around a long time. The very cornerstone of the food combining principles was laid by Ivan Pavlov. That guy was no slouch. Also, there are new as well as old studies.

EW: Do you know of any tests or studies that have been generated as a result of *Fit for Life*'s popularity?

HD: We can point out specific studies in 1902, in 1926, in 1947, and during the '50s, '60s, and '70s, that show that food combining is viable. In that three-quarters of a century, there is not one reference that can be made to any study done anywhere, anytime that proves it not to be effective.

MD: It's just pure prejudice. It's relatively newly uncovered information and it goes against the four-food-group mentality.

HD: The four-food lobby.

MD: Marion Burroughs of *The New York Times* wrote that none of this work was scientifically well-founded and that it had been refuted in other studies. So we contacted her and we said, "What studies? We need to know this." She had none. She had taken the word of some deceased cardiologist who had a very poor background in nutrition, a doctor from the Veteran's Hospital in the

Bronx who is on the board of the sugar industry, and a third doctor from Harvard who's on the board of the egg and dairy industries. And she said those are the people who said it doesn't work.

HD: I wrote to her and challenged her to send me the studies disproving *Fit for Life*. So far, no response. At the bottom of my letter I told her that I subsequently found out that the same month that our book was published, so was hers. And hers hasn't sold a hundred copies yet. I think she's a little jealous.

There will always be detractors for anything. All new information all through history has been attacked. Probably always will be.

MD: In 1850 a medical journal said that the most one should bathe is once a week because it was injurious to health. At that time there were natural hygienists just like us who had been responsible for a great improvement in health just by pushing sanitation and commonsense living. They were saying things that we take for granted nowadays, and they were attacked. They were called quacks. Another example: The medical profession of that era denied water to people who had temperatures. Fever patients died of dehydration at the same time that natural hygienists were pleading to just give them water. And they were attacked.

Give us another two decades and people will be taking food combining for granted because it streamlines digestion. The truth is, this is a reform movement. It is going to take the level of health for the people of this country into a whole new place.

ALAN WATTS

Alan Watts Over Breakfast
September 1972

Alan Watts, "the brain and the Buddha of American Zen," probably was as respon-
sible as any single person for introducing an entire generation to Eastern spirituality
and mysticism. An engaging writer and an articulate speaker, his brand of "spiritual
entertainment" in the 1950s and '60s popularized Zen at a time when it was known
mainly to a small cadre of Beats and academics. The Way of Zen, published in 1957,
and Watts's numerous radio and television appearances provided compelling descrip-
tions of mystical experiences and helped change the spiritual climate of the West.

East West's Roger Alan Jones interviewed Watts on a Sunday morning a little over
a year before he died in 1973 at the age of fifty-eight. True to Watts form, their conver-
sation ranged from Zen communities to the future of humanity, with a stop en route at
his ideas on diet and lifestyle.

EAST WEST: How can we describe your lifestyle?

ALAN WATTS: Well, it is bohemian in the European sense of the word, rather than
beatnik or hippie in the American sense. Beatniks and hippies are Americans,
and that's an American lifestyle. Coming from Europe, I'm a bohemian, and
it's different.

EW: Incidentally, where did you come from at age twenty-three—was it England?

AW: I came from London. Strongly influenced by France.

EW: How does a European bohemian live?

AW: Oh, he's much more colorful than an American hippie or beatnik, or the later
kind, the group that calls themselves "freaks"—they're dowdy. Hippies used to
go in for a certain kind of colorfulness. But the European bohemian rejoices in
good wine, good bread, good cooking, and the relaxed convivial life. And he
loves painting, sculpture, music, likes to sing, play instruments, and all that
kind of thing—but it's a very, very relaxed attitude, and is sexually rather
liberated.

EW: With your background and all your writing, I'm surprised that you aren't a
vegetarian.

AW: I have two principles: I will not kill an animal unless I'm going to eat it, and I won't kill an animal myself unless I'm really hungry and there's nothing else around to eat. Then I'll hunt. But not until then. The second principle is, if I kill an animal, it is my solemn duty to cook it well, and not insult it by serving it on a sloppy platter. The kitchen stove is an altar where one offers sacrifice, and you should do it with all the reverence due an altar. That's my basic philosophy of cooking.

EW: What about the health part of eating animals?

AW: Nobody knows the answer to that. There are vegetarians who have lived to be a hundred, and carnivores who have lived to be a hundred. There are people who smoke constantly who never got lung cancer, people who died of lung cancer who never smoked. There are people who drank, like Bertrand Russell, and lived to be over ninety. There are people who didn't drink and died young. I know a methodist minister who got a very serious illness from drinking too much milk. I don't think we know really very much about this at all. And so I simply follow the dietetic rules devised by the great chefs of the world, the great Chinese chefs and the great Frenchmen.

EW: Do any rules come to mind that you can pass on?

AW: One should never eat boiled onions. Onions should be sautéed in butter first. Never boil vegetables. Never boil meat. Only, at most, simmer them. And thereby one preserves all the energies in them, the vitamins. The best method of cooking vegetables is the stir-fry method of the Chinese, which uses a wok. A very small quantity of sesame oil or peanut oil is put into the bottom of the pan, and when it's smoking hot, the vegetables are thrown in. They're all previously chopped into bite-size pieces, and tossed rapidly with a spoon for about one minute to never more than three minutes. Then they are swiftly dished out. And they are crisp and hot, and they are exquisite. You put certain seasonings in, like soy sauce, or whatever you may use. You first put shredded fresh ginger into the oil, and then the vegetables follow. And go quickly! You have to have everything ready and everybody at the table—and zoom! it's served like that.

EW: You said you liked cushions because then you don't need furniture.

AW: I have very little furniture. I don't have any overstuffed armchairs or overstuffed couches. I don't have any bedsteads. I have pads. Bedsteads with headboards and glass balls on them and all that kind of thing strike me as utterly depressing sleeping machines. I don't even have a bedroom. I have always just curled up on the pad in the living room, or in my library, and usually I sleep under a Mexican blanket. All those bedrooms have struck me as a total waste of space, and they're very depressing places because as a child you would be sent to bed when you were a nuisance. Therefore, the idea of going to bed has never agreed with me, unless I had an attractive lady to accompany me. Or unless I was just plain tired. I always look upon chairs as surgical appliances. They're sort of ungainly perches for people who are not related to the earth.

EW: The reason for the robe is what?

AW: It's comfortable. Trousers are garments for shapely women only. They castrate men, they're impossible for sitting on the floor, they're very uncomfortable, and really ridiculous. They make us look like monkeys. And when the Japanese converted to trousers they looked just horrible because they're not the right figure for Western clothes. They all look like crows or funny birds of some kind, or monkeys running around, and they've abandoned the most comfortable dress in the world.

EW: Roshi Kapleau says that you interpret a certain koan with Basho [the "polishing of the brick"] as zazen not being a necessary way to satori.

AW: There *is* no such thing as a "necessary way to satori," except insofar as you yourself consider that there is a way that's necessary for you. If you have to go through that way, you have to go through that way, and it can't be helped. But you can't program satori, because you can't "get" satori. There is nothing, nothing one can do to "get" satori, and all the disciplines you go through are simply ways of proving to yourself that you can't get it. When you know that you can't get it, and you *really* know it, then you have it.

I practice zazen, but I do it because I like it. I don't do it to get satori. And I'm all for people practicing zazen if they dig it. But I don't regard it as a means to an end. And that's Dogen's teaching, that zazen, properly understood, is Buddha. It's the same thing. I think what is not understood by Westerners, and is also not understood by many Japanese, is that after so many generations every religion undergoes a change because pious enthusiasts, or priests, send their children to study at a young age. And the children aren't naturally interested, especially adolescent boys, or college-age boys who would rather be over the wall chasing girls. But papa says, "You go to the monastery!" So they get all these goofing-off boys in the monastery, and they have to put them into order.

So they develop a certain kind of discipline. It's the same in Jesuit seminaries, it's the same all over the world. I had my fill of ecclesiastical boys' boarding schools in England. I don't want any more of that bullshit.

Westerners who come to the study of Zen are not adolescent boys, they are people with a natural interest, a serious interest in enlightenment, in meditation. So to put them through the militaristic kind of training which goes on in the Zen monastery is perfectly ridiculous.

EW: You're saying this militarism is primarily an order-generator?

AW: It's an older generation's attitude to the boys, who have no natural interest in Zen. So when they meditate, they hit them on the shoulders with a stick, and, to my mind, this is a gross interference with meditation. It's undignified, and it's stupid, but Westerners think, "Oh, it's very esoteric to sit, and it's good for cultivating humility." There's nothing more arrogant than cultivating humility. I'm not of either a Rinzai or Soto "chop-chop" big-discipline Zen school. It's kind of a "cool Zen."

DIET & HEALTH

Gloria Swanson

Michio Kushi

David Goldbeck

Nikki Goldbeck

GLORIA SWANSON

Having a Good Time
August 1973

Gloria Swanson, whose "fabulous face was world famous for fifty years" (as Bill Dufty said in his introduction to this interview) was not only "a very classy lady—a supercelebrity movie queen sex symbol of the roaring twenties" and confidante of the likes of Joseph P. Kennedy, but also an outspoken advocate of a natural foods diet. Swanson, who died in her eighties in 1983, epitomized a life of curiosity and vivacity mingled with conscience and a sense of justice.

In his free-ranging interview with her, East West's Paul Hawken talked with Swanson about natural foods, government irresponsibility, education, the possibilities of life, and "a lot of other things."

EAST WEST: What do you think is the cause of disease?

GLORIA SWANSON: Toxemia. It can be caused by emotional reasons as well as physical ones. We are all a little like Pavlov's dog—we've been programmed—but that is not the way nature wants it at all. I found out that the emotional side can give you toxemia as well as bad foods and the chemicals, like eating from habit. Today there is much toxemia caused by over-medication. A friend went to the Mayo Clinic for arthritis and was told to take twenty-six aspirins a day. What is that going to do to the stomach? What is the use of curing one if you are going to make something else worse? You know, I have had no education whatsoever—thank God!—and I don't believe in colleges because what comes out of them these days is not what I call bright minds. It is all book learning— they haven't a thought of their own. Far better to live, live and not think you are going to make mistakes, and if you do, so what! This too shall pass, and do not cling to it.

EW: If chemicals are a major cause of toxemia, what do you think of our present food laws, which are supposed to protect us from toxic substances?

GS: The government has known about the ill effects of chemicals in our foods for a long time. Dr. Hueper of the "pure" food department (and I put that in quotes) wrote a paper in 1956 for a symposium in Rome where outstanding scientists from around the world had gathered to try to find out what causes cancer. His paper listed some thirty odd things that people used in their homes daily. On top of the list was *all* insecticides, next was *all* detergents, and then it went on to the various types of pots, pans, enamels, plastics, and so on. Do you think this report ever came out in the paper? It is only in the last four years that the papers and the magazines have suddenly come out with this type of story. People would invite me on their radio or TV shows and say, "Please now, don't talk about the poisons in the food because we won't have a sponsor if you do."

EW: Then you believe the government has known about this all the time?

GS: Yes. They could have stopped it. I guess it is better to bankrupt the health of a nation than it is to bankrupt a company that is making the stuff. We can see the power politics here.

EW: The Delaney amendment supposedly protects us from cancer-causing substances being put in our food. It has been called the strongest piece of food legislation in this century, and yet many food processors are trying to scuttle it, calling it "extreme" and "unscientific." What is the story behind this law?

GS: Representative Delaney started getting involved after World War II, about the same time I became aware of the growing use of pesticides. Around '46, '47, '48 there was a group of doctors in a small hospital in Glendale. They decided they could not cure degenerative diseases or children's diseases unless they could give food that was natural. They decided that they were going to have a farm. They bought some land in Escondido not far from Mexico. I arrived in Pasadena the same morning the first truck arrived from the farm bringing the fresh produce. It had come overnight in the coolness. It reminded me of Paris when we used to go to market at 4 or 5 a.m. because we had been up all night. We would have some onion soup and watch the lorries coming in with the fresh produce. It was really the first beginnings of the health food movement there, because up to that time health food stores just had packaged nuts, juices, and what not, but this was real: real fresh vegetables. Not canned vegetables with sugar and God-knows-what to keep it from changing color or spoiling. Fresh vegetables from an organic farm, which meant the soil was healthy.

Around that time I became acquainted with the Delaney committee, which had been out for two or three years going all around the U.S. trying to find out what was really going on, trying to do something about the proliferation of chemicals because our laws were so antiquated, having been passed at the turn of the century. So I got all excited and read three volumes of testimony that had been accumulated up until then. It was a pretty terrifying ten days. I got to the point where I wouldn't eat anything—just yeast and water. At that point I was asked by Bess Truman if I would make a speech at the White House to five hundred ladies of the congressional wives' club.

They assumed I was going to talk about the gossip of Hollywood. I made this speech, and I must say they were shocked. I am sure they wanted to know who Clark Gable was in love with, and I got up and talked about the female sex hormone pellets that were stuck into the backs of chickens. I told them about one vet who said the American public would be happy to know they were eating sterilized pus. So I went on to the next sentence in which the vet was asked how he knew about this, and his reply was that he had seen as much as a cup of pus taken from a chicken carcass and placed in the sterilizer. They were so surprised. It is so incredible! Why, if I came along with a bottle with a skull and crossbones on it and said, "Here's a little lead, do you mind if I give you a drop on your lettuce?" You'd scream at me. "Do you mind if I give you a little arsenic?" They'd put me in jail. "How about a little mercury?" They would throw the key away! Well, that is only three out of thousands.

The chickens today are like machines; they are zombies, they do not get to pick and choose their food. Stuffed with antibiotics and hormones just like our cattle. When I hear of a meat shortage, I say thank goodness, people will be healthier now. Meat ferments and makes people smell. Everybody is so worried in this country about underarm odor and bad breath, and they should be because they eat what makes it. I could leave a bathroom, and swear to God you couldn't tell anyone had been in there.

EW: Do you think the Delaney amendment passed because of your speech to the wives of congressmen?

GS: Rep. Delaney has given me a letter to that effect, and keeps on telling everybody that, because I gave that speech and told them to go home and tell their husbands. "Tell them about it because if you are not worried about it for yourselves, please take care of your children and grandchildren."

EW: Despite the good intentions of the Delaney amendment, the food industry is rushing pell mell towards artificial and synthetic foods. Do you think that there is really any hope, biologically speaking, for this generation or subsequent generations?

GS: It depends entirely on the energy of the generation coming up. Look what happened to you. The worst sinners are the best saints. The young people I have met have given me great hope. And when you see what is happening right now in the establishment! I am thankful for Nader. I would like to see him president. He's training a lot of youngsters and making them think. Many young people detached themselves from material things and got involved with drugs, which became another hell for them.

When you start abusing your body, you are abusing the most awesome thing in the whole solar system. Man did not create it, but he did not come from nowhere either. There is higher intelligence, there is a creator. This is such a precious thing. Our body is so fantastic that it should be kept in the best of condition. Children should be taught that the body is beautiful and they should think of themselves as beautiful so that when they look at someone else, they see their own beauty.

My understanding of you reflects my own horizons and my own life. The bigger your horizon, and believe me you do not get this from college but rather from life itself, the greater will be your understanding. Those who seek should travel—it is one of the best educators. People are always getting stuck. I started traveling when I was eight years old. I was always moving from one army post to another. I first got to California in 1916 and was there for four years. After that, every year I went abroad; then I moved to New York, then to Europe, then back to California, and so I was gaining knowledge. I was like a sponge. As a child I became interested in the smallest things. Once it was even ants. I read everything available on ants. It is so important for children to inquire. Do you know that some children do not even know what a farm is?

I think young people are disillusioned with their parents. Seeing so much strain and stress, I think they want to go back to that common sense. Someone asked me if I thought it was a passing fad, going back to the land. Certainly not all will make it out there. There is a lot of dirty hard work to be done, and only the strongest and most determined people are going to do it. The ones who I think will do it are those who know what hell is like and who don't want that for themselves anymore—and they don't want it for their children or their children's children.

NIKKI AND DAVID GOLDBECK

The Guiding Lights of Whole Foods
April 1988

Since 1971 Nikki and David Goldbeck have worked together lecturing on the issues of food, nutrition, and ecology, and demonstrating cooking around the world—concerns that are distilled into practical terms in their five books. Their 1973 The Supermarket Handbook: Access to Whole Foods *sold 860,000 copies and unquestionably put the Goldbecks on the map as natural foods advocates of national stature. Their investigative thoroughness has ruffled food industry feathers but earned them kudos from food activist colleagues and the popular press. It was the publication in 1983 of their* American Wholefoods Cuisine, *and the success of their several appearances on television, that were instrumental in bringing the 1970s natural foods movement to the mainstream.*

East West senior writer Richard Leviton interviewed the Goldbecks at their home in upstate New York after their two-month, fourteen-city tour across the United States promoting their newest book, The Goldbecks' Guide to Good Food. *Today the Goldbecks continue to transplant the natural foods revolution into conservative middle America, traveling widely to make a case for informed shopping, sensible nutrition, and the joy of cooking.*

EAST WEST: In the *Guide*, you state, "Our food supply is getting better all the time, and though it is still laden with problems, there is a greater selection of whole and minimally processed foods than shoppers have seen in decades." How have things changed in the natural foods industry since you began?

NIKKI GOLDBECK: Supermarkets are selling more bulk foods, but the natural foods stores are cutting back because there are so many new packaged goods. Natural foods packaging is trying much harder to look like mainstream supermarket products to attract consumers who, before, wouldn't look at natural foods or even consider a whole grain cereal. Now it looks familiar to them. But I'm questioning where a lot of the energy is being concentrated. I'd rather buy a potato chip that's unpeeled, unsalted, and fried in a better oil, but, let's face it, a potato chip is still not a whole potato. I see too much emphasis put on natural snacks and candy bars. It's wonderful that we have choices, but there are so many candies in the market now that I'm concerned that kids might be attracted to natural foods through the candy aisle.

DAVID GOLDBECK: To me, the most important issue in the natural foods industry is quality. Unless natural foods stores have quality, they have nothing—they're just vitamin shops or mini-supermarkets. My greatest concern is that some of the new operators seem to think it's okay to carry anything if it's on the label. We start to see white flour products, hydrogenated oils, and occasionally food additives. When the stores diminish the quality of their products, they lose their entire reason for being.

EW: It comes down to a division in stores between what has been called the purist approach, in which the store preselects only the most impeccable products, and the maximum choice approach, in which the consumer chooses among a variety of not-always-strictly-pure items. Would you come down on the purist side?

DG: Absolutely. Otherwise there's no difference between the natural foods stores and the supermarket with its freedom of choice. The natural foods store must continue to be the conscience of the food industry. I praise them highly for carrying the torch for so long, for putting up with abuse and name-calling, and I would hate to see this purity sullied, which would happen if they started putting wrong products in the stores.

EW: You say that even though our food supply is better than ever, it's still laden with problems, and that the future of wholefoods is still under threat from the conventional food industry. What are some of these problems?

DG: Food labeling is one. Although most of the standards have been cracked open and we have almost complete labeling on most products today, there are still some big problem areas, like oils. Oils can be listed alternately if they're not a predominant ingredient. That means you can have palm, coconut, hydrogenated oil, or lard listed, but not know which one you're getting.

Another big problem today is what I call puffery, which is misleading, overblown advertising statements like "all natural, lite, no cholesterol, no preservatives." These terms are used very deceptively.

NG: Certain oils are promoted as having no cholesterol, which is true, but there is no cholesterol in any vegetable oil. You might as well say there's no cholesterol in beer. You see much more of this misleading labeling in supermarket products, certainly. Some products say "all natural" but contain vegetable gums or modified food starches, or some say "no preservatives," suggesting that there are no other chemicals involved, when there are.

Packaging is another problematic area. The proliferation of plastics in packaging is frightening. It's almost impossible to get information about the ingredients in plastics. I'm concerned with the growth of microwave ovens and the amount of plastic packaging going directly into the oven. There has been almost no research on the possible interactions between the foods and the plastic materials. Of all the packaging materials currently in use, plastics present the most concern in terms of human exposure to carcinogens. This is an issue that's not being raised enough. The only lasting solution to the packaging problem is one people don't want to hear: fewer packaged foods.

EW: Isn't your call for a return to this purism somewhat anachronistic in our yuppie-gourmet times?

NG: That's one of the reasons we've done it. Our book was intended to hit the heartstrings of those people who can relate to this way of presenting information and look back into their own lives and see how far off the course they may have gotten. We went to a party the other night in our community where many of our friends are vegetarians and health-conscious. Where it used to be we'd see whole grains, there was lasagna made with white flour and sushi made with white rice. I looked at the foods and thought, "This is definitely a new level of natural foods."

DG: I also take a long view, back to the 1870s, before processed foods. It may take another eighty years to bring the food industry back to this middle ground. We're just carrying on a tradition started by people many years earlier.

EW: Is one aspect of that older tradition the preservation of the family farm and our country's agricultural health?

DG: The organic movement, and the whole idea of growing foods without pollution, has always been the philosophical issue for us and our main goal. The new book, like *The Supermarket Handbook*, is dedicated to the preservation of the family farm. That's our poetic way of reminding people that there is a real connection between how food is grown and what foods they buy.

MICHIO KUSHI

The Macrobiotic Approach to Cancer
March 1983

Michio Kushi (see Family, page 34) appeared on the cover of the first issue of East West *in 1971. The article he wrote for that seminal issue had to do with what he called "the greatest crisis the world has ever faced"—the physical and psychological weakening of the individual. This "biological degeneration" is evident in modern society by the pervasion of cancer and AIDS and other immune deficiency diseases. This interview with Kushi centered on the macrobiotic approach to cancer.*

EAST WEST: Can you summarize for us the key factors which contribute to the development of cancer?

MICHIO KUSHI: There are many theories today about the cause of cancer, including those of radiation, environmental pollution, heredity, and viruses, as well as certain psychological theories; but practically speaking, with all types of cancer, the basic cause is the day-to-day dietary practice of the individual. These other factors such as radiation and pollution can accelerate the accumulation and spread of cancer, but only if the body is already in a weakened state. The reason that some people would be more susceptible to the effects of radiation, for instance, is that the overall condition of their blood and tissues is not healthy as a result of their lifetime dietary habits. Therefore the cancer cannot be changed unless a proper diet is begun.

EW: How do you define cancer?

MK: I would say that it is the ultimate physical self-protection method of the body. The actual process is a localization of abnormal cells which have been created by excesses of certain food factors such as protein and fat.

EW: In the past, you have said that macrobiotics acts to strengthen the whole body to the point at which the tumor, or cancer, is no longer necessary as a focalizing point for the disease, but now your explanation seems to be more that a macrobiotic diet actually dissolves the tumor. Can you explain more specifically how this works?

MK: When a person starts on a macrobiotic diet, the blood begins to change. As the body is nourished by this new blood, some of the abnormal cells actually change to normal cells, as well as some abnormal cells dying as new ones are created. Let me make an analogy with plants.

The leaves of a plant are like the internal cells in a human body, but they are open, exposed, and more visible. The liquid that passes up through the roots and stem to the leaves is like our blood. This liquid actually becomes the cells of the plant, or organs of the body, so if this liquid is not proper for the plant, then the leaves become misshapen and deformed. However, if the liquid that flows up the stem becomes correct, then either the leaves will change to a more normal form or will die, and new healthy leaves will grow. It is the combination of the liquid and plant together that makes the change.

So, cancer in the body usually localizes in one organ, which is like a leaf on a plant. This is helpful because it is saving millions of other cells. The factor that determines which branch or organ will localize the disease is related to the quality of the excess taken in. For example, excess sugar or dairy foods such as ice cream and milk will localize in the upper parts of the body; animal fats and hard, salty dairy foods like cheese will localize in the lower parts of the body, and a combination will localize in the middle parts of the body.

EW: What about the psychological aspect of cancer—is there a recognizable cancer personality?

MK: The body and mind are one. If the body gets sick, usually the mental attitude is unhealthy also. The emotional qualities of stubbornness, egocentric thinking, arrogance, fear, hatred, anxiety, or depression are usually accompanied by physical feelings of tiredness, pain, and other minor symptoms of sickness. These two aspects usually develop together toward a cancerous condition.

But in addition to this, we can also recognize two different types of personalities that indicate different kinds of cancerous conditions: One is nourished and cultivated by overconsumption of animal food and very salty foods, and the other is a personality that is developed by overconsumption of sugary foods, soft drinks, and excess fruit. The first type of person is more egocentric, more aggressive, with a more outgoing type of character. This type of personality may tend to develop cancer of the prostate, pancreas, or colon. The second type is more reserved, more withdrawn, and isolated from other people. These people do not usually participate in social events and gatherings, and may tend to develop cancer such as leukemia or Hodgkin's disease.

EW: What advice do you have for people to more easily make a spiritual or mental change in attitude?

MK: Food is the basis for healing, which then affects our emotions, our thoughts, and our spiritual development. This approach is not symptomatic like taking pills or having surgery. This approach is the self-curing method. In that sense, the person with cancer has to make a psychologically and spiritually deep self-reflection of what he or she has done. That person must admit that the food that has been consumed and the previous lifestyle are what led to his or her present condition. The decision must then be made to change the way of life along with diet. Therefore this approach is comprehensive. Psychological, spiritual, and emotional factors must all be taken together.

EW: It seems to be the common medical assumption that when one has a serious illness such as cancer, it is not time to go on a special diet and risk malnutrition. Can you comment on that?

MK: Most doctors think from the view of nutritional elements, instead of how humans can re-adapt themselves to be in harmony with nature. Our approach is to decide what food is best to develop good humanity.

EW: But is it possible to become malnourished on the diet?

MK: No, not if it is being practiced with the proper understanding—a macrobiotic diet contains all necessary nutrients. Also, the macrobiotic diet is not a limited static approach. It should always be changing with the person's needs and condition; so if malnutrition begins, then a modification is necessary. This is the macrobiotic way.

EW: Once people are declared medically relieved of cancer, are they totally cured as whole individuals, or is there more to it?

MK: As I mentioned before, there must be a psychological change as well. The first stage is symptom relief. Medically, this may be called a cure, however, this is actually just the beginning. Mental processes and social behavior may not necessarily be corrected. The person may begin again to practice the wrong way of life and eating and thereby again attract cancer or another degenerative disease.

I can make three suggestions to help change the mental attitude more quickly: First, we must relax and cease to struggle with ourselves. A reliance on our natural healing processes must be felt. We must realize that we need not worry, and feel a submission, a giving of ourselves to the Universe, that everything will be taken care of. Second, we can look around us and notice how everything in our surroundings is supported and nourished by every other part of nature. In this way, we can become grateful and learn how to appreciate everything in our environment. Third, if we try to return to others what we owe, and do everything for others that we can, then this is the experience of love.

EW: Are there any other recommendations within the macrobiotic approach besides diet that you offer to the person with cancer?

MK: Yes, I always advise my visitors to scrub their bodies with a moist towel every day to accelerate blood and energy circulation, as well as physical and mental metabolism. Also, I advise practically everyone to do some exercise, again to revitalize their whole metabolism. I also suggest that they make order in their immediate surroundings, avoiding synthetic materials, especially in clothes directly next to the skin, to limit or avoid watching television or working under white fluorescent lights. I also recommend avoiding the use of electricity, especially for cooking. Microwave cooking should never be used. Next, I often urge visitors to establish good relations with their parents and families, and in some cases I recommend meditation, or deep-breathing exercise, for a total lifestyle approach.

EW: What about combining the treatments recommended by the doctor with the macrobiotic approach?

MK: When I have a conference with medical doctors, I always advise that the patient should change his diet immediately. Then, if the medical view is that the modern approach is necessary, they may continue to use it for a while, but all doctors and patients know that, although these medical approaches can sometimes work to relieve symptoms, in most cases they will at the same time bring the patient to a very weak condition. Therefore medical treatment should be very well supervised, and not over-used. However, if the dietary approach is working by itself, then it is better to refrain from medical treatment.

EW: Is the macrobiotic approach to cancer expensive?

MK: No, the macrobiotic approach is very economical. Each individual food item may seem somewhat higher than conventional items because of the more natural processes by which it is made and its organic quality; however, because of reduction of animal food and sugar consumption, daily food costs will become one-third or less. This is not even to mention what can be saved on medical expenses. Recently, in meeting with my visitors, I was amazed to learn that among eight of them, there had been around eighty operations. The total that they had spent as a group came to nearly a half million dollars. This included hospital expenses, drugs, and surgery in a span of about eight to ten years. Therefore, on the whole, I should certainly say that the dietary approach is much more economical for the individual, for society, for the country, and for the whole world.

EW: What do you think it will take for macrobiotics to become more widely accepted, instead of just another alternative approach?

MK: We need to de-mystify the words used in macrobiotics and use common Western terminology. In this way, we can show that this is not really a strange approach, but just commonsense principles that we all use anyway, knowingly or unknowingly.

Along with this, there should be a study of the larger view of life and the universal principles of relativity. If we can understand this and learn to express it consciously in our approach to diet and health, then it can begin to make a significant difference in the total approach to sickness and disease. We should also use this understanding to explain other conditions as well, such as our economic, social, and ideological attitudes. Then we can begin to see that this approach is not an "alternative," but includes everything.

Macrobiotics will eventually be the guideline for future generations. It can act as a compass to help us solve many and various difficulties. It does not just cure sickness but helps to realize the absolute maximum health, happiness, and spiritual freedom for an individual, which in turn will create one happy peaceful world—a planet on which we can play from morning to night.

Cancer is just a speck, one small finger of macrobiotics. We will now graduate from this level to other levels of play. We already know it is helpful and effective for the relief of cancer if done properly, so now we can turn to the larger issues of peace, crime, mental illness, and world hunger.

ANTHONY SATTILARO, M.D.

The M.D. Who Cured Himself of Cancer
March 1981

Dr. Anthony Sattilaro, then-president of Methodist Hospital in Philadelphia, has been the subject of much interest since he apparently cured himself of cancer using a macrobiotic approach. In 1980 East West *published the first account of Sattilaro's remarkable odyssey, which was subsequently reprinted in* The Saturday Evening Post—*putting Sattilaro and macrobiotics into the national spotlight. His* Recalled By Life, *written with* East West's *Tom Monte, has been a bestseller. Sattilaro, who was interviewed by Monte, lives in Florida.*

EAST WEST: What changes have taken place in your personal life since 1979?

ANTHONY SATTILARO: Well, it was a profound experience for me to see those x-rays in September, 1979, which showed that there was no more cancer left in my body. The past three years have been a great experiment, which, in a sense, had me defying some of the precepts that I had grown up with in Western medicine—not throwing them away, but realizing that there really is something to nutrition; that health and diet are directly related. Of course I believe that nutrition was instrumental in helping me, even though I can't prove that; that remains to be proven.

　　When you face your own death, you are forced to reflect on your life. And in looking back over my adult life, I realize that I thought of life in terms of luck or the lack of it. I looked at life as if God were rolling dice. I don't look at life that way anymore. I am amazed when I look back on the incredible series of events, the story that took place all through 1977 and 1978, the story in which I changed jobs, suffered the death of my father, faced the possibility of my own death, went through excruciating pain, and felt hopelessness and despair in life, and then suddenly came upon two hitchhikers, whom I have chosen to call angels. Sean McLean and Bill Bochbracher, the two hitchhikers I picked up on August 9, 1978—the day I buried my father—had lifestyles which were really the antithesis of mine. And yet, they helped me change my life. What has happened to me since then I don't believe happened just by chance. I don't think life is directed by chance. I no longer believe that God rolls dice.

What I've tried to do over the past year since I've had the gift of recovery is to love a lot more and appreciate the love that's been given to me. If I've learned anything this year, it is that God calls us, and it's not a one-way street. It's up to us to respond. We don't have to, though, and that's free will. With that belief, I'm trying to build for myself a new life, and I see unfolding before me incredible opportunities.

My life has changed also in that I have found truer values, not in the materialism of the past but in many simple things. Food, for example. In my past life, as an affluent American, I would normally eat prime rib, potatoes with sour cream, and all that kind of stuff. The food was extravagant. Now, when I go out to dinner, I see that kind of food as poison. I cannot believe that God created us to destroy these temples, our bodies. I think he created us in his image to keep our bodies as well as possible. I believe this extravagant food has affected our minds, as well.

Still, one doesn't throw away fifty years of one's life; there are still a lot of other things that are important. There are a lot of people who want to throw away the past, who say all materialism is bad, who want to do away with electricity, do away with automobiles. I'm not suggesting that. I'm suggesting that what macrobiotic philosophy calls yin and yang—we don't have to use those terms, we can just talk about balance—is putting ourselves in a happy medium, whereby we understand that extremes of almost any kind can be dangerous.

As I look at some of the people I deal with who get so proud and haughty with what they're doing—and I'm not suggesting that I've completely shed that either—I can really see why humanity has gotten itself into so much trouble. It's because we're so stuck on ourselves. I think that's the arrogance, the original sin, of telling God that we'll do it on our own. Arrogance is another extreme that will ultimately lead us to destruction.

EW: How did macrobiotics help you open the door to a more spiritually sensitive life?

AS: I think it opened the door to a more spiritually sensitive life by saying that the way you eat and the way you think are just not the way mankind was put together. That was something I had difficulty learning to live with until I suddenly realized that eating brown rice was so much better for me physically than eating meat. The turning of everything upside down, literally of taking all the meat, all the sauces, all the sugar, throwing them out the window and going back to a simpler way of eating was the substrate, the beginning.

I don't say that this in itself was the spirituality, not by any means. I think what macrobiotics did for me was to turn the world upside down, just as Jesus Christ turned the world upside down. The people 2,000 years ago said they were looking for a king, but he came as a different kind of king; he preached nonviolence, loving one's neighbor, and living very simply. That's what macrobiotics is doing. It's simply saying that you should pray before you eat, thank heaven you have that food, live a simple life, appreciate the simple but generous gifts God has given us. This is very much the essence of macrobiotics.

Macrobiotics balances the body; I prefer to use the term centering the body, which goes along with Basil Pennington's concept of the centering prayer. Basil Pennington is a monk at St. Joseph's Abbey in Spencer, Massachusetts. I believe there may be some relationship between centering prayer and centering food, so that the body becomes an open temple for the feeling of God. I also happen to think that maybe the saints had their visions because they spent so much time fasting, literally cleaning out their bodies, to make themselves more sensitive and thus more spiritual.

This is what I'm trying to do in my life.

SWAMI MUKTANANDA PARAMAHANSA

Baba
November 1974

Baba Muktananda, who died in 1982, was an Indian saint of the path of siddha yoga. His mission was to awaken divine consciousness in others by a subtle transmission of energy by touch, word, look, or thought. East West *interviewer Ty Smith said of Muktananda, "I had met a man one hundred percent positive in his being and totally musical in his expression."*

EAST WEST: Do you feel that food is important to health and spiritual development?

BABA: According to the yogic discipline, food is God himself. One should eat good and pure good, food that is fragrant, food that has life in it, food which invigorates the mind.

EW: In your own spiritual practice, what role did ayurvedic medicine play?

BM: Spiritual growth is totally independent of all other factors. However, the discipline and the rules of ayurveda are the same I insist on for spiritual growth. The founder of ayurvedic medicine one day gave his students a test. He appeared among them disguised as a crow, and he put this question: *"Kora ruk, kora ruk, kora ruk.* Who stays free from disease, who stays free from disease, who stays free from disease?" And one student said, "If you were to take multivitamin tablets every day you would not fall sick." And another said, "If you eat a boiled egg each morning you will not get sick." And a third said, "Before you eat you should drink a little, and after you eat you should drink a little, and that will keep you well." And the fourth suggested something else, and the fifth something else, and at last the teacher got completely fed up with them and flew off. He alighted on a tree by a river bank where another of his disciples was bathing, and as the student emerged from the river the teacher again shouted, *"Kora ruk, kora ruk, kora ruk."* The student immediately answered, *"Hita buk, rita buk, mita buk."* Hita buk means eating that which is good for your body, and rita buk means eating frugally, filling your stomach only half full, and mita buk means eating what is suitable to the season. And those are the principles of good health.

MEDICINE & HEALING

Milton Trager

Louise Hay

Ted Kaptchuk

Andrew Weil

Larry Dossey

ROBERT MENDELSOHN, M.D.

The Twilight of Modern Medicine
October 1978

In this interview by East West's *Sherman Goldman, Dr. Robert Mendelsohn (see Family, page 19) discussed the failure of "the religion of modern medicine."*

EAST WEST: How do you view the condition of modern medicine?

ROBERT MENDELSOHN: Modern medicine is already in its twilight years. It is about forty or fifty years old, and by now there's been a chance for the ill effects to catch up with the originally heralded benefits. The breakthroughs have turned out to be breakdowns, and most of the shiny metal has turned out to be tarnished. People no longer have confidence in chemotherapy or radiation or doctors or hospitals or hardly anything else in today's medicine.

Yesterday I noticed that Secretary Califano said we're going to have to rebuild confidence in the flu vaccine; I'd love to see how he's going to do that, because I think that most of the population is aware that the same people who are trying to bring you the flu vaccine this year are the people who brought you the swine flu vaccine last year, and I don't really think anybody else wants to become paralyzed as a result of this kind of baloney.

EW: If it's baloney, why did people believe it?

RM: People believe it for the same reason they believe in anything else—because it's a religion. It offers the services of a religion and has all the paraphernalia of one. I can think of about seven or eight essential components of a religion which modern medicine has, and there are definitely others. It has a belief system—so-called medical science—which can no more be validated than the churches' proofs of the existence of God; a sacerdotal class—that's the M.D.'s; temples—the hospitals; the acolytes and vestal virgins are the para-professionals and nurses; vestments reflecting hierarchical status, namely the length and color of M.D.'s gowns, which indicate their rank; a rich class of powerful princes supporting the church, represented by the formula companies, drug houses, and insurance firms; the selling of indulgences in the form of outrageous fees for completely useless services, which will probably bring down this modern church just as they did the medieval church; and a theological rhetoric of thought—that is, I have confidence in my plumber but I have *faith* in my doctor—the doctor-patient relationship is *sacred*.

Once we realize that modern medicine is a religion, we can compare it to other religious healing systems. Unfortunately, the religion called modern medicine turns out to be worship of a god who fails to answer, who is powerless, and who, in fact, deceives. That, of course, is the definition of idolatry.

EW: You're saying the emperor has no clothes. How long do you think it will be before everyone realizes that?

RM: It won't be too difficult to destroy these old ideas, because most of the ideas have already lost credibility. Right now, for example, the much-heralded antibiotics have turned out to have a negative cost-benefit ratio; we're not sure whether the antibiotics are responsible for killing more people than they cure. The same thing holds true of the other powerful drugs like cortisone. The Pill of course is an outrage, and it's being recognized as such, and the IUD, the various forms of surgery for cancer and heart disease, are being questioned by the public so much that in general I think the public is far ahead of the medical profession in their skepticism.

EW: What will replace the religion of modern medicine?

RM: Let me answer that by telling you what I think are the essential ingredients of a new kind of medical school. A new kind of medical school would have to have two characteristics: One would be a generalist type of approach, which is in sharp contrast to the old specialist kind of approach. The second would be a commitment to ethics, in contrast to modern medicine; the problem with modern medicine is that it completely ignores ethics. Let me just list half a dozen of the major questions in medicine: Contraception, abortion, euthanasia, experimental drugs and surgery, transsexual surgery, the test tube baby, the ethics of tranquilizers. Ethical approaches to these questions are all contained in the traditional religions as well as in the more modern religions.

If you wanted to consider the question of abortion, for example, the medical student of the future will have to learn the approaches of Jewish ethics, Catholic ethics, other Christian sects, the approach of the humanists, the approach of Eastern religions, the approach of secularists, and the approach of people like Joseph Fletcher with his situational ethics. Medical students would learn these ethical systems in regard to each question and as a whole, and then they would have to decide where these fit in with their own systems of ethics.

The most dangerous person is the one who says that he does not make value judgments for the patients—since *he* is making the biggest value judgment of all. Non-ethics is also ethics. That fact has to be brought to the consciousness of physicians so that physicians have to decide what they will do and what they will not do. A physician may have to decide, for example, as I have decided, that I will not accept as a patient any mother who does not commit herself to breastfeeding her child, since as far as I'm concerned there's no mother who cannot breastfeed—with the exception of someone who's had a bilateral mastectomy. It's easy, using proper techniques, to make sure that a mother will be successful in breastfeeding. I will not use tranquilizers. I will not use the Pill or the IUD. I will not subscribe to abortion on demand. I will not condone transsexual surgery.

Most pediatricians and other health professionals I know discourage mothers from taking babies to bed with them for breastfeeding on psychological grounds. Most pediatricians still behave as if God made a mistake when he didn't put Similac in mothers' breasts.

We have two major historical sources in medicine: One is the Greek source, which is reflected in modern medicine, with emphasis on lots of treatment; the other source is the Old Testament, which is reflected in concern with preventive medicine, sanitation, nutrition. I don't think it's any accident that a discipline like macrobiotics comes from a different culture than the United States, because in general the Eastern culture and Old Testament culture have been much more supportive of nutritional approaches. On the other hand, the cultures that derive from the New Testament have had a mixed attitude about it, because if you take a look at some of the statements in the New Testament, such as Matthew and others, they say that what's important is not what goes into your mouth, but what comes out of your mouth. My guess is that those things had an effect on the Christian culture, because by and large I don't see much emphasis on nutrition in Western civilization.

EW: So you feel that the roots go way back before the development of the current medical-pharmaceutical complex.

RM: Yes, I think the roots of the present dilemma are not economic; it's not the fault of the insurance houses or the drug companies or the food industry. I think those are sort of superficial explanations. I think it's a very deep cultural and ethical problem, and I think that until we take a look at the cultural and ethical roots of the matter we will be unable to solve it.

EW: When did the highly technological approach really get started in medicine?

RM: Modern medicine has been on a radical course for the last forty years or so, since the discovery of the antibiotics sulfa and penicillin around the late thirties and early forties. Now the radicalism in medicine fits very well into the political system. I hope you get a chance to read John McKnight's wonderful paper called "The Medicalization of Politics," in which he makes the point that the American political system could not survive without modern medicine, which keeps people quiet and in their place, and without modern psychiatry, which keeps people blaming themselves. As a matter of fact, I have required reading in psychiatry for all my medical students that consists of three sources: everything by Thomas Szasz; Jay Ziskind, *Coping with Psychiatric and Psychologic Testimony*; and the latest book by Martin Gross called *The Psychological Society*. These books, which tear down psychiatry and psychoanalysis, are must reading for every medical student. All my medical students have to read what I call a list of anti-doctor books, so that they know what the other side is saying.

EW: What kind of students would you like to see in the future medical schools?

RM: Number one, they will not be chosen on the basis of any numerical, objective tests such as the present MCATs and GPAs (grade point averages), since my impression is that these tests tend to produce the worst kind of doctors, rather than the best. As a matter of fact, we might do better to reverse and take the people who fail those tests. I have a feeling that the best answer is to simply disregard the tests altogether.

Medical students would have to be drawn on the basis of their family background, and I would pay a lot of attention to whether they came from strong family backgrounds, large families, powerful religious influence, ethical concerns. Most important, the medical school of the future will only serve students from its immediate neighborhood, rather than this ridiculous geographic mix now worshipped by everybody, which wrenches students away from their community ties and exposes them to the dangerous influences of their professors. In our future medical school the students will remain living in their own communities, either with their families or close to their families, and therefore they will escape the monastic influences of modern medical schools.

In the medical school of the future I believe that women will be chosen from those who have successfully raised families, and therefore older women should be admitted to medical school, rather than young women who have proven nothing. As a matter of fact, I consider young women to be in terrible danger from the modern medical school, because most of them end up dehumanized to an even greater extent than the men, and the statistics show that the suicide rate of women doctors is even higher than the suicide rate of men doctors.

EW: Why is the suicide rate among doctors so high?

RM: Almost all epidemiologic studies of physicians have shown that physicians are terribly prone to certain types of socio-pathologic conditions that afflict them to a much greater extent than the rest of the population: narcotic addiction, alcoholism, divorce, unhappy marriages, and suicide. It's no wonder that physicians are such a sick group, when you consider their education.

The first reason is the segregation of medical students from their own communities and their own roots. And the second is the teaching of a new set of ethics. So students may come in having certain traditional notions about contraception and abortion, but they're usually taught in modern medical schools that they are not to make value judgments, and therefore they are presented with an ethical system that conflicts with their traditional ethical system, and this is what leads to the confusion that characterizes the modern doctor.

EW: Could you be specific about the difference between a death orientation as compared to a life orientation?

RM: If you take a traditional system of ethics—Jewish ethics, for example—every aspect of it is life-oriented. If one looks at the Old Testament, one sees that its primary value is life. The very first commandment that God gives Adam and repeats to Noah is "Be fruitful and multiply." Life is the aim, more life, as a good thing, to produce the greatest number of people possible.

Since modern medicine is mostly oriented in the direction of zero population growth, it begins and ends with a death orientation. Modern medicine begins with poor prenatal care, which guarantees the death of a certain number of babies inside the uterus; it also guarantees a high rate of prematurity, and we know that premature babies have a much higher death rate than normal babies. Modern obstetrics, by being oriented toward convenience and so-called pain relief, ensures that a certain number of mothers and babies will die. Bottle feeding is death-oriented. American food habits are certainly death-oriented. The anti-family attitudes of America are certainly death-oriented; for example, the separation of old folks into nursing homes, separation of babies from their mothers into newborn nurseries, thus exposing babies to the dangers of epidemics…one could go through all of American medicine and see the strong undercurrent of death orientation.

EW: Some people get fed up with the game of endless medication, increasing cost, and steady decline in their health. They wake up one day and say, "OK, this is a racket—I'm getting out. I've been played for a fool, I admit it, and now I'm going to see if there's something I can do for my own health." But other people go on being fooled. Why are some people ready to change while others remain stubborn?

RM: In order to switch from one religion to another, something has to jolt you out of that first religion. Everybody has to have some religion. Even atheism is a religious system. I think that other systems, such as macrobiotics and some of the other traditional systems, will gain adherents very rapidly now because people are being jolted by their disappointment in modern medicine. We are going to look back on lopping off breasts with the same horror that we now look back on George Washington's blood-letting; none of modern medicine makes much sense any more.

It made sense when medicines were used for extreme conditions, but now the extreme has become the mean. Penicillin made sense when it was used for meningitis, but it makes countersense when it's used for the common cold. Cortisone made sense when it was used for Addison's disease, but it makes no sense when it's used for sunburn. The application of measures on the average person originally designed for extreme use has destroyed the respect that people had for medicine. What makes people change is disappointment in the present system.

EW: What kind of timetable do you envision for the return to common sense?

RM: First we need to establish the kind of new medical school I've described to serve as a prototype for others to replace the old dinosaur medical school. That can start almost immediately. Of course there will be some resistance; the new medical school will not be welcomed enthusiastically by the old medical schools any more than the medieval church cordially welcomed the ideas of Galileo or Erasmus. But as far as their opposing it successfully goes, I think the political process works: If the people want it, they will get it.

EW: But didn't the people want modern medicine? Or was that a case of mass insanity? If so, what provoked it?

RM: It really got going in the forties with World War II, when women en masse went to work; you know, "Rosie the Riveter." So infant formulas were developed. Then the family broke down. When the family breaks down you get a new religion that tries to take its place. The doctor replaced the wise grandmother, the nurse replaced the mother—after all, who but a blood relation is willing to clean up your vomit?

EW: One last question: Why do people believe in fallacious systems, such as you say modern medicine is?

RM: All religions, even idolatrous ones, have their miracles. You know the contest in the Bible between Moses and the Egyptian magicians who could also perform wonders. Penicillin is a miracle. But the real question, finally, is ethical. Modern medicine has its miracles like other idolatrous religions, but the price in human sacrifice has now become too great.

TED KAPTCHUK

Medicine East and West
April 1983

Ted Kaptchuk, Director of the Pain and Stress Relief Clinic at the Lemuel Shattuck Hospital in Boston, received his O.M.D. (Doctor of Oriental Medicine) at the Macau Institute of Chinese Medicine in 1975. He is the author of The Web That Has No Weaver *and, with co-author Michael Croucher,* The Healing Arts: Exploring the Medical Ways of the World.*

In this interview, Kaptchuk spoke with East West *about his views on the status of Eastern and Western medicine and how they might better be integrated.*

EAST WEST: How do you think Oriental medicine is viewed here?

TED KAPTCHUK: I think we have a fascination with the Far East. In my case, it was basically a rejection of 20th century America that led me to the Orient. But now I think Oriental medicine is put on some kind of pedestal. It's certainly a part of human reality, but it's just a different way to examine illness and to examine ourselves. We have to be critical of this method like any other. Western medicine has a lot to contribute. One thing I learned from being in China was that I'm a Westerner, and I really cherish our religious tradition.

EW: What do you think about the value of the Western medical tradition?

TK: I think the thing I learned most in writing *The Web That Has No Weaver* was the importance of Hippocrates. He was a wonderful healer. While I was writing the book something bothered me, something about a rejection of a thing that was deep inside myself, and inside this culture. I was at the beach one day and I was handed some of Hippocrates' writings. Every page of it was like a revelation. His medical model was so similar to the Oriental medical models that I had been studying. But now this wisdom is forgotten. We reject the Western culture, our own heritage, because it's so much easier to go outside ourselves rather than inside. That's why we are accepting Oriental medicine. So, with the book ready to go to press, I frantically rewrote it with footnotes about Hippocrates.

EW: So, you see a similarity between ancient Western medical practices and traditional Oriental medicine. Can you discuss some of these similarities?

TK: Hippocrates, Paracelsus, and Galen are the archetypes of the classics of Western medicine. I see them not so much in opposition to Oriental medicine, but being very close to Oriental medicine. Their medical role model was the great Arab doctor and synthesizer of medieval medicine, Avicenna. Their way of assessing a human being was different, but not qualitatively different from the ancient Chinese models, which is that a human being is an integrated whole; psyche and soma are one. They didn't dissect a person. They tried to see what kind of image was represented as a whole. A person wasn't a number of quantities, measurable entities such as weight, volume, direction, or force. I would call this view anti-reductionist.

EW: What, then, is the underlying difference between the ancient Western and Oriental approach, versus the modern Western scientific approach?

TK: The Chinese see truth as always relative, a sense of balance. Oriental civilization doesn't say it has to know the truth. The scientific revolution is a result of humankind's cry, "We want a fact." It's something that the Chinese would always hedge on. The Judeo-Christians or the Islamic Christians ask, what's the almighty? What is the creator, or the ultimate basis? The Chinese don't seem to have the need to go to that deeper layer. China doesn't kill its dragon. It can live with chaos. It can live with unclear answers. It can live with uncertainty. The Christian world and Greek tradition both say, "We need certainty." There's a need for an absolute predictability that the Judeo-Christian world has that the Oriental world doesn't seem to have. In the Orient truth is immanent and in the West truth is transcendent.

My real plea is for modern Western medicine to gain access to its own past and examine what is wrong with our scientific mode. What amazes me is how Western science, for ideological rather than therapeutic reasons, totally threw out the old medicine.

RICHARD SELZER, M.D.

Confessions of a Surgeon
November 1980

At the time of this interview with East West's *Leonard Jacobs and Bruce Donehower, Richard Selzer was a surgeon and professor at Yale Medical School. His meditations on modern medicine,* Mortal Lessons: Notes on the Art of Surgery *and* Confessions of a Knife, *were hailed as the literary equivalents of* Gray's Anatomy. *Now retired from clinical practice and teaching, Selzer devotes his time to writing. His* Taking the World in for Repair *was published in 1986.*

EAST WEST: How have other surgeons responded to your books?

RICHARD SELZER: When I first began to write, I encountered a great deal of unexpected hostility and resentment from my colleagues. After all, I was telling the secrets of the priesthood. And surgery is, if nothing else, a priesthood. After all, you go through a long and hard novitiate at the end of which you don special robes. You wash your hands and you enter a place where no one else is allowed in order to perform your secret rites. It's a priesthood, and nothing else. For one member of the priesthood to reveal the secrets is sacrilege. It is inviting a public stoning.

So in the beginning, to my astonishment, I was shunned by my colleagues. It is only in the last few years that I have been accepted. It's been a matter of great joy to me that that has happened.

EW: How do you see surgery relating to the other aspects of modern medicine?

RS: I see surgery as a passing fancy. I don't think surgery is here to stay, and I hope it isn't. It's a rather stupid way to treat disease. A surgical operation is nothing more than an artificial disease that is superimposed on the previously existing disease in the hope that the amalgamation of the two will redound to the benefit of the patient. It is usually a vain hope. Often the patient dies. It seems to me simplistic to think that you can cut open the body and take out an offending organ, and that will be that. I think that's a primitive, archaic way of treating disease. I do not believe it will be here forever. I see evidence of that even within my own professional life. Many of the diseases for which I performed operations twenty years ago I don't do any more because there are now less brutal, better ways of treating them. I like to think, of course, that my specialty, surgery, is the best. Yet I am realistic about it also, and I think it will pass away.

EW: What do you think of the new holistic approach to medicine?

RS: That's a lovely idea, and I would encourage it wholeheartedly. I deplore this overemphasis on technology. It's only because the idea of a personal God declined that people began to look toward science to give them the answer to life. They ask science to answer that question, and science can't do it. Modern technology has just become a monster. Oppenheimer, when he saw the first mushroom cloud, said, "I am become death, the shatterer of worlds." He knew that he had gone too far. I think that this holistic impulse is an honest effort to recoil from the horror of technology and to recapture a kind of purity and simplicity. I'm all in favor of it.

EW: Perhaps what is lacking in conventional medicine is an attempt to educate people on ways to preserve their health.

RS: I think you're right. You know, I've spent my life cutting people open, to put it bluntly, or sharply. Yet I feel that perhaps I am already an anachronism.

I once talked to a Buddhist doctor, the doctor of the Dalai Lama. I asked him, "What about surgery?" He said, "Oh, we don't have surgery. We don't need it." I thought that was quite marvelous. I've never seen a human being so much the distillation of his senses. The Tibetan had shut all of the distractions away. When he feels his patient's pulse, he is isolated from the rest of the world. There is a communion with the patient that is of such an intensity and clarity that it must reveal to him things that we cannot see. His senses are so highly refined as a result of a religious discipline. We don't have that. We have lost the ability to withstand pain. When we have pain, we run and get something done about it. We take a pill. We go to a surgeon. I feel that years ago when these remedies weren't available people could tolerate a great deal more pain.

I think that there is no doubt that stress is the cause of many diseases today. I've seen it happen too often that some trauma in a person's life will trigger the growth of a tumor. Possibly we all have these tumors growing in us all the time, but they never become significant until some mistake on the part of the body, perhaps a stressful situation or poor diet, causes them to appear. But I have no knowledge of this. I have knowledge of surgery, that is what I have done all my life.

EW: Henry Miller once said something about that in terms of literature. He said he enjoyed good books but he equally enjoyed bad books. It was the modern books that had no impact, that caused neither pleasure nor pain, that he wasn't interested in.

RS: In the last part of the Odyssey, where Ulysses comes home and finds the suitors in his house, the place is a shambles and he, of course, is a wreck himself. He's unrecognizable and he looks in and he's filled with fury. But he calms himself and he's led to his wife, Penelope, who doesn't recognize him. Suddenly an old nurse appears to bathe the feet of this stranger and make him welcome. Now forty years before, Ulysses had been taken to an island by his grandfather to hunt boar. During the hunt one of the boars had wounded Ulysses in the thigh. He was placed in the care of this very nurse who now, forty years later, bathes his feet. There she is, and you get the drama of this moment. She has not looked at him, but she is bathing his feet and her fingers run over his thigh and feel the wound and she knows at once who this is. The wound has awakened the buried past. That's the point that strikes me so much. The love between the wounded and the one who tends that wound is so powerful that the nurse knew immediately who this stranger was. It was stronger than the love between Ulysses and Penelope. It was the bond between healer and the one being healed. I feel that's very significant. As I see it, this is the essence of the medical art.

MICHELLE HARRISON, M.D.

Behind the Mask of Women's Medicine
October 1982

Dr. Michelle Harrison is the author of A Woman in Residence, *which chronicled her experiences in residency at a major midwestern hospital and is a vivid condemnation of the treatment of hospitalized women. At the time of this interview by* East West's *Steve Minkin, Harrison was working with Heartspring, a women's health service in Cambridge, Mass.*

EAST WEST: Will you tell us something about what you learned as a resident regarding the childbirth experience and the political evolution that came out of that.

MICHELLE HARRISON: The main thing I learned—and it shouldn't have been a surprise, but it somehow was—was the degree of disrespect that physicians have for women. And I think that's really a key to everything that goes on. I write about unnecessary surgery, and women not being informed, and things being done mostly for a physician's convenience. I realized that the physicians have no respect for women and that's how all that happens. If they basically respected women, then they wouldn't do all those things to them. But if you don't respect people, then you do anything to their bodies.

EW: So, would you say this is more than a general disrespect that physicians may have for all types of patients?

MH: Yes, I think that some of that exists throughout medicine, but Ob-Gyn really lends itself to it, because the patients are all women and the physicians are primarily male, although women physicians do take part in the whole thing. It sort of lends itself to the worst of what's sexist in our society, in the worst of male and female relationships, which have to do with men being in power and women not being respected and having no power in the situation.

EW: Are there any hospitals where, in fact, women do have power?

MH: Not that I know of.

EW: Any in the world?

MH: Not that I know of! There's a lot of talk about hospitals *allowing* more things to happen, *allowing*, *giving* more power. But, you know, as long as the hospital is giving the power, the power isn't with the women, it's with the hospital. In childbirth, for example, the hospitals are now *allowing* husbands in, they're *allowing* labor support people, they're *allowing* friends who are there to help. They're deciding who they'll *allow* in. But everybody knows that, unless those people behave, and behave in the proper way, they're all going to be kicked out.

EW: It's like being under the gun during a delivery?

MH: That's right. And when I was at one of my first home births, I suddenly looked around at all of the people and I realized that the only one there in danger of being kicked out was *me*. I had no power in that situation. I was only there as long as I behaved. And it pointed out to me how powerless a woman is in the hospital.

Another part of that was that if I say to a patient in the hospital, "I'm going to examine you now," then she knows that I'm *going* to examine her now. And when I say that to a woman at home, it's a question, because she might not allow me to. She may have to weigh whether or not it's worth the pain of discomfort or inconvenience or whatever it is and make that decision. It's her decision.

I really think that that's the power that women should have within the hospitals, that somehow the hospitals have to be turned back to the communities and to the patients who use them, and that physicians have to be the people who are technicians and consultants, and, hopefully, trusted advisors, but not the people in power.

EW: Where do you begin trying to bring about this kind of transformation?

MH: Well, I think a lot of things have to happen. First of all, one thing I advise women to do is to bring somebody with them when they go to the doctor, not just to protect them but so that they have some sense of power in that situation of being able to validate what's going on. It's just that you walk out and you don't remember half of what's been said, and you think, "Maybe I misunderstood," or, "Maybe I didn't really ask that question," or you're not sure of what you perceive as the doctor's attitude, and if you have somebody there with you, then you have a chance to validate what that experience has been for you.

R. D. LAING

Mad Wisdom from a Radical Shrink
September 1987

Renowned and controversial Scottish psychiatrist R. D. Laing, who has been called everything from a genius to a schizophrenic madman, has been raising eyebrows, hackles, and consciousness for over twenty years. An almost legendary figure to many, Laing is one of this century's most influential and original psychoanalytical practitioners and formulators. He is the author of fourteen books, the most recent of which, Wisdom, Madness, and Folly, *documents his considerable misgivings about the social powers of professional psychiatry.*

East West senior writer Richard Leviton interviewed Laing in Boston between lectures in Laing's program, "On Myths of Love."

EAST WEST: In *The Voice of Experience* you wrote, "The judgment of what is possible or impossible is often decisive in making a psychiatric diagnosis." You add that most people, sometime, have had at least one "rare experience," or hallucination. Has the definition of what kinds of experiences are "possible" loosened up in the last twenty years with all the new information out on spirit guides, channeling, UFOs, reincarnation, and the like?

R. D. LAING: It operates in two directions at once. On the one hand, many of those experiences find acceptance among a lot of people. Shirley MacLaine's *Out on a Limb* is not dismissed as cranksville by hundreds of thousands of people.

EW: Nor by the television networks, it seems.

RL: No, but once something is on television, you can mix it up any way you like. On the other hand, take *DSM-3*, the *Diagnostic and Statistical Manual, 3rd Edition*, of the American Psychiatric Association, already translated into about eighteen languages. It is one of the most influential documents in the world, the manual that classifies every possible form of mental disorder. It's the standard; you can't get anywhere without it. It's on every psychiatrist's desk.

EW: Is that the book of law for sanity?

RL: Yes. It's an extraordinary piece of work. Any unusual experience is outlawed—clairvoyance, telepathy, the sixth sense, reading another's feelings—and it goes into behavioral areas like inadequate grooming, hoarding food, collecting garbage. Categories like this are necessary for rounding up street people. If you don't want a roof over your head, for example, that is now a sign, an index, or what they call a criterion, of mental disorder.

EW: Even in 1987 the psychiatric establishment is saying that clairvoyant experiences are signs of mental disorder?

RL: Oh yes! It depends on the context, but it's there in the wings to be used against someone if the occasion seems to call for it.

EW: This leads back to your statement that "psychiatric diagnosis is a very political decision," in the sense of whether the individual is removed or not from society.

RL: Yes, that hasn't gone away. The political feature has cultivated for itself a very low profile. There are few people who want to take it up, turn it inside out, and bring it back out front these days. But this mentality is checking-checking-checking away, still operating. One reason it isn't a hot public issue, and why a lot of people think it has evaporated, is that the system eliminates dissidents from its own professional ranks. By the time medical students have reached their early thirties, if they're dissident, they've probably been eliminated by a self-reflecting system as part of the whole mind-police business.

EW: The "politics of experience" haven't changed much in the last twenty years, despite apparent public awareness of other realities?

RL: Not at all. In a master class I gave for mental health professionals and other professors of different varieties, one psychologist from the Midwest had a problem. He was in charge of a number of psychological testing and treatment facilities. He had a number of children referred to his department through PTAs for investigation and recommendation of appropriate action. They had been discovered, between the ages of eight and ten, to be dreaming in color. "Do you think it's abnormal to dream in color?" I asked him. He thought about it a little and said, no, he didn't think so. But that wasn't the point. The PTAs weren't interested in his personal, subjective opinion.

I was discussing this with some professors at Trinity College in Dublin, and one said, "Well, I dream of snooker a lot, so I must dream in color." But the state of mind that will ferret that out and try to determine, "Are we going to allow this?" is what concerns me. The idea remains that you either allow it or forbid it. For philosophical, psychological, statistical considerations we'll allow that, or we will forbid that. The idea is tremendously ingrained. There's no free, anarchist zone. We should be able to declare a principle of experiential anarchy, in which anyone, as a first principle, without any argument, is entitled to experience the universe in the manner he or she happens to. Of course, I'm not allowed to suddenly get up and crush your glasses in order to make a point. But I am entitled to have any transpersonal experience I may be having at the moment, and so are you.

EW: By contrast, if you consulted a Tibetan Buddhist on some of these issues, you would come up with highly supportive views about color dreaming and experiential anarchy. The Buddhists claim we create the world with our minds.

RL: Of course. Absolutely. People are frightened of the possibilities of their own minds. I call this psychophobia. There's a psychophobic trend in our culture that is particularly common among people who are motivated by fear of experiential anarchy and confusion. And these people are the ones who dedicate themselves to policing other people's experiences and minds.

EW: There is a proliferation of splinter therapies today, with nearly everyone hanging a therapist's sign on the door. From your position as a classically trained psychoanalyst, are these therapies helping people?

RL: They do help a lot of people, but the trouble is, it's all fragmented. The ideal therapist ought to be an integral therapist, aware of what contribution he or she can make to help someone find his way in life and balance from a number of different directions—meditation, yoga, acupuncture, massage, talking, music, or martial arts. There are multifarious approaches. But professionals get into one thing and they don't regard it as relevant to know anything, firsthand or even secondhand, about other possible approaches. In the original classical Greek and Roman medicines, before anything else the main thing was a regimen, balancing your whole being twenty-four hours of the day.

EW: In your early books, you describe how the family is often the context and breeding ground for mental disorders. Do you see any changes among today's parents who have passed through the 1960s experience, and may have read some of your books and focused attention on some of these deep-seated issues? Are there psychologically healthier families today?

RL: My impression is that a lot of people who were students in the 1960s and who went through that crisis in our culture have come out of it with a better balance than their parents had a chance to have. They managed to keep it together and get momentum into their lives and live a decent life in their own company. They established their own network, found ways of earning money that aren't indecent, and are coming across now with families and children who are less fraught than they were or their parents were.

EW: So some progress has been made?

RL: I think so. I just hope it builds up to a critical mass. If there are enough comparatively balanced and sane people living decent lives with children today, if that reaches a critical mass, it's bound to affect all of society. One question I ask people who are pretty miserable is, when was the last time you felt happy, if you can remember, or the first time? Or when was the last time you remember enjoying yourself and what were you doing? One man said, when he was whistling. He hadn't whistled a favorite tune for years. If you can just bring yourself to go inside yourself, or have a walk, or try to bring it out in a whistle—it can be anything. For that man whistling was an opening into enjoyment. If you're enjoying yourself, you can't be miserable or frightened. Innocent enjoyment is a chink of light.

JEAN SHINODA BOLEN, M.D.

Gods and Goddesses in Everyone
March 1989

Jean Shinoda Bolen is a psychiatrist, Jungian analyst, and author (The Tao of Psychology, Goddesses in Everywoman, Gods in Everyman). *She is Clinical Professor of Psychiatry at the University of California Medical Center and is a faculty member of the C. G. Jung Institute in San Francisco. With* East West's *Mirka Knaster, Bolen discussed how she uses the gods and goddesses of Greek mythology as metaphors to illustrate the powerful inner patterns, or archetypes, that shape how we behave and influence how we feel.*

EAST WEST: Working with Greek mythology is one of your gifts, but how can deities from over 3,000 years ago serve others in their daily lives?

JEAN SHINODA BOLEN: Myth is a form of metaphor. It's the metaphor that's truly empowering for people. It allows us to see our ordinary lives from a different perspective, to get an intuitive sense of who we are and what is important to us. We have a sense of being in a story. When you think about story as form—it has a beginning, middle, and end—something unfolds. There's a progression, and in that is a working through to solution. Myths are the bridge to the collective unconscious. They tap images, symbols, feelings, possibilities, and patterns—inherent, inherited human potential that we all hold in common. The more I work with people and their dreams and get an understanding of what moves people, the more the reality of the collective unconscious comes home to me. A myth is an expression of that same depth place. That's why we're drawn to a myth. If you listen to someone retell a dream, it fascinates you because even though it's someone else's, the themes touch on that collective unconscious level. We can relate to it as if it were our dream too. That's what happens when you listen to a myth. It's like hearing a dream that has something to say to us personally. When we interpret it, we add the dimension of cognitive understanding, and an Aha! results as myth and personal meaning come together. What I've done with the myths is to express what they could be.

EW: If you're working with a person who is going through a life crisis, do you present a myth to help her to see outside herself?

JB: Sometimes, but not usually, because I am working with their own depth material by listening to their dreams. They are creating their own story in connection with that same level. It's usually not necessary to introduce a myth, but once in a while something happens where a myth example offers another way of seeing the experience. When I worked with a patient who knew that she was possessed by jealousy and that she wasn't acting like herself because of it, I saw her struggling with the goddess Hera in her negative form. When you see that your struggle is with an archetype like Hera, it's a way of understanding that something is taking over, coloring your emotions, and making you obsessed. An archetypal complex has taken you over temporarily or for a period of your life, and the struggle is to get yourself back. If you have a cognitive idea about what is happening, it helps empower the ego to see what is going on.

It helps you to respect yourself, to see that you are struggling with something quite formidable and to see that within the myth, that particular goddess also carries positive traits. It's a means of self-knowledge—understanding what your psychological difficulties are and seeing what positive strengths you might get from this complex.

EW: Do you find that using myth helps move people faster through their process of understanding and out of the complex?

JB: It depends. Not everyone hears a metaphor and gets it. If you do, it's like seeing a picture that's worth a thousand words.

EW: How can this help people to be healthy?

JB: Usually it's much more useful to people who need something to help empower them to do what feels intuitively true to who they are. It's such a relief for many people to have a sense of positive identification with a particular pattern, whether a god or goddess. I have gotten many thank-you letters from women who've read *Goddesses* because they were able to see themselves defined, and from that feel good about choices they're making. Strangely enough, I've gotten the most from women who are like Hestia, who have always felt that there was something wrong with their capacity for solitude, because our society is so extroverted. To say, "I'd rather stay home and put my house in order instead of going to a cocktail party," makes some people wonder, "What's the matter with me?"

EW: Are there limitations in using this new psychology of women? How would black women be able to relate to it, for example? Would it be more helpful for them to have African deities to identify with?

JB: Maybe, and it's not just black women. The archetypal patterns are present universally. They have different names in different cultures.

EW: Then would you have to give readers the panoply of deities from another culture?

JB: Not necessarily. In the first place, metaphor is a very powerful tool for people whose style is to be intuitive. There are also folks who wonder why go through this image of ancient goddesses—it just confuses things. They say,

"Why don't you just tell me which qualities are me?"

EW: Do we have any control over the archetypes within us? Are we born with a set of archetypes?

JB: You see different personality traits in babies in a newborn nursery right from the beginning. There are noisy ones and quiet, relaxed ones. Very often, what you see in the nursery you see reflected a year later, perhaps even ten years later. The Jungian point of view is that the archetypes are present in all of us, but it's clear that some archetypes are naturally stronger in some people from the very beginning. Then the family either encourages or suppresses it.

EW: Could mothers and fathers apply the principles of *Goddesses in Everywoman* and *Gods in Everyman* to raising their children?

JB: Yes, very much so. Parents should know who their children are and try to see them clearly, which is hard. We see children as extensions of ourselves. We need tools in order to understand who they are, and this is just one set of tools a certain group of people will find useful. When I lectured on "Gods in Everyman," a friend of mine in Chicago with two sons began to think of her boys as fitting different patterns, with different needs. What she supports them in, how she encourages them, what she knows of their strong and weak suits are now more available to her. *Gods in Everyman* may be a major consciousness-raising tool for men to realize how the patriarchy has limited who they are, and how being a man in this patriarchy is hard on them, which hasn't really sunk in for most men.

EW: How can men and women during this time of transition use the gods and goddesses to improve their relationships with each other?

JB: It has something to do with being seen and being able to see the other person clearly. It has to do with being interested in really knowing who the significant other is rather than have that person be who you need them to be. So the gods and goddesses as archetypes provide metaphor tools to explain oneself to the significant other. I know that *Goddesses* was used this way. Women said to men, "Here, read about me." I presume *Gods in Everyman* will be used in the same way.

EW: You have a long list of topics you address at workshops, lectures, and conferences—Healing the Psyche, Healing the Earth, Women's Spirituality, The Father Archetype, and so on. What is the fundamental message that you're trying to convey through them?

JB: Two things keep reappearing. One is journey or pilgrimage. I see life as about being on a path, and we need to discover which is the right one for us. I speak of how to do that and what it feels like. The other is that, in the process of traveling along a path that we choose from our intuition, our heart, our archetypal self, we also connect with one another and with the Tao. I have a mystical concept of interconnectedness between ourselves and others and some god, goddess, Tao, whatever one calls it. We are traveling and evolving.

ANDREW WEIL, M.D.

Why Alternatives Work
March 1985

Harvard-educated Dr. Andrew Weil is perhaps best known for his research with psychoactive plant substances and for such books as The Natural Mind *and* Chocolate to Morphine, *which were denounced by the AMA and lauded by many. His more recent* Health and Healing: Understanding Conventional and Alternative Medicine *is a penetrating review of a variety of healing systems ranging from allopathy and naturopathy to holistic and psychic healing.*

What East West *interviewer Bill Thomson found most impressive about Weil was "his range of experience and his openness to experiment with different systems of medicine. What we stand to learn most from him is how to remain open to different ideas, maintaining the freedom to look outside our narrowly drawn boundaries, beyond our accustomed awareness."*

EAST WEST: What will it take for allopathic medicine to open up to a more intuitive style of medicine?

ANDREW WEIL: It's already happening. I think there are many factors that are combining to produce it. The first is enormous patient dissatisfaction with allopathic medicine. But also, for the first time, in the past few years there's been very significant economic pressure on allopathic medicine. That's really the only kind of pressure it responds to, and it's coming from interesting sources—from insurance companies and from corporations that have begun to see that the economics of the present medical system are impossible.

EW: You've said you didn't think that a doctor who was trying to use a system of healing would be able to use it effectively unless he or she had submitted to the treatment and gained some belief in it.

AW: Sure. As I said, I think the physician's belief in the treatment is one of the most crucial determinants of whether it's going to work or not, because that's what can really ignite the patient's belief. And the way you get to believe in things most is by experiencing them working in you.

EW: I understand you to say on the one hand that the body heals itself, and that given the right conditions it can restore itself to a balanced and healthy state. If that is true, would it always be necessary for someone to have faith in a treatment for healing to occur?

AW: I think medical treatments only produce healing if there is an interaction of belief with the treatment. I suppose certain treatments could be helpful even if people did not believe in them. But in my experience the element of belief is crucial.

EW: What is your definition of health?

AW: I consider health a state of balance of all the elements and forces that make up and surround the human being. Not just physical forces, but non-physical ones as well. And I think that health is a temporary dynamic state of balance, a temporary equilibrium that has to break down periodically in order to reform as conditions change.

EW: Could you comment on the role of diet in your practice and in overall health?

AW: Diet is an important factor in health but I don't think it's the be-all and end-all, as some people feel. It has a special importance in being the only factor that we—at least potentially—have total control over, because when it comes down to it, you really are the final judge of what goes into your mouth. You can't so control most other variables. That gives diet an importance out of proportion to its actual role.

EW: What do you think in general about holistic health?

AW: There's a lot of inconsistency in the holistic health movement. It ranges from ideas and ideals that I think are solid to very unscientific acceptance of procedures just because they're unorthodox. I see this even among some M.D.'s who call themselves holistic. The health field has always attracted a lot of exploiters. It's an easy area in which to take advantage of people. And also, because of placebo responses, it's very difficult to sort out what's valid and what's not. It's easy to invent some system of therapy that appears to work both because of placebo responses and, maybe even more importantly, as you said earlier, because many conditions tend to go away by themselves. I get inundated with mail about this scheme and that scheme that people promote as the one way to health, whether it's some kind of electrically-charged water or the latest supplement you can't afford not to take. An example I mentioned in the book and will mention again that bothers me very much is applied kinesiology. Until I see evidence to the contrary, it looks to me like a suggestive phenomenon. There are ways you can make people's arms go down if you want them to, whether by deliberately pushing them down or by giving subtle unconscious cues in the way you initiate pressure.

EW: You mentioned in *Health and Healing* the idea of patient-dependence in chiropractic. Would you say there is such a thing going on generally in the holistic health field, even though it purports to be self-care?

AW: Yes, it's a potential in any system of treatment. At the same time, I meet occasional practitioners in all systems who don't encourage it, who do really go to the roots of problems. But I think the general trend in all forms of treatment is to make people dependent. Look at the way homeopathy gets used today. In classical Hahnemannian homeopathy, you give one dose of one remedy and wait to see what happens. Now you see people buying homeopathic preparations in health food stores and taking them several times a day for weeks and months as though they're some kind of vitamins.

EW: One thing that may inspire faith in allopathic medicine is that there's someone to tell patients what to do, to give them the placebo, and so on. When somebody says you have to take care of yourself, that's a big order for some patients, isn't it?

AW: Absolutely. In fact the message I put out—you are responsible for your own health; there are no quick and easy answers—is not very popular. It's different from telling you that if you eat this vitamin and that vitamin you'll live to a hundred and never get sick. There's enormous fascination in our society with quick and magical answers that involve substances or external procedures. A lot of people want to be relieved of responsibility, not just for health, but for living. They want to surrender authority, and that's a very dangerous trend. It's not only what leads to getting hurt by medical practitioners but also what leads to religious cults and political fascism.

EW: What role does spirituality play in your concept of health?

AW: I don't think you can make a distinction, really, between life and non-life. The things that we call non-living, looked at on a fine enough scale, seem to have all the characteristics of living things, including motion, a kind of inherent activity, and luminosity. That fits in with Eastern ideas of consciousness being the basic stuff of everything, that matter is crystallized energy or crystallized consciousness, and that whatever it's made up of has self-awareness and shares some of the characteristics of life. That kind of connection with everything I consider spiritual. A feeling of connectedness is an important aspect of wellbeing. People who don't have that sense tend to feel much more cut off, isolated, lonely, and despairing than people who have some sense of being connected to a creation that is larger than themselves.

EW: You said in *The Natural Mind* that alcohol in your opinion was the most harmful drug we use. Yet you now say tobacco is.

AW: At the time I wrote *The Natural Mind* I was not as aware. I still was under the spell of cultural biases. I feel alcohol is a more toxic drug and a stronger drug, and it has much worse consequences on behavior. But it's not as addictive and it's not something we're forced to pay for with our tax dollars. It's not something we force non-users to consume.

EW: What role should drugs have in our society? And which ones?

AW: First, they're going to be here whether we like it or not. They've always been a part of human cultures. I've looked at drugs as they're used in very ritualized ways in traditional societies where they don't cause any harm. In those cultures drugs often serve to bring people together and promote communication. That is certainly a function they perform in this society as well. Coffee breaks and cocktail hours serve as a ritualized, socially-sanctioned means of relaxation and recreation, which people need. It's advantageous to know how to relax without using drugs too, of course. Potentially, at least, I think drugs, by altering consciousness, can both aid people in the exploration of their minds and in attaining other states of consciousness where they can change their outlook on the world and on themselves. A major use of drugs in traditional societies is in connecting with healing rituals, as in shamanism, for example. That's a potential for drugs that may not be for everyone, but it's a potential. The question of which drugs, I can't say. That really depends on the person's own taste. Whether the drug is legal or illegal is not the most important distinction to me.

KENNETH PELLETIER

The Healing Mind of Kenneth Pelletier
May 1988

Dr. Kenneth Pelletier is a Ph.D. in psychology and associate clinical professor in both the Department of Medicine and the Department of Psychiatry at the University of California School of Medicine in San Francisco. He also directs the University's Corporate Health Promotion Research Program and is the author of Healthy People in Unhealthy Places: Stress and Fitness at Work, *among other books. Research with corporate executives, and his long list of credits—advisor to federal and international health organizations, consultant to major corporations, author of professional journal articles, TV talk show guest—have helped Pelletier to legitimize preventive care (including meditation and relaxation techniques) that might otherwise have been dismissed as too unorthodox. To his effort to bridge the gap between science and spirituality he brings the influence of his own adherence to a spiritual practice that is essentially Tibetan Buddhist in orientation.*

East West *contributing editor Mirka Knaster interviewed Pelletier in Hawaii during a talk he gave to the Mental Health Association of Maui.*

EAST WEST: What do you do when you feel a little off balance? For instance, do you use homeopathy, acupuncture, massage?

KENNETH PELLETIER: Nothing that I could say by way of a prescription, because if you think about it, each potential for you to become ill is different every time it happens. Because of that, what I do each time is something very different, except for going inside and trying to sense what it is I need, and getting rest. I think it's critical, at least for me, to rest in some fashion, through a meditative practice or simply by sleeping. Other than that, sometimes it's homeopathic remedies, sometimes antibiotics, sometimes an herbal tea or an acupuncture treatment, whatever seems to be needed at that point. How I determine that, I'm not certain, except that it's a feeling or an intuition that tells you, out of all the things you've been exposed to, what you need right now.

All of us feel out of balance sometimes. We get truly sick when we continue to ignore the minor feeling of imbalance because we think there is something better to be gained. So if we have a clenching in our stomach, we carry on the conversation with someone we don't like because we want to get something out of the conversation. We stay up too late in a happy situation because there's some reward in it for us, even though we have to get up early the next morning. There is always information, but we ignore it. When we override this system, the signal that tells us we're out of harmony will get louder and louder. That signal is what we call the symptom. If you feel a little tension, it may become lower back pain. If you feel your heart rate accelerating because you're under a lot of tension right now, perhaps that's tachycardia. A slight tightness in the temples becomes a tension headache. If there is any trick, it's to realize that those signals are there and to know yourself well enough to know when you are getting the first early detectable indication of disharmony, and then to restore the harmony.

EW: What do you think is keeping people who are sick all of the time from doing that? The way you present it, it seems extremely simple. You listen to the message, you pay attention, and you act accordingly. Yet, people all around us have back problems, migraines, indigestion, hypertension.

KP: Unfortunately, there are a billion reasons. Some of the reasons are cultural. We are very externally oriented—toward things, money, achievement, position—and anyone who is introspectively oriented is suspect. It is profound how distrustful our culture is of looking internally, of "knowing thyself." Lack of self-knowledge is perhaps one of the major and most profound causes of many diseases. Certainly the way we generally eat is monumentally unhealthy. And we are profoundly sedentary. We have a half-million-year-old biology that is oriented toward physical activity, yet most people don't move unless they have to. We owe our survival as a species to the ability to be mobile, and yet on a daily basis we immobilize ourselves. Certainly the kinds of lifestyles and workstyle conditions we've created are extremely stressful for ourselves and others.

Another factor that I think is becoming increasingly interesting is the idea of the importance of social support systems. There is an abundance of research indicating that, when individuals are estranged from family, friends, animals, plants, they have a higher-than-normal incidence of disease. A group of men having the same blood pressure and cholesterol readings, who are estranged from a social support system, will have a heart disease rate six times higher than a group of men with the same readings who report having a supportive environment. In a group of women, all with the same risk factors, those who do not have a social support system will have a cancer incidence four times higher than those who do. There's no question that there is a genetic predisposition to disease, but to me the much more challenging question is: What is everything that happens after the sperm and ovum unite, exchange genetic information, and in effect create the template for a biological organism? That "everything" is something over which we have an immense degree of influence. The challenge is to find out what that is. Our failure to do so has resulted in what we call the "afflictions of civilization." The director of the World Health Organization calls the results of our failure the "diseases of indulgence" and points out that no nations on the earth could afford to be so unhealthy as the post-industrial developed nations. The persistent destruction and contaminations of our physical environment is clearly a predisposing factor to disease, particularly to cancer, and I think that is becoming clearer over time. *The Journal of the American Medical Association* stated that, based on the Surgeon General's report, two-thirds of all death and disease prior to age sixty-five are preventable if we apply what we know right now about hazardous lifestyle and environmental conditions which lead to disease.

I think the challenge right now and for the foreseeable decade is, if we have gained better insights as a result of various meditative practices or inner searching, whatever those forms might be, we should be able to solve all problems in better ways. We should have a better approach to government, medical care, hunger, and warfare. I really do think that, fundamentally, that is what is occurring right now.

EW: Are you basically optimistic then?

KP: Unquestionably, because I have met enough people in every single area that you can point to—global ecology, economics, politics, business, peace—who are working on the same values, who have a new, more humane, less destructive way to solve these old problems. The evening news or the front page of *The New York Times* may not make me optimistic, but knowing how hard these people work and how well-positioned they are to accomplish things—like successfully getting millions of acres of rain forest in Brazil designated park areas—makes me very optimistic.

EW: You've said that talking with people in business and government, you were surprised to find a commonality of values, that they're not all the Machiavellian figures they were supposed to be.

KP: Absolutely. About six or seven years ago, working with individuals at high levels in major corporations, I kept being surprised that I liked them. "Something's radically wrong here. Why do I like these people? They're supposed to be bottom-line monsters." They weren't. I'm not wearing rose-colored glasses. There are a lot of people who do run on a purely power-oriented model and are successful at doing it. That's unequivocal. However, there are major corporations that are equally or more successful that are run on a different set of values by truly visionary people who have a sense of purpose or mission in the world and who genuinely want to improve the welfare of humankind in every sense of the word—physically, mentally, spiritually, environmentally. And that's wonderfully refreshing to me.

EW: How do you cope with working with people whose political values are different from your own? Doesn't helping them to become healthier also enable them to better accomplish goals, such as building missiles, that you're not in agreement with?

KP: Actually, I've worked with Lawrence Livermore Laboratory and Lockheed and on occasion I've been criticized for that involvement. I'd like to reiterate that my experience is one of working with individuals within these impersonal organizations. There are many people in the defense industry who share peaceful values, people who are really afraid of the consequences of not handling these enormous energies properly, people who maintain a humanistic conscience in a very hostile environment. When individuals from the outside come in and reinforce or help them shore up these values, it's a real boost to them. It gives them the support and courage to ask, "Why are we doing this?" at a board meeting, to add a word of caution, to take a stance that might be unpopular, to try to throw their weight into the argument in a positive direction. These are the people that I encounter when I go in. I've come away from my work with them glad to know there are people like that in the industry. The feeling afterwards of having helped them represent these values in a very dangerous industry is rewarding.

EW: What is the most fascinating thing you've learned in all your years of research? What has struck you more than anything?

KP: Part of my early research in the seventies was to study people who could control bleeding and pain to a remarkable degree and to verify that they could accelerate healing and affect their immune systems. But independently of those particular phenomena, there are things that, as soon as you asked, came to mind. One is the birth of a baby. Seeing a child born under Lamaze-like conditions is a most moving, extraordinary event.

Another one was swimming with Joe and Rosie, John Lilly's dolphins. It was not what I was expecting. It was a paradoxical experience of feeling utterly different from them and totally the same simultaneously.

And the third was when I was visiting a friend who is a pathologist at the University of Rotterdam and he asked me to attend an autopsy with his medical students. I thought, "Are you kidding? This is not what I do for pleasure." "Just come to this autopsy," he said. In the course of the autopsy he looked around at these new Dutch medical students and asked, "What killed this man? The cause of death I'm listing is this cancer, but I tell you that this cancer could not have killed this man, and there's no other evidence of organic pathology." And with that—he was opening the chest cavity—he took a chisel and smashed it against the sternum, as though it were a piece of granite, and right at that second there was a sense of how unbelievably dead and inanimate this body was, that without human consciousness, without the spirit, how stone-like and thing-like we are. It came sharply into focus how absurd it is that we mistake human beings for these things and reduce people to these objects, because it's like saying a stone has a creative thought.

The Buddhists admonish us not to confuse the finger with that to which it points. Not only have we forgotten that the finger is pointing, or toward what it is pointing, but we believe that our reality can be resolved and understood by dissecting the finger, by breaking it down to its atoms and molecules as though somehow that is the ultimate reality and that's going to answer those questions for us. It's not that it's wrong, it's just incomplete.

LARRY DOSSEY, M.D.

A Conversation with Dr. Larry Dossey
June 1982

In his first book, Space, Time and Medicine, *Larry Dossey, M.D., explored the possibilities that our cultural perception of time might indeed affect our health. Any device or technique, such as hypnosis, biofeedback, and meditation, that expands one's sense of time can be used as an analgesic, he feels, and spiritually aware people who reach a certain level of consciousness achieve the same feat that primitives and children have managed, namely, they live in the "continual present." In contrast, we moderns race around dominated by our watches, which Dossey refers to as "symbols of death." He also authored* Beyond Illness—Discovering the Experience of Health, *and his newest books,* Mind Beyond Body *and* Medicine and Meaning, *will be published soon.*

Dossey has been chief of staff at Dallas Medical City Hospital and is currently medical director of the biofeedback department at the Dallas Diagnostic Center. Interviewers Leonard Jacobs and Tom Monte tested Dossey for "any lingering time-sickness" by being an hour late for their meeting.

EAST WEST: You begin your book with the metaphor of a hex to show how consciousness has a strong impact on health. Can you elaborate on this?

LARRY DOSSEY: We now have studies that show that consciousness is a terribly important factor in what evolves in healing and illness. This is the battleground of the classic mind-body problem. It is the old body-mind relationship in reverse; we have always struggled with trying to understand how consciousness evolves out of biochemistry and now we are trying to go backwards and answer how the body's immune system absorbs the impact of consciousness. The phenomenon is the same; the direction is in reverse, that's all.

EW: Can you give us some practical examples of how this phenomenon is being used today therapeutically?

LD: The work you're probably most familiar with is that of Carl and Stephanie Simonton, authors of *Getting Well Again*. [The Simontons have pioneered the use of positive imaging and the importance of the mind in combating cancer. Through a variety of techniques, the Simontons help the patient marshal the immune system's healing forces against the cancer. They have had some success with these methods.] The Simontons do clinical research, and don't do basic research, but their work in getting patients to visualize an end to their illness seems to be extraordinarily effective. We know that their patients treated for the same stage of cancer live twice as long as those treated in traditional ways. The critics from orthodox medicine say the patients are selected in a special way; they are self-referred, they go there because they think it's going to work, therefore it does. As a result, the critics maintain that they are taking advantage of a kind of placebo effect and the data are meaningless. There are no double blind trials that doctors want to see. However, I think we should be terribly open and encourage this kind of work because what the Simontons are doing is trying to bring into play those mechanisms that we know in the laboratory affect immune function.

EW: Would you discuss your ideas on how our perception of time affects health?

LD: The classic example is with coronary heart disease; people who suffer from this illness are possessed by time—they have what is called hurry sickness. Time for these people is constantly running out; this is their felt sense of time. This has all sorts of concomitant effects. It is much easier for these people—because of the effect this attitude has upon the heart—for them to fibrillate, to have a heart attack and die. We know that anxiety affects the immune system. Time sense affects our ability to handle stress. In fact, time sense can create stress, and stress has been shown to affect our body's immune system. People who are bereaving the loss of a spouse—an extremely stressful state—suffer a weakening of the immune system and two to three times more death in their respective age groups. The immune system is affected by our time sense or the level of stress in our lives and thus cannot withstand or fight off insults from without. I don't know of any illness that is not affected by our sense of time passage.

EW: What about childhood illnesses?

LD: I'm not sure that they differ physiologically; it depends on what age, because the time sense changes with age.

EW: Could the child's sense of time have something to do with its development of language? This would seem to be the case, since the development of language is associated with the left hemisphere of the brain, the logical and analytical side. The right hemisphere, which is associated with the intuitive, holistic view of life, would seem to give rise to the more cyclical, cosmic view of time. Have you looked at this possibility?

LD: Those are interesting speculations, but it's more complex than that. There are cultural and historical factors that may or may not be related to language. Western society was not possessed by a sense of linear time until a reliable pendulum clock was developed in the seventeenth century. Before that time, we had a rather primitive notion of time in the West as a sense of an eternally returning phenomenon. And this domination that Western society experiences now from the clock depended upon the emergence of the clock. Moreover, adults from other cultures, such as the Hopis, are able to think in very precise left brain fashion and maintain a complex ordering of their lives, yet live in the sense of the now. The Hopi's language has no tenses. Australian aboriginal children learn to tell time with great difficulty. They have difficulty adapting to a watch, yet even with conventional ways of assessing intelligence they are equally as intelligent as children in the surrounding Australian society. It would seem that our ability to assess time, therefore, is an extraordinarily complex one and goes beyond our abilities with language.

MEIR SCHNEIDER

The Healing Vision
February 1988

Born legally blind, at the age of eighteen Meir Schneider effectively restored his sight with the help of the Bates vision method. He subsequently developed his own theories of self-healing and to date has helped over 3,000 people cure themselves of such ailments as vision difficulties, scoliosis, arthritis, polio, and even multiple sclerosis and muscular dystrophy, all of which is chronicled in his autobiography, Self-Healing: My Life and Vision. *Currently, Schneider trains therapists and works with clients using movement therapy and counseling at his nonprofit Center for Self-Healing in San Francisco, which he founded in 1977.*

Schneider was interviewed for East West *by freelancer Joe Vitale.*

EAST WEST: You were declared legally blind. You were told it was hopeless. Yet you persisted. Why?

MEIR SCHNEIDER: You know the saying, "Pain leads to growth." For me it was painful not to be able to do what other people could do, to be an exception. What happened to me is that I met a sixteen-year-old genius. He told me to take my glasses off. I could see light and shadow with them. He told me to see light and shadow without them. See them fuzzier. Start there. That's the first thing he taught me, see what you see, possess your eyes. Blind people eventually become more blind because they aren't expected to see. Just because somebody has one percent of vision, that shouldn't be dismissed.

EW: I always understood blindness to be total blackness, total nothingness, but you're saying there are degrees of seeing?

MS: Exactly. And 90 percent of blind people do see something, even those who have guide dogs. The point is, we have criteria: "What do you see on the eyechart from twenty feet?" If you see less than 20/200 with corrections you're considered legally blind. That's not good criteria.

Let me give you an example. A friend of mine came here from Austria recently. She's blind and has a guide dog. She had non-functional vision. Yet she had a sense of colors and she could sense some objects—she did not know this actually until I met with her. Her vision was so non-functional nobody paid attention to it, including herself. She came here and I spent a whole day with her, walking to places and showing her that she could see signs and objects, but in *her* way. Her vision isn't like mine or yours. But I taught her to use what she had and to coordinate between her body and what she sees. She called me from Austria the other day and said, "Meir, I have something very important to tell you." I said, "What is it?" and she said, "I'm not blind. People think I'm blind, but I'm not. I see. I see the moon, I see the sun, I see some colors."

And she told me about an incident from the day before. In Austria blind people wear a yellow tag on their arms. She was in the supermarket, shopping. I had taught her to move toward what she could see, and she slowly moved to the yogurt. She had a sense of boundaries—she might not see it the way you and I see it but she had a sense of the shape of it. She knew exactly where to extend her hand so she took it and placed the yogurt in her basket. An old woman standing behind her suddenly screamed, "You have no right to wear that yellow tag when you can see!"

It's interesting the kinds of teachers we have along the way. Some of them are positive and some of them are negative. But the thing is, she learned that she could see.

EW: You taught her to be aware of what she could in fact already do?

MS: Yes. And one of the things I learned is that we need to nurture our eyes. That was something that wasn't my original intent. It was never introduced to me that eyes need to be nurtured, that *you* need to be nurtured by *you*. That was very new. That's what made me change my life. That's what made me understand that there's a dimension in our life that is missing.

EW: So you're saying, work with what you can see, develop that?

MS: Yes. Or with what you can hear, if you have hearing problems, or with what you can smell, if that's a problem. Or with the amount of movement you can make if you have paralysis. The biggest difference between me and physical therapists is, they'll say, "your arms work, so let's work with your arms." I'm saying to hell with that. If you can work your arms, we don't need to know that. Let's see if something moves in your legs, something of insignificance, but let's see if it moves. You'd be amazed how much movement most wheelchair patients have and they don't even know it. It was never encouraged. What happened to me was that I was encouraged to possess my own vision.

EW: There is a statement you made in the introduction to *Self-Healing* that I imagine provokes some response. You say, "No ailment is incurable, and hope should never be given up." Why do you say no ailment is incurable?

MS: I have not proven it by any means, but I think it's really interesting that the statement appears so bizarre to the world. People don't even take it as a possibility. That's one of the reasons for my making it. In this world we have AIDS, cancer, heart attacks. We have all kinds of problems. We believe that ailments are inevitable, and maybe all we do is touch them a little bit. But I think that if we could learn the resources we have in our bodies, we could create a healing process. And if we collectively heal ourselves, we create a healing atmosphere. And that healing atmosphere would create a situation where there would be no ailments. With time the world may evolve to be free of disease. I cannot prove it or guarantee it, but for God's sake I think some people should think that with me. I find myself pretty much alone in the world, thinking that way.

I have seen muscular dystrophy patients—not become Olympic runners—but be able to walk, which is something totally unbelievable. I've seen MS patients recovering or improving or changing the process of decay to a process of growth. I've seen, on the other hand, normal people who restrict the movements of their bodies. Tensing up, being confined, jailing themselves. Those normal people could end up being ill just from what they're doing. But I think that, when they become much more open, when they breathe more deeply, when they are less confined, they change themselves and they change others.

EW: We're talking about self-healing—your book is called *Self-Healing*—but when I asked you how people could self-heal themselves, you suggest they find a teacher. Why do you advise looking outside ourselves for self-healing when you say the power is inside?

MS: We have not been educated to heal ourselves. The education we have says you have no power, you don't know anything, and, if you try something, it is merely an experiment. That's why you need somebody who has a good education in self-healing. I also think the personal touch of a practitioner can be a vehicle for improvement. Massage and bodywork can help you break your holding, break your tension, so the exercises become more effective. Some people read the Bates book and can toss away their glasses. Other people can take my whole training course and not give up their glasses. Most likely, though, if you do meet an instructor, you'd have more chances for improvement than if you tried it with just a book. Because the instructor might have an insight into what you need to start with.

The way I work with a student is this: You come to me with a tension and I work with you. Then you invent work for yourself. You come back to me and show me what you've invented. I give you exercises and you say you did them somewhat differently. I'd say, "Great!" and I'd give more suggestions. We'd go back and forth until eventually you teach me much more than I know about you. I started you. You actually brought me more knowledge, though.

EW: What are the basic elements of self-healing?

MS: The requirement is that you believe you are worth your time. Most people don't think that way. They have to provide for their family and so on. You should be responsible for your family, yes. But you also are responsible to your problems. You are not responsible for your disease but you are responsible *to* it.

EW: Could you explain the distinction you make in *Self-Healing* between the brain and the mind?

MS: I believe we have a mind separate from the brain. And the brain reflects what the mind thinks. What the mind does patterns us. Those patterns we have are a result of habits. The mind regulates those habits. There is another mind, that I might call soul, that knows right from wrong. Sometimes we can meet this mind and life will change in an instant, in a split second. What we are trying to do in our work is to get to that larger mind or soul.

I feel there is a world mind, too. We are a reflection of that world mind. The dualism within us is a reflection of the dualism the world has within it. That world mind conceives of poverty and wealth, illness and health, of all situations. When I help an MS patient improve, I help the whole world. Because in that particular moment I teach the world its strength.

LOUISE HAY

Keeping Good Company
June 1988

Offering the simple message, "Love thyself," Louise Hay has skyrocketed in popularity during the last four years as author (You Can Heal Your Life *and* The AIDS Book: Creating a Positive Approach, *among others), AIDS lecturer, and now publisher (Hay House). Her infectious faith in the power of self-acceptance and forgiveness has helped thousands of people with AIDS and ARC begin a journey back to full health.* East West *publisher Leonard Jacobs and staffer Cynthia Smith met with Louise Hay when she came to Boston to lecture and present one of her popular healing workshops.*

EAST WEST: What does it mean to love yourself?

LOUISE HAY: To appreciate who you are, to stop criticizing yourself, to stop making yourself wrong, and to just allow yourself to be. If you feel that you care for yourself, then you relax into life a lot more. But if you don't trust yourself, because you're not there for yourself, you get into trouble. You scold yourself or go out and get drunk or overeat. It's because there's a part of you that doesn't trust you and that's not good company, usually.

EW: Is it possible to love yourself without having a relationship to others?

LH: The way you feel about yourself will determine the sort of relationship you have with others.

EW: Couldn't we end up with a lot of people who love themselves but don't give a hoot about anyone else?

LH: When you really love yourself, you cannot hurt yourself or another person. I'm not talking about narcissism or arrogance, or anything like that, because that isn't love—that's fear. I'm talking about cherishing the being that you are. Out of that comes feelings that you want to help other people. And you're not doing it out of a "should," you're doing it out of "I care. I really care."

EW: Why does it seem that there are a lot more unhappy people than there are happy people?

LH: Because so many of us were raised by frightened or angry parents. We have this cultural way of looking at life. It's socially acceptable to worry, to get ill, to see the worst. The way we look at life is the way we're going to find it. People in the human potential movement are not necessarily more loving, either. I think I've taken every workshop that's around and I remember being in one group and I was just appalled at how they treated their own people. I thought, "My God, these are your people! I'm not talking about the workshop people who are supposed to be getting some message, but the people who work with you. You treat them this way. That's awful!" It's not my way.

EW: Has your popularity surprised you?

LH: Yes, it surprised me. I knew the work would increase. I didn't know it would come the way it did and of course I had no idea that AIDS would pop up on the planet. I was one of the first people to take a positive approach to people with AIDS, and that increased my visibility a great deal.

MILTON TRAGER

Moving with a Bodywork Pioneer
January 1988

Seventy-nine-year-old Milton Trager is the founder of the Tragerwork Approach for Psychophysical Integration—an astonishingly successful and largely intuitive method of body-mind healing with over 1,000 trained personnel and many more students in eighteen countries. Using his simple Tragerwork tools: "hook-up" (a meditative state), "Mentastics" (mentally directed movements), and "the best hands in the business" (he places far more credence on demonstrating his techniques than trying to explain them), this former boxer, acrobat, dancer, and general practice physician has had consistent success in treating a wide range of ailments, from migraine and lower back pain to autism and sciatica. His first authorized book, Trager Mentastics: Movement as a Way to Agelessness, *was published in 1987.*

Interviewer Richard Leviton said of Trager, "...you know you are in the presence of an original healer, a professional peer of such luminaries as Ida Rolf and Moshe Feldenkrais."

EAST WEST: In recent years what has been the most dramatic turnaround you've experienced with a client?

MILTON TRAGER: It happens every time. I don't find anyone who doesn't respond. Anybody, with any kind of condition—they'll be better when they leave my office. They walk out of here differently. It's a matter of reaching the unconscious. My direction now is completely towards the unconscious mind. I pick up restrictions, areas that are not working in the body, and release them at the source, which is the unconscious mind.

EW: Are you saying that we unconsciously choose all our illnesses?

MT: We don't choose anything. It's a happening. It's stored in the unconscious and remains there, hardly ever getting better. You're stuck in the pattern. Doctors will say, "By all that's holy, he should be well. I've done everything I should, so he should be well, but we're going to lose him." That's because the pattern can't be changed by those doctors. They can't do anything with the pattern because they're not trained to know of the existence of a pattern. Yesterday I made the statement to a student here, "My job is to develop more sensitive therapists so they can pick up these restrictions and release them."

EW: How can you develop that sensitivity in somebody?

MT: By making them more proficient in the manner in which they work and feel. We're talking about the most important thing in the work: feeling. Whenever you use the words feel, feelings, felt, you are talking about the unconscious mind. The conscious mind does not feel.

EW: In terms of what this says about an illness, it sounds as if it is just a matter of degree whether you have lower back pain or something more intense like asthma.

MT: No, it's not that at all. The psychic and emotional part enters all of those conditions and breaks down the immune system. Gastroneurologists often say, "If I could cut off his head, I could cure his ulcer." That's how powerful the mind is.

EW: So a particular disability becomes stored in the unconscious and, in a sense, is maintained there?

MT: Maintained in the unconscious in the pattern that exists there. In the Trager approach we break down your resistance patterns, the locks, as we call them.

EW: How does this differ from verbal-oriented psychotherapies where the goal is to remember what happened and why one is so uptight?

MT: I had two years in psychiatry so I'm acquainted with the psychiatric approach. But I don't have to know what happened a long time ago. After experiencing my work the pattern isn't bugging the person anymore. That's all I give a damn about. I won't work at digging stuff out of people. My model is finding the restrictions, working with them, bringing positive feeling patterns to the unconscious mind where I can break up the old patterns. That's the whole story.

EW: Is there a disease your system might not work with?

MT: I don't work with cancer patients because they're not coming to me but going to the medical doctors. I think that, regarding the immune system, which is involved with cancer, AIDS, and multiple sclerosis, if we can break up the block and develop the immune system better, these people will be on the way to being cured. I haven't involved myself with this mainly because I have all I can possibly do with the neuromuscular field, which is where I've been working all my life.

CULTURE

Anaïs Nin

Tom Wolfe

Salvador Dali

John Denver

Yoko Ono

Keith Jarrett

JOHN CAGE

Zen Composition
May 1979

John Cage, the first American composer to have gained international recognition in avant garde music, is famous for his use of "chance operations" and multi-media audio-visual devices in composing, and for introducing into music the "all-sound continuum" including silence and so-called environmental "noise." Cage has been associated with Merce Cunningham Dance Company in New York since 1943. He was interviewed by freelancer Maureen Furman.

EAST WEST: You mentioned that the busiest you ever were except for now was twenty-five years ago. What was happening then?

JOHN CAGE: I made a decision in the early fifties to accept the sounds that are in the world. Before that I had actually been naive enough to think there was such a thing as silence. But I went into an anechoic chamber in Cambridge at Harvard University, and in this room I heard two sounds. I thought there was something wrong with the room, and I told the engineer that there were two sounds. He said describe them, and I did. "Well," he said, "the high one was your nervous system in operation and the low one was your blood circulating." So that means that there is music, or there is sound, whether I intend it or not. Silence is the change of my mind. It's an acceptance of the sounds that exist rather than a desire to choose and impose one's own music. That has been at the center of my work ever since then. I try when I make a new piece of music to make it in such a way that it doesn't essentially disturb the silence that already exists.

EW: People talk about the "music of the spheres" as the sound of the universe, almost like an ideal that musicians should strive for. What do you think of that idea?

JC: I think that rather than searching for a perfect music, or a fully resolved something-or-other, that we should live with gratitude in a world of greater multiplicity than we have ever had before; and rather than searching for *the right* answer for a problem, I think we should take all the answers and use them *all*—because some of them will benefit some people and others will be more accessible to other people.

Some people are color blind. How could they benefit from a particular kind of painting? So, you can imagine someone who simply would not be able to hear a particular kind of music but could hear another one which a third person might not be able to use, and so on. I don't think, in other words, that rightness exists; I think this situation we're dealing with is really as Suzuki said, "purely subjective." It is received differently in different centers of creation.

EW: What about the role of music in furthering world understanding and peace?

JC: I'm not entirely optimistic about the effectiveness of art as a means of changing people's minds and bringing about this change for the better. I think that it certainly can be used that way, but I don't think that it is automatically effective. People who are going to live in a destructive way can be brought into an auditorium where beautiful music is playing and they can leave just as destructively inclined as they were when they went in. I don't think music will change those people until they are, so to speak, ready to change.

I think that diet has a more immediate and universal effect, but even there those people who are destructive (or self-destructive) are not inclined to change their eating habits. In my own case I know I wouldn't have changed unless I had been in pain.

However, the need to change my music was evident to me earlier in my life. I had been taught, as most people are, that music is in effect the expression of an individual's ego—"self-expression" is what I had been taught. But then, when I saw that everyone was expressing themselves differently and using a different way of composing, I deduced that we were in a tower of Babel situation because no one was understanding anybody else; for instance, I wrote a sad piece and people hearing it laughed. It was clearly pointless to continue in that way, so I determined to stop writing music until I found a better reason for doing it than self-expression.

I finally found the reason in Oriental traditions; however, a friend of mine found it expressed by an English composer as late I think as the seventeenth century. It was this: "The purpose of music is to sober and quiet the mind, thus making us susceptible to divine influences." I then determined to find out what was a quiet mind and what were divine influences. I found through further study of Oriental philosophy, first Indian, then Zen Buddhism, that a quiet mind was one that was free of likes and dislikes. So I set about to do that—it led me to making my music, so to speak, silent—that is, not imposing my intentions on it.

My ears hear everything as music really. All of these sounds you hear now, all the street sounds, I enjoy as acoustic phenomena. I enjoy that more than *any* music, including any of my music. And I do that all day long.

KEITH JARRETT

Dancing on the Edge
October 1981

Keith Jarrett is a jazz pianist who has been playing since the age of three. According to East West *interviewer Meg Seaker, "He discussed his unique and complex improvisational technique, which has won him the acclaim of critics and the almost fanatical devotion of a large, international following." Jarrett played with Charles Lloyd and Miles Davis, among others, before forming his own quartet. In 1983 he made his debut as a concert soloist with the Philadelphia Orchestra and the San Francisco Symphony.* East West's *Richard Lehnert and Merridee Shaw were co-interviewers with Seaker while Jarrett was in Boston for a solo concert celebrating Bach's birthday.*

EAST WEST: What do you see as your primary responsibility as an artist?

KEITH JARRETT: Dylan said that "beauty is a razor's edge." That to me is exactly what it is. You have to just keep dancing on the razor's edge. To me that's my primary responsibility as an artist.

EW: Can you describe what it means to "dance on the edge"?

 KJ: The edge is knowing it. The edge is when you are not here and you know it, but you have to be here on time, with the flow.

EW: Two different things are going on at one time and both are true.

 KJ: But in this case you know which one is the bigger truth. You love the earth and there's something that needs to be done. You know that no one else is doing what you do. In my case, I don't know anyone who does what I do. So if I don't do it, who's going to do it?

EW: You once mentioned that death hovers around quite a bit at a solo concert. Do you feel like you're in more danger as you become more sensitive?

 KJ: Yes, but the danger is greater when you want to remain on the edge. Everything that helps you to stabilize yourself anchors you in this dance, keeps you from flowing. The danger of that is it's crystallizing, like wanting to make a liquid into a solid, so that you know where it is, and it won't go into the next room. You solidify—you take it with you and put it down on the table. Everyone crystallizes, but the earlier you do it, the less you are alive. And as

145

soon as you're crystallized it's not life anymore. It's an attitude toward life. You're not living. You're putting your own stake down; instead of your two feet on the razor you have a third thing: Your attitude toward what's around this edge and how to deal with it. You decide how to deal with life. Then, if you're an artist, all you portray is your way of living. And it could be real hip, depending on the time, or it could be considered very avant-garde, or it could simply be where your anchor goes down—it's just a slightly different place, making a different angle.

EW: How have you kept yourself from crystallizing?

KJ: I think you have to be completely without mercy with yourself. You can't say something like, "I did this yesterday before I played the concert, and the concert was great! Therefore, I should do that again." Anything that creates a pattern creates an anchor. First it's conscious and then it's unconscious. When it's unconscious, it isn't only an anchor, it's a habit.

It's something everyone does at times. But for me the difference is—no matter what the beneficial effect of the thing—I *cannot allow* it to take the place of the dance. So it's the only way that the music is going to keep coming out. The music is dancing more than I am. I have to keep up with it by not having an anchor, so the music can take me somewhere. And that's where death comes in. You're choosing to be blown around in the wind. It's bad to be blown around in the wind if you don't know it. Then it's very important to have some center of gravity. In art that would be a style, the way you want yourself to sound. You've got your own sound—your own way of playing. But then you've got to throw it away and be blown around. That's where real art begins, and for most people, they've never even thought of that.

EW: How do you feel your music may be in terms of healing qualities? More and more musicians seem to be getting involved in that.

KJ: Those are the people who will never heal anybody. If you look—and it would take a lot of looking—at the music most capable of healing, the sounds that seem to be most enlightening and healthy and vital, are sounds that come from people who just make music and consider it a responsibility. There are no extra-curricular considerations such as "I can do this with this" or "I'm sure this will happen with this." These are all anchors again. If you were a musician and you were unconsciously dissatisfied with the music that you played, you would start wondering whether it could be used in a certain way. If it said everything you needed it to say, you wouldn't mention a word of it. Because it would heal if it needed to heal and it would not in other cases—it would do whatever needed to be done, automatically. The minute you think, "I would like to be involved in musical therapy," you are giving yourself a raise and promoting yourself. You are not only a musician, you are also a musical therapist. That's the problem: What do you think of yourself, instead of what do you do. It is the lack of attitude completely that allows the whole thing to be there, which is the only attitude an artist that I would put a capital A on should have.

RAVI SHANKAR

An Interview With Ravi Shankar
November 1972

Ravi Shankar, master of the sitar, is the man most responsible for bringing the traditional music of India to Western audiences. Aside from his association with Beatle George Harrison in the late '60s, which secured the sitar's place in the pop music of that time, Shankar is a renowned musician and composer in his own country. He has composed many film scores, most notably for Gandhi, *and is active in Indian national arts programs while continuing to perform concerts throughout the world.*

East West's Ed Esko and Philadelphia radio station WXPN's Barry Mike conducted this interview prior to a Shankar concert in Boston.

EAST WEST: What is the background of your tremendous rise in popularity?

RAVI SHANKAR: When George Harrison became my student in the end of '66, all of a sudden the whole thing became, as I like to call it, the "sitar explosion." Young people discovered our music for the first time, which was very good. I think that was good for our music in a way, only there was the other side, which really was a great strain for me for all these years, and still now I have to face some problems when I go to new places. And that is because these kids became familiar with the sound of sitar through George Harrison and other pop musicians. They had a wrong attitude and wrong approach to our music. And invariably the drug association, which was very annoying. Even now I face problems when I ask people to stop smoking when I'm performing.

So that was the negative side of it, but on the other hand, I think we did well. Of course that fad period is finished now. What has remained is something beautiful. I like this, because now whoever comes to our music I find to have a much more serious approach, and in places like Philadelphia, Boston, New York, Washington, San Francisco, Los Angeles, London, Paris, and I could go on, for we have been performing for quite a while, I find not only appreciation, but a certain amount of understanding also, which is fantastic. It's almost like playing in Bombay or Calcutta now. Only you have union rules where I cannot go on playing for hours, as many people would like.

EW: If you were playing in Bombay you might go on for four or five hours?

RS: Yes. When I play in certain places, like smaller places—when I say smaller I mean the number of people might be as many as 1500 or 2000—these are the music circles we have in India, and they all sit on the floor, and there are a lot of chairs in the background where some older people sit. And I play as long as seven hours, eight hours, nine hours, with just one short break. My fingers start bleeding, but I don't feel it. I enjoy it because I have all these people in the front who are either musicians or music students or connoisseurs. It's a great ecstasy, because our music is improvised. There's no fixed duration for playing a raga. It depends upon the mood of the artist, the listener, the situation.

EW: Could you explain the role of emotion in Indian classical music?

RS: All of our art forms, not only music but also painting, dance, drama, are based on *nava rasa*, which means literally "juice" or "nectar," but in this case it means mood or emotion. There are nine principal moods or emotions, like *shringare, veera, hasya*, or the tranquil, the pathetic, the heroic, the erotic, and so on.

EW: Is that because the Indian people express themselves more through emotion than through precise scientific means?

RS: That's the beautiful combination. Emotion, of course, is a very important thing, otherwise, you won't have any reaction from the listener or the viewer. But don't think that it is all emotion and no intellect. We have to learn complex ragas and complex talas which form the scientific basis of our music. Our music is balanced between both.

EW: Most Westerners have little understanding of what a guru is, how he relates to music, or the whole system of study under which you learned to play. Could you explain it for us?

RS: "Guru" to us is something so very special. Guru is not just a teacher, but is like a teacher, a master, a preceptor all in one. We look up to the guru sometimes as a god, even more than a god. And it is not just the technique or the craft that the guru teaches his disciple, but it is the whole way of life, the philosophy, the spiritual, the religious; in fact the whole cultural heritage of our country is passed through the guru.

EW: Given the very improvisational nature of the raga, and at the same time the improvisational nature of jazz, do you think that there is some sort of natural relationship between the two?

RS: I wouldn't say relationship, but a resemblance, which is very superficial. The only things that are similar is the improvisation, the individuality of the artist, and the excitement of the rhythms.

EW: But aren't those things very important modes of expression?

RS: Of course, but what I'm trying to say is that these are the only resemblances. If you go deeper into it you will realize that our system has a history of almost 2000 years, even more than that, and it has a very scientific and precise system of discipline. The fact that we improvise on these ragas and complex rhythm cycles shows the precise root of our music.

EW: In your book, *My Music, My Life*, you mentioned that when you were in

America in the 1930s, you saw Louis Armstrong and Duke Ellington.

RS: Oh yes. In a way they were my musical heroes; the same with Casals in his prime, or Segovia in his youth, and even Yehudi Menuhin. All these musicians were my heroes, and in the world of jazz I was so impressed by musicians like Duke Ellington and Armstrong.

EW: Did you notice then any feelings of similarity between jazz and Indian music?

RS: I was more moved by the earthy effect of those jazz musicians. They weren't the same as the Western classical musicians. They were more personal; they could bring out so much more warmth. But jazz has changed tremendously. Now it is more intellectual, more cerebral, very atonal, and very much like modern avant-garde music. That is something I find a bit difficult to appreciate. I react much more to the earlier jazz where there was so much, I'll use that word again, earthy feeling, and so much poignant sadness, or happiness. Very childlike, and at the same time tremendous musicianship.

EW: In India is music thought of as a healing power?

RS: Yes, we don't exactly have practicing doctors who are musicians, but it has always been said that music has tremendous healing power. Just the fact that it relaxes the body produces quite an effect. There is a theory that certain combinations of notes and certain scales produce different effects on the body.

EW: What is the role of *prana* [ki] or life force in Indian music?

RS: Well, it's a very involved thing, and it takes a number of years to get into that. But a raga is only a raga when it is alive, otherwise it would be just a succession of notes, a dead raga. It is the prana, the life, that is given by the musician or the guru. It cannot be found in books; and no matter if it is computerized and told that this particular wavelength is the correct *shruti* [microtone]. You get that special thing that is alive from your guru, which he got from his guru; and this is the only secret that is passed down from guru to pupil.

YOKO ONO

A Woman Inside My Soul
February 1973

Avant-garde artist, film-maker, songwriter and singer Yoko Ono is the widow of former Beatle John Lennon. East West interviewers Ed Esko and Jessica Chambless remarked of Ono and Lennon's New York apartment, "inside the feeling is relaxed, yet with an air of activity." Currently Ono is involved in projects of her own and travels widely, supervising them.

EAST WEST: Do you believe that music has a medicinal effect?

YOKO ONO: Yes. This is something we've been working on for over ten years. I started to see that there is something about vibrations that you can't limit to thirteen sounds. The more delicate vibrations come across only when you're in a certain state of mind. I used to fast for five days before I would do a concert so I would be in a certain state of mind for the vibrations to be right. Finally, the concerts became more and more involved in vibrations you can't even hear, and they came to be called concerts of the mind. There was no sound. It was music created and communicated within the mind.

So I went into all that vibrational thing, and what I found was that for people who are completely square or who don't have enough freedom of mind, you can't talk to them because they have a barrier there. But what if you make a record that has a certain vibration in it that they can't even hear? That was my big project when I first met John.

I asked my assistants to look into the scientific side of it. What sounds and combination of sounds produce vibrations that cause people to feel more loving and peaceful rather than violent and miserable? They came to the conclusion that the music (like some of the Beatles' songs, for instance) is naturally reaching that point. If it is analyzed scientifically, it goes back to that. I realized, then, that I was going in the right direction through fasting and producing a state of mind—not scientifically, but through a mental process—to create sounds with healing vibrations.

EW: So the state of mind that you approach music with influences the nature of the music?

YO: That's right. Most of my free things happen when I go into the studio and just do it, and don't go over the line, to use a Japanese expression. When I go into the studio and do something, I'm aware that every voice that comes out of me is from thirty-nine years of experience, and you can't get that from any other instrument.

EW: It seems that your music goes from the very basic up to the highest spiritual levels—you can feel something that's very melodious but at the same time you feel an element that's very lamenting.

YO: In Zen there's a way of going, "crack!" It's all yin and yang. Not just being sweet, but giving a little shock as well. I'm perfectly aware that we could probably create music that could kill somebody who was just listening to it. But if we have that power we have to control it and be aware of it. And if you have that power then you also have the power to soothe and heal, as well. It's like poison—it's the way you use it.

When John and I recorded *Cambridge '69* it happened in a sort of unusual way. Cambridge University invited me to do some music. I told them that I was coming alone with my band—of course I didn't tell them that my band was John. So we did about an hour's worth of music and completely used our energies and completely exhausted ourselves. It was very strong stuff and I don't think I could do it now. Now it's sort of a resting period for my voice. In *Winter Is Here To Stay* I show a more quiet side. I might come back into that again, though. It's like breathing: You inhale and then you exhale, and then find balance.

EW: Do you and John feel that balance?

YO: Yes, definitely. I think it just happens naturally. When I'm strong he tends to retire and vice versa. Sometimes we both have this vitality going.

EW: In certain songs on your album you take very simple situations and get to their basic feeling, especially in "I Want My Love To Rest Tonight."

YO: Oh, yes, that was naturally coming from our togetherness. John had to go through this female liberation thing too, being with me. It was difficult for him in a way. You must understand what kind of environment he comes from—Liverpool—then immediately being King of the World, everyone around him catering to that situation. In a way it was difficult, but he's very aware of things. He's one of the most understanding men in that sense. Intellectually he understands, but emotionally it must be difficult. So we went through all that, and I felt his pain too. I understand why they have to go through that. I just don't feel that they're male chauvinist pigs and that's all. It's like they're victims of society too. So there's that side of it.

Anyway, we were out in the country at a farmhouse, resting for a weekend. We were coming back to New York, and he was getting sort of frightened, thinking, "We're going back to New York, back to life again!" Then he fell asleep in my lap in the car. That's when I was writing this:

Sisters, don't blame my man too much,
I know he's doing his best.

I know his fear and loneliness,
He can do no more, no less.

He was brought up by us women,
And the world that told him to be a man.
He reached and stretched to be someone,
While millions more tried to be the one.

Cho: I want my man to rest tonight,
So he can face the world tomorrow.
I want my love to sleep tonight,
So he can deal with tomorrow.*

EW: Now that this album is out, what do you see ahead of you?

YO: There are many more songs that I have written that are not on this album, so I may do something with them. But I think right now both John and I want to rest.

*Copyright 1973 Yoko Ono

JOHN DENVER

Healing the Earth with Country Love
August 1981

John Denver, whose songs, including "Country Roads" and "Sunshine on My Shoulders," skyrocketed him to world celebrity status, has had a lifelong concern for the environment and humanity's role on the planet. He is the co-founder of The Windstar Foundation in Snowmass, Colo., which is dedicated to the appropriate use of technology through conscious choice in a spirit of community and peace.

Denver was interviewed in Boston by East West *freelancer Ann Fawcett.*

EAST WEST: Your early songs affirm the positive side of things, but I've observed in recent albums such as *Rocky Mountain High* and *Autograph* that there's an increasing concern for preserving our natural environment.

JOHN DENVER: I never intended to take people away from life. I really prefer to put them in touch with life. And more in touch with the life that I find most real and honest as opposed to the superficial existence which we have created for ourselves. Even though we live on concrete, I would prefer to have people touch the earth. Many of us have so taken the environment, nature, for granted that we really have lost a big part of ourselves—where we come from and who we really are. I intend to keep bringing people back to that, to the degree I am able, through the music. Within that context I don't know if the songs are prophetic, but they are getting deeper and more pointed.

It's a very interesting thing. I'm involved in a conflict between my career and my conscience. Yet I recognize that the greatest way to do the work of my conscience is to keep my career alive and vital. Through being a celebrity I have a chance to speak to as large an audience as I am able about the things I care most deeply for.

EW: Your music has a great capacity to touch people on a personal, political, and spiritual level. You possess a great deal of personal power and influence. How do you feel about having that kind of influence?

JD: I treat it as a responsibility. It is not necessarily something that I was working for. From the very beginning of my career I didn't just want to entertain people. I wanted to touch them. I just want to acknowledge and express my appreciation of nature and the world around me. We're all talking about the same thing. I just find it easier not to get caught up in any specific form. I don't want to be too caught up as being macrobiotic either. I don't want it to become another way of separating ourselves from each other.

EW: How do you respond to criticism?

JD: People can say whatever they want about me. I'm going to be myself. I'm going to grow, learn, and do everything I can to complete the cycle. I'm not just going to take from life. I'm going to give back to it. And whether it's effective or not, whether I'm making a contribution or not, I will learn and I will change.

You know, I'm a very wealthy man. I have my own Lear jet. I'm a pilot, and I'm involved in all these kinds of projects. I use those things as tools. They make my life a lot easier, but I don't feel bad about it one iota. I'm using all of this to further projects I feel deeply about. I wouldn't have been able to come up here today without my own airplane or leave for Paris tomorrow to do a special appearance in tribute for Captain Cousteau. All of these things have come my way and I intend to make use of them. The parable of the five talents is one of my favorites and reflects what I mean about responsibility: One guy got one talent and he hoarded it over here and lost it. The next guy got two talents. He did the same thing but a little bit differently. The third guy got five talents and look what he did. He did this, this, and this, and came back with ten talents. Now that's what I want to do. I have incredible opportunities, and I want to use each and every one of them in order to realize the age-old dream of peace on this earth. The future is ours. It's up to *all* of us to keep that dream alive.

KAJI ASO

Etchings in Moonlight
May 1980

Japanese-born artist Kaji Aso teaches at the Boston Museum of Fine Arts School, but devotes most of his time to the students at his own Kaji Aso Studio. Aso organized the Living National Treasures of Japan exhibit, which toured the U.S. in 1982-1983. He is an avid runner, and when interviewer Christina Haftmann asked about it, Aso replied, "Running is a natural thing; it's cooperating dynamically with nature. Art is a completely civilized act, and running is very primitive. It's a good thing for a human being to have a double character."

EAST WEST: Did you have a vision or dream about your studio?

KAJI ASO: No. It just happened. As far as I can, I do things which I have to do. That's all. However, even in the beginning I recognized the value and meaning of these activities. When we started, the commercial art of Newbury Street in Boston and Madison Avenue in New York was completely stupid, very chaotic. It was conceptual art and all this sort of junk, but still I respected painting, so I thought I had to defend the sanity of painting. Without sanity, painting doesn't exist.

I wanted to work with truly intelligent, naive, innocent, yet capable people. These people are usually the foundation of a society, the basic energy, yet they are always neglected by the other people. I was standing on the borderline because I could be socially and superficially successful, but at the same time I had a conscience and a basic idea of my capability. I could see both sides and so I really felt strongly that I have to save this aspect of human beings.

EW: What do you think an artist can do for society?

KA: If you are just painting to impress people for fame or money, there is no hope. Society has no values, so how can your painting exist without a foundation? An artist cannot perform art for society, because if he did it would just be entertainment. The relationship between an artist and society must be upside down. The function of an artist is to be a priori; he must always be far ahead of society. To have an advanced vision without society's approval or negative limitation is very important. If you are truly painting, here is life and here is hope. Maybe this painting won't help anyone in the society, but the philosophy or attitude of this painting—the fact that I paint, I do exist—if this attitude is perceived by a large number of people, then there is hope and more life. That is actually what I'm doing.

EW: Do you think it's an advantage or a disadvantage for an artist, male or female, to have a family?

KA: The condition of your art comes out of the condition of your life. If you haven't suffered, how can you have sympathy for others? It reminds me of Basho's poem:

> First autumn rain
> Looking for the straw raincoat
> A monkey too.

Basho himself felt cold, miserable, sad, and needed a straw coat. When he saw the monkey, he felt sympathy for him. So here is a poem. Actually, Basho himself was the monkey. That's life. People believe that art is just technology, but that's not true. Art comes from life. To transform your life into a certain object such as canvas or words, you need some technology, but basically you need maximum human contact.

Art is a life environment; in art people can grow, people can live. For example, in haiku we squeeze out short verses and it becomes the essence of the human spirit. That means getting from a lot of things. And that means everyday life.

EW: What about your own life?

KA: In my case being alone always reminds me of the real condition of life. Even if you are married or in love, you are basically alone. In my life one side is Paradise, a flower garden, and the other side is a deep valley. The reality is both. If I miss a step, I fall. That is life. Being an artist is really walking a tightrope, because you have to be a human being or no art comes out. But if you are just living, then you have no idea how to bring out your life into art, so you have to be conscious of what you are doing. Being alone keeps me clear and in perspective.

Generally, a human being should be just like an animal: Born in this world, eat enough, sleep enough, run enough, and when he gets old he should die. Nothing is wrong with that. To be an artist you have to have life *plus* this other business. Living alone for me is good because one side is a warm spring breeze and the other side is a cold north wind. But that's not necessary for everyone.

To be an artist is not really a question of whether you have talent or not, but to see this basic human vulnerability and transform it. That involves more heart than mind.

My instruction is simply to pay attention—open your eyes and see what nature is doing. What happens on the canvas is the process of your recognition of nature. It depends on the stage and condition of your life. Painting naturally shows your life process. And there is no doubt you are there. You don't have to make up anything like a trademark.

EW: You have the ability to say something to a class that touches everyone on a deeply personal level. To what do you attribute that?

KA: I think it's simply that no fragmentation has been going on inside of me, which means I'm not specializing in any one thing. Any knowledge that comes from me comes from my simple life. For example, you can never start a painting from painting. A painting has to come from living. You have to paint from your place, which will take you any place. What is your own place? I teach the most basic knowledge of painting, then a student can go anywhere. I give them the universal value.

SALVADOR DALI

Hello, Dali
February 1974

Surrealist artist and designer Salvador Dali, who died in January 1989 at the age of eighty-four, can perhaps best be described in the words of interviewer J. Richard Turner: "He was born some years after a brother who had lived and died of meningitis. When Dali himself was born, he so resembled his dead brother that his grief stricken parents through an incredible, morbid transference totally identified him with their first, deceased son. He was even given his name—Salvador. At every moment of his life, he was not the living Salvador Dali, but the embodiment, the physical extension, the unique connective of his dead, previous, other self. Salvador Dali existed in the duality of two worlds: The dimension of death—the other side—and this dimension—the physical reality. And so, his work constantly flows between the two."

Turner, with Bronwyn Feeney, "interviewed" Dali in a darkened cocktail lounge at the St. Regis Hotel in New York.

EAST WEST: Do you think that it is possible for an evolution of consciousness to occur on this planet?

SALVADOR DALI: I will not discuss metaphysics! Only what is in *Scientific American*.

EW: What is your definition of Reality?

SD: Bits of information. What is important is to copy exactly, copy as in a history, or tradition. Creative, tradition.

EW: Your work seems to break down our conceptions of limits. What do you see beyond the worlds of time and space?

SD: Time is relativity, and time and space is one single thing. When you approach the speed of time, you become more young. That happens to space...everything is the same...the anus has the spiral—35 or 36 wrinkles...with the speed of light your anus contracts!

EW: It has been said that truth is stranger than fiction. What is truth?

SD: I will not discuss the truth! Never tell the truth, because today is not the same as tomorrow. Everything is always changing, so truth can never be static. It is always moving!

EW: This seems to be a time when the institutional superstructures...

SD: There is only one structure!!! That is the spiral!! In the beginning, Dali was concerned with the psychoanalysis of Dr. Freud—the darkness of the subconscious, and now through bits of information, this becomes more luminous. In one little atom, there are bits and bits of information...every fragment of matter carries within it the potential for immortality...each cell contains within the complete genetic code of the whole organism. Through DNA, Dali conquers death!

EW: What is God?

SD: God is a little less than one meter! God is very little; this proves that God is condensed substance. The last particle invented only energy, and probably the only substance exists and is condensed in God.

EW: Senor Dali, where do you get your inspiration? Why paint? Why create?

SD: Dali's inspiration comes through playing, not working or thinking. The worst model is Rodin's *Thinker*. This only makes for defecation! All thinking makes for defecation! Painting is one way to show a little part of my idea. The painting is a very fragmentary part of my idea.

EW: Do you consider yourself a twentieth century alchemist?

SD: No! Not in those words! But, in words that mean that!

ROBERTO ROSSELLINI

On Film Making
February 1974

Italian film director Roberto Rossellini, who died in 1977, is credited with having created, in the '40s, a new style of film-making called "neo-realism," marked by socially concerned themes and the use of locations rather than sets. Setting Rossellini apart throughout his career was an overriding spirituality, a sense of the beauty and harmony in the world even amid destruction and struggle. Perhaps his best known films are Stromboli...Land of God *and* Fear, *which he made with Ingrid Bergman, his wife at the time in the early '50s. He went on to use nothing less than the entire history of the world to express a vision of the unity and inner balances of existence in such works as* The Rise of Louis XIV, Man's Struggle for Survival, *and* The Acts of the Apostles.

Rossellini was accessible and amiable in this interview by freelancers Eric Sherman and John Dorr.

EAST WEST: In a talk you gave at NYU, you referred to essential images and how they relate to bringing about a universal discourse. Would you please comment on this?

ROBERTO ROSSELLINI: What we call images are really just illustrations. Our mechanical, mental way of thinking is purely verbal. When you prepare to make a film, the first thing you do is write a script. Writing a script is absolutely verbal. After that, you go back and use the technique of images to illustrate your thoughts.

Now, when we first appeared on the earth, having a brain with the capacity of observation, the capacity to store reflections, experiences, and so on, our sense of the world came from our own eyes, from the images, the "essential images." But to remember what we had recorded we were obliged to invent a technique—the invention of a language. And so, our dialectical mind is built on words instead of images. The image was, at the beginning, the only way to understand things. Now that we have the possibility to build images (make films), we build images for a mental proceeding, which is verbal. So, those images become illustrations and not an essential image. An essential image must say everything in itself.

What I am trying to do is reestablish, to find for myself, that sort of essential image. You must be trained to discover all the messages there can be in a single frame. Instead of demonstrating something, I want to offer an image through which you discover things yourself. Normally, the technique of film is underlining everything. "Look at that, look at that, now observe that." If you want to recreate the truth, you must not underline anything. You must offer an observation.

EW: In order to retain a spontaneity of image, you said you would not reshoot scenes.

RR: No, never. If you search for perfection, you're involved, and want "to show." It's you in the first person who talks. Sometimes I want to disappear totally. My films can be very bad, horrible, disgusting, anything you want. But one thing I am almost sure, they are very true. Even if I do something historical. And the truth comes out from the non-perfection, I think.

EW: It seems that the essential image is something we started with, but words then interfered. Now you're getting back to this.

RR: You must, if you are to reach a total innocence, if you are to be really like a child. If you can reduce yourself to the level of a child, with all their enthusiasm, and no more than that, that is the essential thing to living.

EW: No rigid expectations.

RR: That's right, no message, just to be continuously in search.

EW: Can the general audience...

RR: The general audience—what is it? If you want to do something, you must do it. Who cares if you don't have success now? If you want to be really like a child, the only thing that is important is enthusiasm, and no more than that. Otherwise, you become immediately a victim of the system. You are tied with a certain kind of mental procedure, which is conditioned.

EW: The translation of your ideas into your art is so amazing.

RR: But art, what is it? It's a certain kind of capacity for thinking. The main thing is to think, to have the capacity to express yourself if your ideas are clear. If your ideas are clear, you'll find a way to express yourself.

EW: Do Italian filmmakers have much freedom?

RR: Yes, they have freedom. You know, freedom is something absolutely personal. You are free if you have the courage to fight. You are not free if you are scared. That's the thing. Everyone tries to reduce your freedom, but if you have courage nobody can reduce it.

EW: How do you feel about not getting the recognition that most people, especially film students, think you deserve?

RR: I'll tell you one thing. When I get the success, I get scared. I know something is wrong. Because if you do something new, you must not have success immediately. My main goal in life is to always be in the adventure. If you get success, it means you are doing something not so new.

JOHN GARDNER

America's Dostoevski
February 1974

An innovative and highly talented writer, John Gardner represented a developing "new age" consciousness, full of reverence, intuition, wit, imagination, and compassion. He did a great deal to revive what some felt was a dying art form—the novel, with such works as The Sunlight Dialogues, The Resurrection, Nickel Mountain, *and* Grendel. *Gardner, who was killed in a motorcycle accident in 1982, was the recipient of the 1976 National Book Critics Award for fiction for his* October Light.

EAST WEST: As a successful novelist, could you say something about creativity?

JOHN GARDNER: There's a great desire by a lot of writers, painters, and musicians to be original—and that's the least creative thing they can be. Particularly now, when all cultural options are open to us—we can hear music from Ireland as easily as music from New York or St. Louis—the thing is to explore traditional forms and find the ones that suit you. Express yourself through an imitation of the form, because then you're getting a balance between what is yourself and what's universal. I think as long as you're following forms from clear traditions, you can't go wrong, because always the individual stuff will come out.

EW: Would you say that currently everyone stresses individuality so much that no one thinks form is important?

JG: It depends on what you mean by form. Take the different modes of music; there are hundreds of modes that you can write in—different ragas and so on. The form is the notes of the scale that are in that raga. But then what you do with it is *you*. You have to make it work. It has to sound good with those notes.

Another way of saying it is this: When a culture goes bad, as every culture does—Eastern, Western, or whatever—it usually goes bad because people decide that as individuals they're the all-important thing. Think of classical wrestling and modern show wrestling. The idea of show wrestling is that each guy has a different thing: Gorgeous George, years ago—what pretty hair, the angel tries to look like a monkey. Whereas, in classical wrestling, the whole point is to get exactly the same holds that one used for centuries and make them work. Same way with classical ballet as opposed to modern dance. All ballet dancers try to look like all other ballet dancers. They may be better and better and better at the particular step, whereas with modern dance your total purpose is to express your own individual body. There are times when you need modern dance and times when you need classical. But this is a time, I think, when we need classical.

EW: Do you feel that everyone has artistic ability in one way or another?

JG: Everybody has imagination, but artists have an ability to snap into *theta* at any moment. You know, the *theta* brain wave pattern, measured by electric impulses. Whereas a yoga master snaps into *alpha* at the drop of a hat.

EW: Would you describe that?

JG: There are different brain cycles, measured electrically. They happen to be named *alpha*, *beta*, *theta*, and so on. The *alpha* is the state that's involved in transcendental meditation. It's a state of extreme quiet. Ultimately, pushed to the very end by a yoga master, you can stop your heart or whatever. The *beta* state is the state that a lawyer has when he's cross-examining a witness: All intellect, very sharp, the adrenalin is way over-pumping. The *theta* state is a state in which imaginative functions are at top level. Where you can see, make up a character; you're sitting in a room looking at people, and you make up a character, and he's more real than the room and the people. Everybody goes into it and out of it from time to time, but an artist is a guy who is specialized in it. Artist, at this point, means a creative chemist, or anybody else—anybody who can create a reality greater than the reality around him.

ANAÏS NIN

Out of the Labyrinth
July 1974

Anaïs Nin, who died in 1977, was a self-educated writer and psychoanalyst. She was the author of Under a Glass Bell, Winter of Artifice, *and* The House of Incest *(a study of D.H. Lawrence), among others. Nin was what she termed an underground writer. She consistently defined herself as a woman artist, uniting the conscious world of time and the eternal unconscious.*

Nin was interviewed by freelancer Jody Hoy.

EAST WEST: Your works often evoke symphonic form. Do you feel that music has influenced your writing?

ANAÏS NIN: Very strongly. I even said as directly as that in the diary that my ideal would be a page of writing which would be like a page of music. There must be a language, a way of expressing things which bypasses the intellect and goes straight to the emotions. I wanted to evoke the same reaction to writing that I have to music.

EW: I'm interested in the creative process itself, how you move from the interior vision to its exteriorization in literature.

AN: My concern was for exterior reality as holding a secret of a metaphor. I would never describe the city or the rag-pickers or a person without looking for the inner meaning. When you are concerned with the metaphysical meaning, everything becomes transparent. I never described a city for its own sake but immediately had to find what its spiritual qualities were. Its symbolic value is what makes it seem transparent, people would even say dreamlike, but that wasn't what it was.

EW: How do you explain the almost universal identification of your women readers with the characters in your novels?

AN: I believe that what unites us universally is our emotions, our feelings in the face of experience, and not necessarily the actual experiences themselves. The facts were different, but readers felt the same way towards a father even if the father was different. So I think unwittingly I must have gone so deep inside what Ira

Progoff calls the personal well that I touched the water at a level where it connected all the wells together.

EW: Is part of your uniqueness as a writer due to the fact that you venture into realms that relate specifically to women's situations and experience?

AN: My own subjective attitude towards reality was all I really knew, what I could see and feel. I read a great deal, but I didn't imitate men writers. I wanted to tell what I saw. So it came out a woman's vision of the universe, a highly personal vision. I wanted to translate man to woman and woman to man. I didn't want to lose contact with the language of man, but I knew that there was a distinction of levels.

EW: In your writings you express a profound belief in the human capacity to grow beyond neurosis. What is the source of your optimism?

AN: I never thought about the source. I always felt that impulse in myself, the way plants have an impulse to grow. I believe that what happens are accidental interferences and blockages. We all have that impulse, but then it gets damaged occasionally. It's in children, isn't it? They use their strengths, their skills, and explore everything, all possibilities. I believe that we can take notice of the damage that most of us sustain somewhere along the line and we can overcome the damage. We all have interferences, discouragements, and traumatic experiences. I have met young writers who have stopped at the first rejection notice. So it's a question of how much we are willing to struggle in order to overcome the impediments.

EW: Would you say that one of the major themes in your works is the conflict between woman's role as a dependent and loving being and the artist's drive toward transcendence?

AN: Yes, I think that is a very great conflict. The creative will pushes you in one direction while you have guilt about using time and energy which is supposed to be devoted to your personal life. It hasn't been a problem for man because the culture incites him to produce, he wants to be obsessed with his work, he is blessed for it. But woman has really been told that the primary concern is her personal life, she hasn't been encouraged to create; in her case it is accidental phenomena.

EW: How does it feel to have achieved recognition as a major literary figure?

AN: Well, I never imagined that. It's a lovely feeling. You lose your sense of isolation. And you can live out your universal life. You're in contact with the whole world, which is probably the wish of every writer.

TOM WOLFE

The New American Letters
October 1973

Tom Wolfe's first book, a 1965 collection of magazine articles titled The Kandy-Kolored Tangerine Flake Streamlined Baby, *was seen by many as "a dangerous literary mutant," according to interviewer Phil Levy. "It was a bunch of wild stories about hot-rodders, doormen, megamillionaires, jet-setters and others, and many readers assumed that not only was it half-fictionalized but that it was socially worthless." Wolfe, however, continued to author works of "instant cultural history" and "pop sociology" that came eventually to be called "new journalism." He is the author of* The Electric Kool-Aid Acid Test, The Right Stuff, *and, most recently,* The Bonfire of the Vanities, *among others, and contributes articles regularly to magazines such as* Esquire. *Wolfe recently won the Columbia Journalism and John Dos Passos Awards.*

EAST WEST: Do you think your writing could, or *should* do anything to help eliminate the division [social status, class conflict], or mediate at all between the two sides in any one scene?

TOM WOLFE: Possibly. But then it wouldn't do the things that I want it to. When I wrote *The Electric Kool-Aid Acid Test* I was constantly criticized—by some—for not condemning the use of LSD [Wolfe took LSD once while researching the book], for not condemning hippies, and so on. I think if I had done any of those things it would have involved giving up all the *power* that I want my writing to have. I want to be able to bring the reader inside the lives of the people I'm writing about, and to do this you've got to some way let the reader experience through print what the people themselves experience. You can't constantly be pulling back to effect some kind of moral point, or some political position. The thing can be a real process of discovery for the reader, rather than something to bounce his opinions off.

I'd like to, if I can, subvert the whole process of having opinions, and draw, if I have the skill to do it, the person into the experience that I'm writing about in such a way that he can't even use his opinions any more; they become valueless to him. To me the whole process of discovery is much more important.

One of the things that fascinated me about Ken Kesey and his group was that they seemed to have a vision of what I call "beyond catastrophe." We're so used to thinking of threats as the only serious subject because throughout human history these *have* been the only serious subjects. The Four Horsemen were the serious subjects. War and Pestilence and—well, if you add enslavement to those you've still pretty much got what are considered the serious subjects. The thing I like about Kesey and his group was that they were saying, here we are in post World War II America, a great many of those threats have been met, or they seem to have been met. People are not in danger of starving, they're not really in danger of dying off in plagues. They didn't *seem* at that time to be in danger of being brought into war, so after you've checked all the threats, and given yourself a sort of blank ticket to do with what you want—in other words you're presumably stopping all these threats in order to do *something* at the end of the line, then...what do you *do*? As a matter of fact, you can see this in terms of mental health. The psychiatrists went out of business in Leningrad during the siege because everyone felt a sense of purpose and they got all organized around a threat. I think psychiatrists get busier when people are left with their free ticket and they have to make something out of it. This is what intrigues me when it comes down to it about politics, and the reason I can't really get excited about politics is that politics deals with threats. The only thing they offer to you is that they're going to save you from a threat.

What would you do if all these threats really *were* met, including the threat of class and status? Let's say that by some magical formula the considerations of class and status—by some magical synthesis—had been overcome. Then everybody would really be up against it. They'd have to say, "Now what am I *really* going to do with my life?" They'd really have to face up to the question, "What does it all mean? What am I here for? Am I here for *any*thing?" That's a scarier frontier, really.

EW: How does your writing reflect this?

TW: It could be, you know, that my writing makes these things *worse*, to tell the truth. I probably have pointed out differences in status, particularly the symbolism in status, that people never really thought of before. And once it gets into your brain that, for instance, you speak in a way that people look down on, it starts preying on your mind. But I still think it's worth it. I think the best thing you can do as a writer is just lay it out on the table as completely as you know how, capturing the whole experience, and then people can decide *what*, if anything, they want to do about it. Most of the things that I've chosen to write about, the vast majority of my fellow writers consider worthless.

JEAN AUEL

Back to the Past
November 1985

Jean Auel is the author of the immensely popular "Earth's Children" series, which includes The Clan of the Cave Bear, The Valley of Horses, *and* The Mammoth Hunters. *Auel told freelance interviewer Cary Groner, "Can you imagine anything more fun than learning anything in the world you want to learn, and earning a living at it?"*

EAST WEST: Is Ayla [the protagonist of "Earth's Children"] a reflection of an inner path traveled by you and by other women?

JEAN AUEL: I suppose, yes. Her ideas are my ideas. I am a product of my culture, and I am a feminist. I'm not a militant.

When I grew up, there weren't any role models. There weren't any stories with female heroes, instead of heroines. Heroines are always those women who wait for Prince Charming to come and save them. I wanted to write an adventure story about a woman, but I didn't want her to be a carbon copy of a man. I wanted her to be a strong *woman*. So when I started writing about this period, I wanted to look at those elements in human nature which are constant and basic. And if they were the same as we are in these basic ways, then some of the problems we suffer with they ought to have suffered with, too. I can't write about a woman engineer back then, but I can write about a woman making discoveries. It's a way of looking at ourselves from a different perspective. Women have always been strong. Women have always been independent. It's a fairly recent myth of the last 4,000 years—remember I'm writing 30,000 years!—that women are weak and subservient. Native American women were strong, but they were not written about in the same ways. There's a new book out called *The Hidden Half*, which is about the Plains Indian women, and the fact that so many of the Victorian anthropologists ignored them. They saw them as second class, not because Native American society saw them that way, but because the anthropologists' society saw them that way.

I wanted to write an honest picture of humanity. I'm a feminist, but I like men. I don't love my sons any less than I love my daughters. I wanted to write about people. If you write about prejudice against blacks, that has just too much emotional content for most people. If you write about prejudice against Neanderthals, you can begin to explore what is prejudice, what causes prejudice. So it's not just feminism. It's not just modern women. It's humanity.

EW: Do writers of fiction have social responsibilities?

JA: I don't know that they do. I think they have a responsibility to write a good story. I think that too often if you assume a social responsibility in the beginning, then you end up writing polemics, instead of stories. I think what a writer of fiction has a responsibility to do is write honestly. Sometimes that can be very hard. If you want to experiment, then write experimental fiction. Write what comes from yourself. I'm writing these stories to please myself. I had no idea they were going to be bestsellers. That's a hard question for me, because I think that a writer of fiction has the same kind of responsibility that a human being in society has. We all have a certain responsibility to be as human as we can be. What is survival of the fittest for a human being? Is compassion a trait of survival of the fittest? Is the most compassionate the most fit? It's not all tooth and fang.

SOCIETY

Liv Ullman

Tristan Jones

Jonathan Kozol

Fritjof Capra

Jeremy Rifkin

Hazel Henderson

EDGAR MITCHELL

Inner & Outer Space
June 1976

The sixth man on the moon, Edgar Mitchell was an astronaut with the Manned Spacecraft Center at NASA from 1966-75. His lifelong interest in philosophy and theology, and the insights he had in space ("The crew of spacecraft Earth is in virtual mutiny to the order of the universe.") gave impetus to his study of parapsychology and transpersonal psychology. Mitchell now travels throughout the world lecturing and trying to inspire scientists to examine the field of human consciousness. He is founder of the Institute of Noetic Sciences in Sausalito, Calif. and is currently writing a book.

Mitchell was interviewed by East West's *Tom Goldwasser.*

EAST WEST: What is the cause of man's problems on spaceship Earth?

EDGAR MITCHELL: I suggest that the one thing that keeps this planet from functioning in the harmonious, coordinated fashion one would think it should, is the limited purview of its people. Now, how do you change the limited purview of people—we have been trying for several thousand years. I don't know that we can, but if we can, it has to be through the study of the basic nature of ourselves. I hold the thesis that as human beings we know virtually nothing about ourselves. And certainly in a scientific sense we know virtually nothing about ourselves, about the functioning of the mind, what we are, how we are, are there external forces, is there a God, if you will? What are these things that we call paranormal? What is intuitiveness, what is creativeness, how do we get to these things? In my opinion, if there is a fundamental lasting solution to the enigma of mankind, it lies in the study of mind, or the study of consciousness.

EW: On looking at the earth from space, was there a sense of alienation, and did that give your experience its height and sense?

EM: The perspective of earth at that distance was merely a trigger to consciousness, to a new perspective, a new view. I submit to you that you can gain that perspective without ever going there. I happen to be a little slow to learn. Like the mule, I have to have a sledgehammer between the eyes. I think all it takes is concentration and meditation on these things, and at some point in time you will get the trigger necessary to get that feeling, but I had to go into space to get it. I'm sure that from my point of view, getting out there, physically knowing I was two hundred and forty thousand miles away from the planet I call home was an extremely powerful stimulus.

FRITJOF CAPRA

A Quantum Leap from Science to Society
March 1982

Austrian-born scientist Fritjof Capra's bestselling The Tao of Physics *explored the spiritual implications of a new, dynamic view of reality and became a mythic text for a generation seeking alternatives to an impersonal and mechanistic view of the world. In* The Turning Point, *Capra described how the holistic view of physicists and mystics is now emerging in the other sciences, from biology to economics. His newest book is* Uncommon Wisdom: Conversations With Remarkable People. *Recently Capra has founded the Elmwood Institute, in Berkeley, Calif., which researches the relationship between science and spirituality.*

Alex Jack conducted this interview.

EAST WEST: What is the main theme of your new book?

FRITJOF CAPRA: Over the last few years I have been very impressed by the parallel between the crisis that physicists went through in the early 1920s and our general social and cultural crisis today. I have come to believe that our current social crisis is very much a crisis of the same kind. When I talk about our social crisis I mean all the various manifestations that we can read about every day in the newspapers. We have an energy crisis, high inflation and unemployment, a rising wave of violence and crime, an ecology crisis, a crisis in health care, the threat of nuclear war. All these I think have to be seen as different facets of one crisis, which is essentially a crisis of perception. This is how I make the link between the crisis that the physicists went through when they went from Newtonian to quantum physics.

Our current social institutions are all basing their activities, policies, and planning on a world view which is now outdated. The world view of the seventeenth century—the same classical world view that physicists had when they were studying atoms in the first three decades of the century—could not adequately describe all phenomena in terms of cause and effect, or explain the nature of space, time, and matter. They were struggling with the limitations of the Cartesian world view, the mechanistic view of reality proposed three hundred years ago by the French philosopher and mathematician Descartes. And this is what we are doing now as a society and as a culture. The Cartesian concepts which govern our understanding of other sciences and areas of life, including medicine, psychology, and economics, have lost their validity. We have now reached the limitations of this seventeenth century world view and have to go, and are going through, a very profound cultural transformation. We are now undergoing a shift of paradigms.

EW: Could you describe the old paradigm?

FC: Descartes had a mechanistic vision of reality. He based his whole world view on a very fundamental separation between mind and matter, assigning each to independent and separate realms. The material world was to him a machine, a mechanical system where fundamental parts work together as in a human-made machine.

EW: What was the crisis which quantum physicists went through and what were the limitations they encountered?

FC: During the first three decades of the century physicists were able for the first time to penetrate into the world of atoms and subatomic phenomena and what they found there was totally surprising. Their conventional concepts, their classical concepts, were not adequate to describe this new reality. These very basic concepts involved space, time, cause and effect, and the nature of matter and energy. The situation was very dramatic. The handful of scientists went through a profound intellectual—and emotional—crisis because their very ability to understand reality, to understand nature, was seriously challenged. This had never happened before in science. There had been scientific revolutions like the Copernican and Darwinian revolutions, but the concepts were not difficult to understand. Now with Bohr, Heisenberg, and Schroedinger the concepts themselves were extremely difficult to understand, and the physicists did not know whether they could ever be understood.

EW: What is the new paradigm that emerged from these discoveries?

FC: The shift is toward a world view that you can call a holistic view, an organic view, an ecological view. That's actually my preferred term, an ecological perspective. Ecological because it is characterized by the notion of the fundamental interdependence between all phenomena. The very essence of the science of ecology is to show how all phenomena in the natural environment are interdependent and mutually interrelate. This fundamental interdependence appeared first in physics, when quantum theory and relativity theory were finally worked out by around 1930. As Niels Bohr emphasized, the main consequence of these theories was that you could not separate any part of the material universe from the rest without making an error. When you got down to the smaller and smaller dimensions, the larger the error became. Heisenberg's Uncertainty Principle actually shows you precisely to what extent you can apply classical or Newtonian notions of separate objects to this atomic world.

The new world view is a view where the universe appears as a web of relationships rather than separate objects as in a machine. There is a second important aspect of the holistic world view and that is the notion that the universe is intrinsically dynamic. This web of relationships is not a static grid. It is a dynamic network of events. What we call things are really patterns in an overall cosmic process. We have found that everything is connected to everything else and that everything is always changing, always in motion, in transformation. In *The Tao of Physics* I related this world view of modern physics to the views of mystics, especially Eastern mystics. Mystics also have this organic view that things and phenomena are profoundly interrelated, dynamic, and that the web of events includes the human observer and his or her consciousness in a very essential way.

EW: Wasn't the complete separation between subject and object on the psychiatric couch also a result of the Newtonian model?

FC: Yes, one of the principles of Newtonian science is that you have to be objective. The observed phenomena are separated from the observer, especially from the consciousness of the observer. As a result there is supposed to be no influence, no mutual interaction. You can objectively observe what there is out there in nature. Freud was very eager to follow this objectivity. He admonished psychoanalysts at one time to be as cold as a surgeon. But Freud somehow made a distinction between his theory and his practice. He acknowledged that in his practice the influence of a therapist on a patient was very strong. Here I might say that usually the great founders of new intellectual developments are more flexible than their followers. Descartes was much less Cartesian than the people who came after him, Newton much less Newtonian, Freud less Freudian, Jung less Jungian, and Marx less Marxist. This is a very interesting phenomenon which you can always observe.

EW: How has the Cartesian model influenced economics?

FC: Very often the Cartesian and Newtonian principles just didn't work for the social sciences. This can be seen quite clearly in economics. Like most of the social sciences, present-day economics is fragmentary and reductionistic. Most economists separate the economy conceptually from the natural environment and from the social environment in which it is embedded. They define their basic concepts like profit, GNP, and efficiency in a narrow way, without taking into account how economic activity is related to the social fabric and the natural ecosystem.

EW: Could you give us an example?

FC: In the valley where I grew up in Austria there was and still is a huge paper factory. For decades they just dumped all the waste into the river and messed up the environment. And children swim in the river, at least I used to. The pollution has an effect on the fish and on the people who bathe in it, and it has an effect on the people who breathe the air. All of that creates costs, not only from the human point of view but also from the economic point of view in that health costs are generated. And those health costs are not taken into account when the paper factory does its profit and loss accounts.

EW: What do you see replacing the Cartesian view in economics and the various natural and social sciences?

FC: There is now emerging in biology, medicine, psychology, and the social sciences a natural extension of the concepts of modern physics and that is the framework of systems theory. It is a view that deals with integrated wholes—or systems—that derive their essential properties from the way their components are interrelated and interdependent. The systems view is complementary to the Cartesian view. Where the Cartesian view focuses on the parts, the systems view focuses on the interdependencies and on the interrelations between the parts. It also emphasizes the primary importance of process. It emphasizes that every structure is the result of an underlying process. Systems theorists study principles of organization that are characteristic of various systems, particularly living systems. These include everything from the single cell to the human organism. Furthermore there are social systems, like a family, society, or a community, and there are ecosystems where individual organisms and inorganic matter combine in a mutually interdependent network. All these systems, ending with the planet as a whole—which is the global system or global organism—satisfy the same or very similar principle of organization. From the point of view of science, the new vision of reality is a systems view. It is an ecological view. It is a natural extension of the concepts of modern physics. It takes into account how we are imbedded in larger networks, in social networks, and in the network of the natural environment.

EW: So from your own experience you could say that the new view is also a spiritual view.

FC: Yes, the new vision of reality is a spiritual vision in its very essence. And that personally took me quite a while to understand. In writing *The Tao of Physics* I started out making the connection between modern science and ancient spiritual traditions, but I understand this relationship much better now and can put it in a broader context. The human spirit, as I've come to see it, is that mode of consciousness in which the individual becomes aware of being connected to the cosmos as a whole. That mode of consciousness is much broader than a rational mode; it is an intuitive mode. It typically occurs in meditative experiences, but can also occur in many other settings. Psychologists nowadays call these experiences transpersonal experiences. Some people have experienced them while playing tennis or other kinds of sports. You can have them in art, in a deep sexual experience. Meditation is the one that is the most continuous, systematic, and goes the deepest.

EW: In the history of science it's interesting to observe that most of the great discoveries were made during meditative experiences, not through the logical reasoning process in the laboratory. Take the case of the apple falling on Newton's head while he was sitting in contemplation under a tree. What has been the reaction of scientists to *The Tao of Physics* and your attempt to unify mysticism and physics?

FC: It's a slow process. The comparison I made with mysticism was a severe threat for many physicists. It takes a certain maturity of view and personality to accept it.

EW: What about Niels Bohr?

FC: Bohr went to China and was very much impressed by the yin and yang termi-nology and the Chinese notion of complementarity. And vice versa, the Chinese were very impressed by Bohr. There was a real mutual exchange but no direct influence on his work. He had already worked out his ideas on the model of the atom at that time, but he did adopt the yin yang symbol in his coat of arms when he was knighted in Denmark.

EW: How about Einstein?

FC: Einstein is a very interesting case. Einstein certainly also was very intuitive and a very religious person. There is an interesting connection, that I think I'm the first one to point out, in my new book, between Einstein and Descartes. Des-cartes' whole idea about nature was that there was a system of separate objects out there. Einstein adopted that from Descartes. In the historic debate between Einstein and Bohr the debate centered around the question of whether there is a reality of independent separate objects out there or not. Einstein could never bring himself to give that up. So although Einstein went far beyond Newton in his relativity theory, somehow he could not bring himself to go beyond Descartes.

I think the very essence of scientific discoveries is always intuitive. The very core of scientific activity—as in any other activity—is always intuitive. I think that what makes a good scientist is the proper blend of the intuitive and the rational. It reminds me of one of the great sayings of Chuang Tzu, "Life is the blended harmony between the yin and the yang." Although the rational part is a very important part in science, it is overemphasized in our educational system. Science is presented as something very dry and logical, but in fact, the reason why we do research ultimately is because of the joy of the scientific discovery, the breakthrough, the sudden flash of insight.

EW: Have you had such flashes in your laboratory?

FC: Oh yes, every scientist has that. It is interesting that typically the flashes do not come in the laboratory where you work on your problems. Typically they come during periods of relaxation after intense intellectual work, you know, when you take a shower, or walk in the woods, or switch off and the cycle goes on, and you put things together.

WILLIAM IRWIN THOMPSON

A Planetary Civilization
April 1973

William Irwin Thompson has been called "one of the most exciting of all the contemporary global thinkers." The author of At the Edge of History, *and featured in both* Time *and* Harper's, *he became a herald of self-realization as the most effective tool for social reformation. Founding director of the Lindisfarne Association on Long Island and editor of* Gaia, *Thompson has recently authored* Pacific Shift, *in which he explains his theory of a global cultural shift from the mechanistic economic influence as epitomized by New York, London, and Paris, to the more humanist, spiritual direction of California and the Far East.*

Interviewer Tom Lloyd was editor of Order of the Universe *magazine.*

EAST WEST: In *Harper's* a little while back, you did a book review on Gopi Krishna's *The Biological Basis of Religion and Genius*, which is about the awakening of the kundalini. This introduces an interesting aspect of the transformation of mankind that you did not mention too much in your books: the biological, evolutionary aspect. You point out that his theories of human evolution parallel in some respects those of Sri Aurobindo, de Chardin, and others as well, such as R. M. Bucke. But I didn't feel you took a well-delineated position on his theory, except to say that mystics "are looking for a lofty class of men to watch over the race."

Might these philosophers see a development of an elite as an interim situation at most, until the evolutionary process as a whole is carried out, and the race as a whole goes through its sea-change?

WILLIAM IRWIN THOMPSON: One has to be careful in that. You must not allow yourself to do things in the present by imagining the future in which those limited events will be made good. They must be made good in the present. If people say, "We know what is best for mankind, so give us power now," but when you look at them they have all the characteristics of the enemy, are full of violence, hostility, and rage, then you should not trust them. The people you should trust are those who in the present show joy and transfiguration, and are *already* living in the new age. So if a class of men, no matter how mystical, come in and say, "We have to take power momentarily, in the interest of those who have their kundalinis up, to protect those who have their kundalinis down," I would say don't trust them. I would take my stand with Christianity against that kind of crypto-fascist mysticism. I would say that that is very similar in structure to what the Nazis were trying to do, very similar to the idea of the temporary dictatorship of the proletariat until we have the "withering away of the state"; it didn't work in dialectical materialism and I don't think it will work in mysticism.

My own roots are in the American concept that if each person is to go through an elevation of consciousness in the new age, he has to be free; he can't be compressed as a unit in some homogeneous mass; he has to be allowed his selfhood, so that his lower-case selfhood can be raised to capital 'S' Selfhood. The only way to do that is through his own unique integrity and freedom. In this case, the concept of democracy as it is mystically expressed in Walt Whitman is very much a part of our American heritage, and I think it is closer to the spirit of the new age than a rerun of the pyramidal structure of ancient Egypt or of ancient India. I don't think we want a rerun of the caste system. The basic point is, you can only trust people if they give evidence of the new age right now; if they tell you, "Wait a while and things will be all right," don't trust them.

The freedom of the individual is the means by which the unification of mankind is going to occur. This is in Teilhard de Chardin too, but he tends to take the other point of view, to apologize for collectivization, saying the more we collectivize now the more later on we'll be uniquely free, or in de Chardin's phrase, hyper-collectivization leads to hyper-personalization. You have to be careful of that, because that can be an apology for tyranny.

The Catholic Church attempted to express those institutions *in time*, and to hold power under the aspect of eternity, and it created a tyrannical, collectivizing, totalistic institution, and generated the Inquisition. And remember that the inquisitor torturing a man believes that he is doing this for the good of his soul—saying, "If I torture you for a few minutes, it's nothing like the torture you would have in Hell for all eternity."

So, you take that attitude of the Inquisitor and put it into a politician who says, "Look, I'm going to give you ten years of tyranny, but what's coming up is an eternity of bliss," you've got to distrust him. All evil is created in the name of good. No one would support it, otherwise.

I operate from day to day with an imagination of the future, a sense of the new age, the new possibilities, but I back away from making predictions, and I think those who do are vain and arrogant. They lead us in the direction of power-tripping and error.

EW: In a state of affairs that's potentially anarchic, that is, with things falling apart, disintegrating, how would you see that we make sure that the crystallization which occurs is not off in the wrong direction? Since we're pretty much eradicating many of the traditions which no longer hold true, and building anew, how do you feel that we keep our orientation? It seems to me that this is an individual development.

WT: I agree. There's anarchism and there's anarchism. I use anarchism in a positive sense, the same way that you're using it—as opposed to chaos. I consider myself to be a conservative Christian anarchist. I think the change will occur through the individual, that the transformation going on now makes a lot of our institutions unnecessary; as I have said before, you can't go to the university to find wisdom, or to the church to find holiness—that all our institutions are becoming obviated by the immediacy of the energies that are everywhere present. They are not locked into centers of learning and holiness; they are available in hundreds of different kinds of forms. The important thing is to internalize the experience and by the immediate flowering of these values, "ye shall know them."

E. F. SCHUMACHER

Changing Knowledge to Wisdom
November 1976

E. F. Schumacher, an economic advisor to the National Coal Board in Britain from 1950 to 1970, was the originator of the concept of intermediate technology for developing countries popularized by the phrase "small is beautiful." He was also the founder-chairman of the Intermediate Technology Development Group in London, and director of the Scott-Bader Institute. Schumacher, who died in September, 1977, was the author of the popular and influential work, Small Is Beautiful: A Study of Economics As If People Mattered. *He was interviewed at his residence outside London by* East West's *Sherman Goldman and Bill Tara.*

EAST WEST: How did the title of your book, *Small Is Beautiful*, occur to you?

E. F. SCHUMACHER: This phrase, as you can readily appreciate, is stolen from the blacks—"Black is beautiful." In a speech that I gave in Switzerland quite a few years ago I reflected upon how deeply imbedded in the language is "big is beautiful"; "great" and "grand" also mean something good. The same occurs in German, my native language. Maybe this usage developed at a time when human means were so limited, most things were pretty small, and anyone who could do something big (and big at that time was something we would call small now—it's relative) was valued. But now we have really so grossly overshot the mark in this direction that, I thought to myself, maybe we ought to do what the blacks are trying to do. Everybody was saying, "White is beautiful," so they just turned it around. So we ought to say that "small is beautiful." That's the way it happened, and it turned out to be a catchy phrase. I start off with a title, and immediately a subtitle follows to define what it's about: *Small Is Beautiful: A Study of Economics As If People Mattered.*

EW: When and how exactly did people first adopt this prevalent notion that big is good or beautiful?

ES: There are not many basic things that have been so totally overlooked over the last three hundred years as the relevance of *size* to everything. Aristotle was aware of its importance; all ancient and traditional cultures knew this. But it is one of the things that has been totally forgotten in modern times. Now people will debate all sorts of questions—saying, "this is good" and "this is bad"—but then if you do only five minutes' thinking, what *size* are you talking about?

Let's say we are praising the virtues of private enterprise, understanding by that, a man who runs a business. Well, are we talking about a business employing twelve people or twelve thousand people? Some people say, "Private enterprise is good." Others hold the opposite opinion: "No, we have to have a socialistic or communistic kind of thing." Well, now, are we talking about the little garage around the corner which employs five people or are we talking about General Motors? They don't say.

Now it may be—and this is what I claim—that some kinds of private enterprise are the ideal system when a business is small and involves real face-to-face contact, where the outstanding entrepreneur means something. (He may, of course, be inclined to exploit his twelve employees, but we have the trade unions to look after that, there's no problem. Leave him free.) But when you talk about Anaconda Copper Company in Butte, Montana, the whole community hinges on this, and you can't pretend that this is private enterprise, even if the shares are held by all sorts of people. If they now want to move the whole town, which they may in fact want to do because they now want to extract copper from underneath the town, well, that's rather something different. Because it's so *big*. So whether something is social or private cannot be discussed unless you find the *size*.

EW: In the economic planning for the Coal Board you were dealing with things on a very large scale. Was it then that you began to think, "Well, perhaps something very fundamental has been neglected, and this large-scale planning is leaving something essential out of the picture"?

ES: When I got this job at the Coal Board in 1950, we were in a great state of enthusiasm. Here was the chance to build something really new and decent. The coal industry was in an absolutely shocking condition, and nothing could be done. There was, I mean, no option. You couldn't just say, "Well, now let's try to improve it on the old bases," because the coal owners had been neglecting the industry for thirty years. So we thought, "With nationalization we really have a chance of bringing into business proper ethics. We should manage it." And we had an excellent crew of people, really outstanding people on the board—a hothouse of ability and intelligence.

I remember—it must have been 1952 or thereabouts—I went down to Wales; I was asked to give a lecture there, and after the lecture I was sitting with these very vain, very attractive Welshmen who had a peculiar kind of human warmth, and a fellow who was quite a well-known lawyer said to me—with a Welsh accent, which I cannot imitate—that the Coal Board was a "cri-mi-nal or-ganization." Now, this hit me below the belt, because I knew we weren't—certainly not at Hobart House, the headquarters—and I got very hot under the collar. I must admit I really lost my temper: "How can you say such things!" And he said, "I am taking one case after another of widows whose husbands worked in the pits, and all the Coal Board does is bring all the big guns to bear on this little work widow to do her out of a pension by proving that in fact the fellow contracted pneumoconiosis [a lung disease common among miners] long before he joined the pits, or that he never had pneumoconiosis." He was speaking from his experience.

Then I increasingly realized that if a thing is beyond a certain size, it doesn't matter what your intentions are, because you have to translate it into such legal jargon, and you have so many lawyers, that by the time it reaches our little man, the Coal Board man who has to look after compensation cases, he does his best for the Board, you see, and he comes home in the evening and tells his wife, "I have saved the Board five thousand pounds!" He feels he has earned his salary. Well! This damn thing is a frightful thought, and soon it made me despondent, because I found that you cannot do both.

You don't draw these conclusions very quickly—because at the same time I knew that the only way to rescue the Board from total perdition was to put it all under one roof and do it with the planning. That's real life, you see; now we're beyond theory. That's real life, suspended between these two opposites: You need the size for doing certain things, and with the size you cannot do it decently.

EW: How do you combine the two?

ES: In this particular case, you find a chapter in my book about the theory of large-scale organizations: If you can't get away from the big size, then at least see if you can't structure it in such a way that inside the bigness you can achieve a human scale again. That was, in fact, my real act all through the '60s, when we gave the Board a new structure which led to phenomenally good results.

You can learn about the right size no doubt more easily when you are in a thing that is too big than when you are in a thing that is too small, where you are dreaming about getting bigger. Then I began to notice many similar things. What I am now thinking of is many years later. As you may recall, in California people became very interested in a little island in the Caribbean, Anguilla, which was part of some larger country. Anguilla wanted to get away from this giant and do their own thing, so they declared their independence, an island of two thousand people! Anguilla wanted to become a member of the United Nations, and they just wanted to do their own thing. All the wise guys said, "Ridiculous. It won't be viable." But the Anguillans said, "We don't want to be run by this bunch of exploitive politicians in St. Kitts." Then finally, because this all was still under Britain, we had to send some troops there, also to stop St. Kitts from threatening Anguilla. An island of two thousand people!

One thing that struck me was that they never had any crime there. I don't know the Anguillans, but I have no reason to believe that they are any different from the Jamaicans or anybody anywhere else. There is not suddenly an island of saints there! Then it was brought home to me that when things are on the human scale, you don't have crime. Yes, occasionally you have a misdemeanor, but it's never a problem, so they have no police there. Occasionally somebody really does something wrong and sometimes he is sent to prison, but on Anguilla there is no prison, so he is sent to St. Kitts. Now, when he comes back, what do you do with him? "Yes, oh, Joe, he needs something to do, so we find him some work, and he needs somewhere to live, so we find him a room," and the problem is solved. He gets reintegrated. Islands are always particularly interesting to study because they are so directly defined. With a big continental mass you don't notice the way things happen.

Then I thought, let's say one person a year comes out of prison in Anguilla, and he is reintegrated with no problem. Now I live on an island, called Britain, which is twenty-five thousand times as large—it's not two thousand people but fifty million, and it is not one person a year coming out of prison but twenty-five thousand, so the ratio is the same. In school I learned that 2,000 to one equals 50 million to 25,000. But I tell you—it *doesn't* equal. Because 2,000 to one is a solvable problem and 50 million to 25,000 is not. In Britain we have the home office, we have the probation centers, we have any number of private organizations, and the reintegration just does not work. We can study why it doesn't, and it can be explained. In connection with the atom bomb, in atomic reactions you have the factor of critical mass; this is where the mere change in *quantity* changes the *quality* of the situation. The stuff is quite harmless—relatively speaking—until it attains the critical mass, and then it becomes extremely dangerous.

EW: By what means can a deep change occur on a broad level, and also in a lasting, not just a superficial or fanatical way?

ES: I think one has to come to some view on what is really the mechanism of big change. This is a very testing question, because I find myself raising so many objections to the approach of many scientists and others to this whole thing: Manipulation, brain-washing, all that—the "hidden persuaders," and so on, which I think is antihuman. Nothing is worth having in this sphere unless it comes from the *inside* of you.

If I come to the conclusion that "I don't want to be a manipulator," then I state my opinion and I don't force it on anyone. Thank God I haven't got any power. If people adopt the same opinion, then it is because they have seen the truth of it. But if anyone comes to me and says, "Yes, but many people don't see the truth, and you must force it down their throats by getting clever television producers to present it," then I say, "No, without me." But what is the proper way, the mechanism of change? I believe that it is everyone's personal task to try to demonstrate in some way, by word or deed, what he considers to be true, adequate, right, etc., and not look over his shoulder whether people follow his example or believe what he says. When people then start ridiculing him as a crank, and say, "Well, you know what you are doing is all nice and dandy, but we haven't got time. You know, after all, you have been at it now for x years, and time is running out." Then you say, "Yes, thank you very much. I hear what you say." You just carry on.

It is not so easy to maintain this sturdy attitude. In India they call it karma yoga; you just do what you consider right, and you don't bother your head with whether you are successful or not, because if you don't do what you consider is right, you're wasting your life!

JEREMY RIFKIN

Who Should Play God?
December 1984

Political activist, economist, and author Jeremy Rifkin has in the past fifteen years challenged orthodoxy of all stripes. In the 1970s he was instrumental in the formation of the alternative Peoples Bicentennial Commission and the Peoples Business Commission. During that time he wrote several books on the general theme of how people can regain political and economic control over their lives. More recently Rifkin, who founded and directs the Foundation on Economic Trends, has broadened the scope of his interests while retaining his roots in radical economic thought. In his book Entropy *he proposed an innovative definition for energy efficiency, in* Algeny *he called for a searching public debate on the new "age of biotechnology," in* The Emerging Order *he explored the Christian evangelical revival, and in his most recent* Time Wars, *Rifkin continues his attack on conventional thinking in the new field of "chronobiology" —our conception of time.*

Since this interview, in which he discussed with East West's *Mark Mayell the philosophical implications of genetic engineering, Rifkin has become a leading critic of genetic engineering technology. He has recently filed suit against the National Institutes of Health in an attempt to block the first authorized gene implants.*

EAST WEST: What do you mean by "algeny"?

JEREMY RIFKIN: Many people think that genetic engineering is just a group of products or a set of technologies. It's much more than that. The only thing comparable in historical terms to this technological revolution is the harnessing of fire. We are a Promethean creature and we have been using fire technology for thousands of years. We have been burning, soldering, forging, and melting together inert materials from the earth's crust, transforming them into all kinds of combinations, such as steel, glass, and synthetics, that do not exist in nature. In fact, the final culmination of the fire technology revolution is the nuclear bomb. We've been trying to harness fire power for thousands of years and we've finally managed to harness so much fire power in one product that all we need to do is drop that product and we can recast the earth as the fire ball that it was at the beginning of the cosmic story.

In the 1970s, two scientists did something in the world of living material that is comparable to fire technology in import. They took slices of genetic material from two totally unrelated species and combined them, getting a new form of life on a molecular level that does not exist in nature. Recombinant DNA is a technology that now allows scientists to cross all species boundaries. In metaphorical terms, we can now heat, solder, melt, forge together living materials across all walls, creating new combinations in shapes and forms that never existed in nature.

The whole idea of the sacredness of a creature becomes archaic once you can eliminate species boundaries at will. We now can do that with recombinant DNA. The sacred unit used to be the organism, the species. Now the sacred unit is the gene. In fact, the sacred unit isn't even the gene now. With computer synthesizing techniques, the sacred unit is now the unit of information coded within the gene. So we are witnessing a new form of "desacralization" of life with this newest technology.

EW: What might be some concrete effects of this new attitude?

JR: To decide in advance how the genetic makeup of living things ought to be planned and executed is to raise the specter of eugenics, the inseparable philosophical wing of genetic technology. Eugenics is the philosophy of using genetic manipulation to create a better organism or a better race or even a master race.

When we think of eugenics, we normally think of Nazi Germany, although I'd hasten to add that the United States supported a massive eugenics movement from 1900 to the Depression. Many American opinion makers and politicians embraced eugenics. States passed sterilization laws, and 70,000 Americans were sterilized because they were deemed biologically unfit.

When we engineer changes in a plant, an animal, a micro-organism, or a human, there is at every step of the way a conscious decision that has to be made as to what are the good genes that should be bred into the species and what are the bad genes that should be eliminated. What are the criteria we establish for determining good and bad genes—efficiency, health, profit, utility, national security? These are very thorny social and political questions.

EW: Is there a real danger of a Hitler-like figure abusing genetic engineering?

JR: My concern is not with the re-emergence of social eugenics but with the new commercial eugenics. There is no evil party here. It's not that the corporations are evil, or the scientists, or the capitalists or the socialists. The fact is, we human beings want perfect babies. We want perfect plants, perfect animals, predictability and organization in our lives. We want to maintain some control over our future. There's one last reservoir of spontaneous, erratic, unpredictable activity on this planet, and it's living systems.

EW: How do we go about organizing opposition to what seems to be an incremental acceptance at this stage of genetic engineering?

JR: The way we relate to other living things comes to reflect the way we relate to human beings, and if we see all other plants and animals as simply matter for manipulation, simply information to be coded for some utilitarian or productive ends, then there's no doubt in my mind that we will bring that same conditioning to our activities with human genetic engineering.

Every species has an inherent right to have its own gene pool remain inviolate from contamination. The most cruel form of behavior towards animals and plants is to attempt to change their nature by superimposing genetic traits of unrelated species into the hereditary makeup. From an ethical point of view, I think it's impermissible. From an ecological point of view, it's potentially devastating.

If we begin taking genetic traits and crossing species borders for short term, utilitarian gain, we're likely to undermine the delicate relationships between species in the ecosystem. The process could be irreversible and catastrophic in the long term. Earlier this year in England, they took a sheep cell and a goat cell and they created a mature "sheep-goat." Those are totally unrelated species in nature. This is truly algeny, isn't it? Do we have a right to unravel the identity of a species and change it for whatever our interests happen to be? I don't think we have that right.

We have to understand that with human genetics, as with all the other areas that genetics might apply to, there are tremendous short term benefits—animal husbandry, pharmaceuticals, agriculture, medicine. The question is not whether there are short term benefits, but whether the short term benefits exceed the long term risks.

EW: How can you impress upon people the long term risks, which are more abstract compared to the short term benefits?

JR: We can start off with a lesson from past history. We have big problems now in animal husbandry and agriculture because of monoculturing. Over the past three decades, we have attempted to locate and preserve pure strains, or the most lucrative strains of animals and plants, with the expense of eliminating genetic strains that we felt were not lucrative or productive in the marketplace. As a result of monoculturing, we have lost much of the genetic diversity of our various plant and animal species and now are facing the prospect of extinction of whole strains and breeds.

For example, we have created super wheat and super corn and eliminated many of the so-called less profitable strains. And now there's not enough genetic diversity in our corn and wheat fields to withstand simple assaults from the ecosystem. In the area of animal husbandry, the same thing has happened. We've eliminated all the so called un-lucrative breeds, leaving only a very few super breeds. As a result there are disease patterns to which these breeds are not immune and it is conceivable that entire herds could be wiped out. Every species has to have a certain amount of diversity in its gene pool so that when the environment radically changes, these diverse strains, or breeds can be called upon to adjust to the changing conditions. If you eliminate all of the various strains in the long run you risk the extinction of entire species.

Take sickle-cell anemia. As a recessive trait it helps arrest malaria. Do we want to eliminate that trait from the gene pool? These are hard decisions.

EW: You say that the next generation offers some hope, but in *Algeny* you imply that there's going to be even less hope for the next generation because they're speaking computerese, the language of technology.

JR: If they choose that over the ecological approach, yes.

EW: Will their exposure to computers commit them to a worldview of knowledge as power?

JR: Futurists say there are two great high-technology futures: computers on one side, genetics on the other. The information sciences and the life sciences. But they're really only a single mode of production. The computer will be used to organize the life sciences. Because the products of the next age of history will be biological. They'll be made of living things. Just like most of the products in the last few hundred years have been made of fossil fuels. The computer is the way to organize genetic engineering products because genetic structures are so complex and have so many characteristics that they require sophisticated computer management to program them.

We now reduce living things to positive and negative feedback. We see living things in cybernetic terms, as programs or instructions. Once we have fully grafted the information language onto the life sciences, then we will be ready to manipulate the life sciences, using computer technology to design and produce biological products.

With regard to your question about children, if children are sitting in front of a computer from the time they're able to conceptualize, organizing their whole world and manipulating their entire environment from a computer screen, sooner or later they're going to start to think that the physical world they're manipulating must be constructed by principles that are remarkably similar to the ones they're using on the computer screen. What happens is that the defining technology of a civilization sets the context for how we redefine the totality of our cosmic existence. So that if we are in front of a computer screen, sooner or later we are going to think that nature, the environment, the universe, must run by cybernetic feedback loops and self-organizing programs. Instead of the old mechanical reductionism we relied on during the industrial era, we now substitute the new information reductionism for the biotechnological era.

EW: How does this change our view of life?

JR: What is sacred about life if it's reduced to information flows? If life is only a matter of programs that can be edited, changed, deleted, added at will? When I was growing up, to give a compliment to a person one would say that person is very knowledgeable. Today we're likely to say that person is very well informed. That's a revolution in how we see ourselves. To be knowledgeable assumes that there are certain truths that have some immutability to them. To be well informed is just to be constantly updated and to be able to change as conditions change, but without any reference point, value orientation, or underlying principle behind it. What happens if a whole society starts to see itself merely as well informed? Where is the reference point for judging what is important and what is sacred?

EW: And you think our relationship to technology will be a key factor?

JR: Instead of questions like, "How can technology be used for good rather than bad?" we need to ask the new question, "How much power is appropriate?" If all technology in history represents increasing influence and power over nature, is there ever a point where more power is simply inappropriate, because it either undermines the concept of life or the survivability of life? Is there a point where power is so out of scale, so uncongenial with our relationship to the rest of the planet and the universe, that it's simply wrong to exercise it?

EW: Doesn't it depend on who controls the power?

JR: Certain technologies, by their inherent nature, are inappropriate regardless of whether they're controlled by the people or not. Genetic technology is inappropriate philosophically to our definition of what life is all about. It should not be used.

We've never said no to any increment of power that increased our advantage technologically. We've always believed that if it can be done it will be done. Now we've got to ask the question, "Is there any point to stop?" If we haven't reached it with the bomb and engineering life by design, if we haven't reached it with splitting the atom and splitting the DNA nucleus, chances are we won't reach it until we've destroyed ourselves.

EW: And computers are an integral part of these inappropriate technologies?

JR: The computer's prime function is to find ways to use things faster, quicker, more efficiently. It's a dramatic leap forward in our ability to use up more of our endowment and to disravel the creation of the ecosystem that we live in. That's my feeling. I know that that's going to very unpopular.

EW: You seem to be a lone voice.

JR: Just temporary.

EW: Are there other organizations that are involved?

JR: Many groups are caught up in fighting the final pressing and critical battles of the petrochemical and nuclear age. These are hard, challenging issues that must be dealt with. So when I ask them to address an entire new epoch in history—the age of biology—it almost seems overwhelming in terms of fitting it into the agenda, since resources are scarce.

EW: Who are your natural allies on this issue?

JR: The environmental movement. The right to life constituency, because of all the new human reproduction technologies and their impact on the desacralization of life. Feminist constituencies are becoming involved, again in the area of reproductive technology, because of the loss of control over human reproduction to a male-oriented scientific and corporate culture. The animal welfare and animal rights constituency is going to be increasingly concerned about genetic engineering of animals. The alternative agriculture constituency, which is fighting for organic agriculture and for developing appropriate technologies on the farms, is going to be increasingly engaged in confrontations around these issues. The labor movement, because of the issue of genotyping workers. Minorities are going to be increasingly interested as we fight the nature/nurture battles and as the [William] Shockleys of this country continue to press their claims that certain races and ethnic groups are biologically inferior on the basis of genetic make-up.

A lot of people in the industry say Jeremy Rifkin is the only problem. If I go away, the problem will go away. I'm here to tell them that I am a little twinkling of what's about to happen. Genetic technology will have an impact on civilization like no other technology in history. It raises the most impressive social, moral, and ecological questions we've ever had to deal with. Because it raises the specter of us designing life in its totality. There can be no more pressing, no more challenging, no more important problem on the human agenda than the question of whether we become the architects of life.

EW: What's a worst-case scenario for the introduction of genetically-modified organisms?

JR: It could be catastrophic. An analogous situation would be the introduction of exotics from their native habitats. Gypsy moths, Dutch Elm disease, starlings—these are all examples of organisms that, placed in a new habitat, went amok. The damage we have to the fauna and flora of North America totals billions of dollars a year. The introduction of genetically modified organisms is an analogous situation. If you take a look at the long term, cumulative impact of introducing these thousands of organisms, some of them are going to do big damage. But we'll never be able to recall them. Every time we introduce a genetically-modified organism into an environment, we play ecological roulette.

EW: Would avoiding such "ecological roulette" require a political change as well as a change in consciousness?

JR: In a sense. The Iroquois Indians, who were a very advanced civilization from whom we borrowed a lot of our ideas of democratic government, had a very interesting practice for decision-making. When the council of elders had to decide on a political course of action, they first had to trace their decision to several generations in the future and ask how will this decision affect them? Only after they had tried to speculate, using foresight, as to what the implications of the decision might be on those generations did they feel that they were prepared to choose a course of action. They saw themselves as part of a continuum. That continuum stretched out in both directions, back to the past and toward the infinite future.

We have yet to embrace that kind of concept in Western civilization. We have to, for the survival of future generations of plants, animals, and human beings will depend on the decisions we make now.

HAZEL HENDERSON

Making a Living Without Making Money
March 1980

English-born economic analyst, independent futurist, and political activist Hazel Henderson travels worldwide giving lectures and conducting seminars that "redefine development." An advisor to many national and international associations, including the Worldwatch Institute, Henderson is the author of Creating Alternative Futures *and producer of the video series of the same title. The newest edition of her* Politics of the Solar Age, *which, with its practical arguments for appropriate technology, has become a handbook for activists and an underground text for students of economy, is just being released.*

East West's Alex Jack and Stevie Daniels spoke with Henderson about the future of development and the world economy.

EAST WEST: Do you feel we're headed for total collapse of the economic system?

HAZEL HENDERSON: It's unclear, really. One aspect will be the continual gentle deflation of the "prosperity bubble" as inflation begins to manage the system. You know, if human beings don't manage their affairs, the natural system of balances will provide some way of doing it for us. At the moment, inflation is managing the industrial economy and taking everybody down off the job ride simply by making the currency more and more worthless. All of those so-called external variables economists label as inflation will be flooding back across the artificial boundaries of the "economy," that is, the whole GNP funny-money game, and it will be swamped with social costs, whether for cleaning up Love Canal or Three Mile Island, or dealing with the stress of cancer epidemics.

Then there will be those other external shocks that will arise, some of which we caused a lot earlier, such as the situation in Iran. At the same time, a lot of air is getting taken out of the bubble by investors having their paper stock certificates, bonds, and currency written down more and more. That's a fairly orderly process—that's what happens in the stock market. So people who enjoyed the ride up and all the funny money will now have to take their lumps on the ride down. There's no way out of that.

EW: Could you describe what you call the informal economy, and project its possible growth during the next few years?

HH: In the total world economy, well over 50 percent of all of the world's production, consumption, and maintenance activity is outside the monetary system. This includes production, consumption, and savings for local use. None of this ever gets into the economic maps. So start there and realize that economists have only mapped half of the economic reality that has always been going on, the GNP half. Take that as sort of the baseline data, as Scott Burns does in his book, *The Household Economy*. He says that the production, consumption, and economic activities that go on outside the monetary economy in the average American household by men, women, and children, as well as cooperative activities, add up to about $300 billion a year if they were equivalently monetized. He says that this amounts to more than all the wages and salaries paid by all the corporations in the entire economy.

Then there's another way of looking at the informal economy involving the number of people who see themselves being read out of the funny money game by inflation. They question the point of earning these more and more worthless dollars and are beginning to live more communally out of pure practicality. They say, "Why shouldn't I have more than a half- or part-time job in the cash economy and acquire the rest by sharing with a group?" Many people are doing things that way now. That economy, according to Peter Gutman at New York University, is equivalent to about $200 billion, and it's completely off the books every year. Now some of it is old-fashioned tax dodging, or people playing games with their taxes. But a lot of it, I suspect, is that people are being driven out of the cash economy by the absurdity of trying to keep up with the game, and are turning to real sharing and bartering.

EW: What's the government's reaction to this development?

HH: The bureaucrats in Washington are reacting just the way you'd expect them to. They're trying to hound down the people who are in the underground economy. For example, they just brought suit against a food coop in Minneapolis, saying that the members will have to pay taxes and social security on the work credits. Coop members, as you know, get a discount on food in return for the amount of time they put in working. This crackdown, of course, is an attempt on the part of the bureaucrats who are toppling from their little niches, which they created in order to save themselves by keeping up the flow of taxes.

You can't check human beings in that many ways. We're still incredibly ingenious creatures, thank God, and we'll continually find ways around the system. In fact, the only way you can possibly get through a period like the eighties will be by making new pathways and fighting off the IRS when they try to interfere. Congress now is trying to pass a value-added tax (VAT), which institutionalizes inflation. It's a tax on consumption. Basically, that's the last play, where the system tries to shore itself up with one last round.

To me the denouement of that kind of funny money economy is just a matter of time. The more people who know about this, contemplate it calmly, and rearrange their lives around it, the less of a problem it will be. The faster all of us get into something real, the more pressure we take off the big system. It's going to be a bumpy ride, but because of the complexity of the institution-alization that's gone on—Social Security health care payments, unemployment insurance—we cannot go down the way we did in 1929 and 1930. We may go down, however, from other external shocks that won't be predictable, because of the increasing militarization of the planet. But I don't think that we have to fear the 1929 kind of situation, unless we press third world countries to the wall and won't give them any way out of the box we've put them in with so many huge loans at impossibly high interest rates they can never repay. I suspect that we are going to learn from the experience with Germany's inabil-ity to pay reparations in the 1920s, not to up the ante to the point where we exclude so many players that the whole game disintegrates.

EW: You describe economics in your book, *Creating Alternative Futures*, as a "pseu-doscience" and as "a form of brain damage." Why are economists so myopic?

HH: It's because they have a neat, linear model of the world. It's totally divorced from the basic laws of physics, biology, bioproductivity—the real world of nature. Economists have their little models of supply and demand, input and output, and all those simplistic ways of viewing the world so that anything else that goes on will be an "external" variable. So if you have a nonlinear system and you're using such an inadequate map, it's like using a little flashlight stab-bing away at the dark, and there's no way that any policy directions can flow out of that approach.

It's a great danger to let those people stay in charge. That's why I have felt so missionary about the need to defrock the priesthood that bestrides the resource allocations process in most industrial countries. The economists have to be exposed as charlatans. We have to have much more complex interdisci-plinary policy models, and those will not emerge as long as we have the economists telling us that they know what to do.

EW: What is the requirement, then, for a new, more realistic type of economist?

HH: One of the problems of macro-economics has been the level of data averaging. Remember, first, that economists are only looking at the one-half of the econ-omy that happens to be conducted in cash. They collect all the data from that side and then they average it to such a heroic level of abstraction that it doesn't fit any local real world case anywhere. I remember that Hubert Humphrey used to say, "I just came from Detroit, and I saw 16 percent unemployment. Now, they tell me in Washington that it's 8 percent." He said, "I go to Los Angeles and it's 12 percent. I go to New York black neighborhoods and it's 40 percent among black teenagers." If you have policy directives coming from that level of insane averaging and abstracting, you lose all the fine detail. I mean, politicians and economists who have been trained like that obviously wouldn't even know how to grow a cabbage, or any other complicated activity where one has to deal with the real world.

IVAN ILLICH

Learning is Unlearning
April 1976

Vienna-born scholar and ex-Catholic priest Ivan Illich is the author of Deschooling Society *and* Medical Nemesis, *among others. Throughout his writings and his life there runs a current of opposition to rigidified institutions—whether the church, the educational establishment, or the medical profession—coupled with an affirmation of the living values those institutions claim to represent. Illich is the founding director of the Center for Intercultural Documentation in Cuernavaca, Mexico. He was interviewed by Sherman Goldman during a visit to Harvard University.*

EAST WEST: In the *New York Review of Books*, July 2, 1970, you wrote: "Equal educational opportunity is indeed both a desirable and a feasible goal, but to equate this with obligatory schooling is to confuse salvation with the church." What is real education?

IVAN ILLICH: Looking back now, I am sorry to have written that sentence, using the term education. At the time I wrote that, in 1970, I was not aware of how recently the word education has entered the language. The first mention I find of the term education as a noun occurs in French in 1836, and the dictionary definition is taken from Voltaire, who in turn probably had it from Lope de Vega. Education is an ugly neologism used by schoolmasters to give importance to their trade. I, therefore, would like to amend the sentence by substituting the term "equal learning opportunities."

EW: By equal learning opportunities you mean equal access to...

II: To books, to tools.

EW: What is the basic difference between the current institution of education and actual learning?

II: Let me put it this way: Education is inevitably—the way it's being used—an anal concept.

EW: By anal, you mean an attitude that stresses control?

II: Yes. It refers overwhelmingly to the channeling, accumulation, and acquisition of knowledge stock. It is conceived as a heap made up of the mental excrement of our best and brightest, which can be packaged by so-called curricular plans, delivered through educational institutions to people who then acquire not *knowledge* but certificates of their *knowledge stock*. People then interiorize the belief in knowledge as a commodity that can be earned by a sitting activity called "school attendance."

At the time of writing that article in 1970, and while writing *Deschooling Society,* I was not sufficiently aware of the way that school baiting would allow the least personally concerned and dedicated schoolmasters to drop out from schools—for the purpose not of becoming learners but of becoming "adult educators."

A schoolmaster is restricted to school, as a priest is kept within his chapel. His aggression is limited by society to people between the ages of six and sixteen, to the part of the day before three o'clock, only on certain days during the year, and only within the curriculum. An "adult educator," however, is somebody who goes out on the street and believes himself competent to define everybody's educational deficiencies, for which he can supply remedies in the worldwide classroom.

By my lack of precision, which you saw in that article from 1970, I contributed to rendering school baiting radically chic, a mao-maoing activity, and I'm sorry for this. I became sorry about it even as the book *Deschooling Society* was in page proofs, and therefore I sat down and wrote an article, "Alternatives to Schooling," which was then published in the *Saturday Review* in '71, simultaneously with my book on deschooling. In that article I called attention to this "hidden curriculum" known as adult education.

EW: Many North Americans involved in the biological revolution are also moving toward greater awareness and respect for the people of the so-called third world. How would you advise them to go about developing that awareness?

II: In your *Journal* I have the chance to answer without offending. As for awareness, there is, of course, nothing wrong with that. But awareness, when it becomes a goal among rich people, almost inevitably becomes an excuse for people to exercise license.

Ten years ago, I saw hordes of well-meaning North Americans, in the Peace Corps and so forth, go to Latin America to help the natives; and now for the last few years, I have seen hordes of North Americans—admirable people who have renounced considerable privileges—flooding to Latin America to get education from the peasants there. Because these North Americans believe that they themselves have become poor, they impose themselves on people in Latin America; they are down there living off the charity of native people, requesting to be fed by them while learning witchcraft from them. The North American who believes that his New Consciousness entitles him to charity from northeast Brazilians, who believes that his interest in Castaneda permits him to disturb village life, is, in a way, an even more subtle pest than the conceited Peace Corps members I saw ten years ago.

JONATHAN KOZOL

A Capacity for Rage and Compassion
November 1975

A graduate of Harvard and a Rhodes Scholar, Jonathan Kozol taught in the Boston public schools in the early 1960s—only to be fired for his civil rights beliefs. He described this experience in his first book, Death at an Early Age, *which won the National Book Award in 1968. A year later Kozol joined the parents of his former students to create one the first successful Free Schools in the nation.* Free Schools, *his chronicle of that period of struggle, became a basic handbook for urban schools. His latest book,* Rachel and Her Children, *is about homeless families in America.*

East West's Sherman Goldman conducted this interview.

EAST WEST: Sociologically, you come from the same background as the liberals who copped out of the struggle against the Establishment at one point or another. Why, in your opinion, are you different from your peers? What kept you going?

JONATHAN KOZOL: The one thing I find difficult to view with equanimity are the people who came and did their bit for a while and then disappeared. Those people offend me. I do not think this represents inherent evil in anybody. I don't think there is much that is inherent in human nature, period, but rather, these people were well conditioned, as I say in the book, to move from one thing to another. We are all involved in trying to be good consumers. I think that what has happened to many who are really of good heart and spirit is that they have been trained to trade in one social cause for another, just as we learn to trade in a Ford for a Chevrolet, or Kellogg's for the newest brand of cereal.

EW: Do you think guilt can ever lead to a really sweeping revolution?

JK: I certainly do not allow for the kind of crippling guilt that binds people up in helpless knots of self-hatred. This is the sort of emotion that leads nowhere except into mental hospitals and more often to paralysis. There is another type of experience which I call guilt but could perhaps be much better described as "ethical upheaval." This does not function like a prison cell, but rather is the kind of experience that we identify with Saul on the road to Damascus, or

Moses in sight of the burning bush, or Gandhi when he began to see how the lower castes were treated on the trains—the kind of upheaval that so many of the white kids in the 1960s felt when they went down south to Greensboro and Selma and suddenly recognized the sheer fact of rural poverty such as they had never seen before. This type of experience does not enslave people the rest of their lives. This is a catalytic experience, which is comparable in religious terms to a moment of conversion such as the kind of experience St. Francis underwent.

In political terms in the United States, I think it is similar to the experience of the young inheritor or heiress of a wealthy family, who went through an enormous upheaval at some point during the 1960s, got rid of the $100,000 inheritance that came of being born of proper Anglo-Saxon stock...and threw it into a printing press for *Resist* or for SNCC or CORE, and this seems to me to be healthy. These people lead lives filled with energy and even joy—and not joy of a fatuous kind but joy that identifies with the farm workers, for example, exhilarating in the sense of struggle.

EW: Why do people know what is right but do not do it?

JK: The standard liberal answer would be that it is human nature, but I don't believe there is any such thing as human nature. I think what we call human nature in the United States is a certain type of well-inculcated behavior pattern that serves the interests of the people who own supermarkets and automobile factories and so forth. In China, I suppose if they someday lose the clarity of vision that seems to be very sharp right now, they might tend to say it is human nature to have communal generosity. I don't think it's human nature. I think it's up to us to decide what we want to be; and, unlike animals, we have a great deal of choice as to what type of entity we want to be. Why, then, do we have this particular phenomenon, not just in the United States, but probably in most of Western Europe and I suspect in the Soviet Union also? I think it is because our education trains us to separate the word from the deed. We are so accustomed to this approach that most people take it for granted, that the word is one thing, the deed another.

In school, I think, for the first time in a child's life, knowledge gets broken up into two separate items known as thought and feelings. And ethics becomes divided into two separate items known as intention and realization. The school is compartmentalized from top to bottom: periods, semesters, two credit hours, 45 minutes for thinking about starvation, and then 32½ minutes for doing geometry, and then the bell rings; on to your next subject. I think this compartmentalization, when it comes down to this particular question of action versus deed, is very effective, is cataclysmic. There is the classic line of a professor of religion in one college that I visited who said to me, "Look, it's my job to teach ethics. It's someone else's job to go out and act upon what I teach."

EW: Why is life such a difficult thing? The stage is set, with all the scenery fake.

JK: Although I'm not a disciplined or a dogmatic socialist, I do believe that economic structures have a great deal to do with the kind of lives we lead and the kind of people we can be. I do not believe it is to the advantage of the people who control our society and who perpetuate their values through the public schools to educate zealots like Thoreau, and I think the schools take great pains to ensure that we do not turn out this way. I don't think the schools take any chances. The schools go to considerable effort to make certain that we do not grow up to question, to inquire, to know.

Thoreau pointed out that most people acquiesce in the kind of lives that have been prepared for them, and he described their state of acquiescence as a form of mature resignation. They cease to recognize it as a defeat, as a surrender. He said something to this effect, that "most men lead lives of quiet desperation." What is resignation but confirmed despair? It is a kind of despair that most people don't perceive, and if they get used to living a life of unreality and a life of self-serving, and even self-despising, they blur into this sort of genteel resignation.

EW: There is another possibility...involving things like an interest in meditation, natural food, back to the land, alternative communities, planetary culture, and so forth. In your opinion, how much of it is a viable effort to create an alternative to the present society, and how much of it is a retreat from social involvement by young people who were discouraged by the efforts directed against the peace and integration movements toward the end of the '60s?

JK: Those who try to find ways to reconcile biological needs with a larger ethical dream of collective existence seem to be very definitely on the right track. Those are people who have really thought beyond the closed world of the imagination.

On the other hand, those who wish to experiment in various lifestyles, including communal existence, but attempt at the same time to rule out all political action and all recognition of the larger economic framework of a society that enslaves many for the benefit of a few and, to go still further, torments millions in order that people such as themselves have the luxury to experiment—people who forget *that*, it seems to me are then creating a potential utopian existence surrounded by a kind of living nightmare, which is almost as grotesque as the image of Nero fiddling while Rome burned.

I said in a previous book that an idyllic Summerhill in the mountains for the children of the rich, serving exclusively all white children, while the children of the Bronx are starving and the people in Harlem are dying in the streets, is too much like a playpen for the children of S.S. guards. This offended many people in Vermont, in New Hampshire, and California. I received about ten thousand letters in response to *Free Schools*, not all of them angry, but an awful lot of people were very upset and said, "Just because our Summerhill school up here in the country only has white kids, only has rich kids, doesn't mean we're doing anything bad." What can I say? Of course, I don't mean you're doing something bad, but you should know that what you are doing you could not do if other people were not suffering greatly.

One thing doesn't exist *near* the other, in a separate compartment. One exists *because* of the other. The very lovely little experiment which just happens to enroll only the children of lawyers, doctors, and career women, this little school might be as benign and gentle as Thoreau or Rousseau could have dreamed, yet the money that it takes to run that school, sooner or later, is money that comes out of the pockets of poor people someplace. As Chomsky has said, all money in an unjust society is inherently corrupt; the question is what efforts at justice we make out of the money we get hold of.

I think the whole syndrome of collective experimental existence represented by food collectives, and all the other attempts which fall into this category, are benevolent in intention and wise, and perhaps will prove to be prophetic, but are literally flawed if they do not somehow incorporate in them a constant effort to redress the injustice without which they could not exist, whether this means making careful efforts to include poor people in their ranks or—if that proves, as it sometimes does, impractical or unfeasible because poor people aren't interested in the type of life they are living—at least making sure that when there is severe trouble in the fields of California, they break out of their relatively reflective existence and pick up some picket signs and add some strength to Cesar Chavez's struggle. If they are living near a city like Boston and see black people being tormented in the streets, let them put away their life experiments for a day or a month or a year and get out and turn the mimeograph machine to help to get out the crowds that it takes to form a good protest march, or, by their skills if they are writers or filmmakers or polemicists or skilled in any way, help to publicize the truth. In other words, it seems to me we are not faced here with an either/or: "either we experiment with new ways of living or we fight for social change." It seems to me that good people can do both, and the healthiest rebels in an unjust nation are those who learn to do both.

LIV ULLMANN

Putting World Hunger on Center Stage
September 1981

Scandinavian film actress Liv Ullmann has for the past ten years been active with various world hunger relief organizations. She served as Ambassador of Goodwill for UNICEF and was vice-president of the International Rescue League. Interviewer Karin Stephan spoke with the actress after Ullmann's tour abroad to such hunger and drought-stricken countries as Bangladesh, Somalia, and Ethiopia.

EAST WEST: Did you feel that your work has somehow affected real individuals?

LIV ULLMANN: I feel that everything you do, good or bad, is somehow affecting individuals. Obviously the work I did this past year affected me and I affected others through more what I was than what I wanted to do, and they affected me through what they had been doing for a long time.

EW: It must have been very hard on you.

LU: Obviously, I don't really think that. I am so much a richer person because of what has been given me by the people I met. This doesn't mean that we should say that the poor are wonderful because they're poor. Rather, it's that we who are living in this materialistic society have lost something. We have forgotten the splendor of the touch, you know, that innocence is the best way, as with people living close to the earth. There is such a pleasure to meet eyes that look at you, that hold you, and the enormous generosity and grace given by people who really have nothing. I think that this is something very beautiful, but it is almost dangerous and difficult to say because people romanticize it, and it is not like that.

Those people should not be poor. They should not live like this. But as much as we can give them, we should know that the real value of life is something they give us. They have stayed much closer to the land, whereas we simply have lost it. Not that they did anything to stay in touch with it, but we are losers at birth.

EW: I felt the connection between the individual and humanity after having read what you wrote about your daughter in *Changing*. I felt your relationship there had a very deep effect on your ability to perceive the children as you travel.

LU: Yes, I feel that children are so real and direct. On these travels I met children who didn't get Barbie dolls, cars, and things at an early age, but children who have found reality where reality is. It's close to what even we had as children. I remember growing up we played with stones and had a farm and the country was so much more part of our life. This has been taken away from children today. These children still have it because they don't have another place and they have to create their own world. That's why the kids can say such fantastic things, like this girl who said she wanted to show me everything that was wonderful in her life. She wanted to show me her home, her family, and everything that grows. She's living in a village in Bangladesh and her house is made of mud. Inside there were ten or twelve people and dogs and only one bed, and this little girl had something to show that is good—she has a home to show, she has a family to show. I don't know how many twelve-year-olds in our part of the world would even approach a stranger and in happiness want to share this, even if they are only growing potatoes in the garden.

TRISTAN JONES

Modern Ulysses
July 1979

Tristan Jones, about whom Motor Boat and Sailing *editor Jeff Hammond said, "He is living an odyssey of such immensity that it is difficult to imagine," has been inspiring readers with the chronicles of his exotic adventures for many years in books such as* Ice!, The Incredible Voyage, *and* Saga of a Wayward Sailor, *to name just a few. Long before his grizzled face appeared on* East West's *cover with this interview, Jones was solo-sailing small vessels around the world. Now in his "second fifty years of sailing," Jones has recently completed what he calls his most difficult yet worthwhile adventure—the crossing, in a small wooden boat, of the treacherous Isthmus of Kra in Thailand with a crew of three physically handicapped young Thais and a young German. As this book goes to print Jones, who himself is missing one leg, and his crew are sailing up Southeast Asia's Mekong River to continue to "show by example what fellow amputees, especially youngsters, might do given the opportunity and the will."*

Jones tried to teach interviewers Leonard Jacobs and Sam Weiss the almost forgotten art of "idling," keeping them enthralled for three hours with his Welsh wit, passion, and storytelling.

EAST WEST: What factors in your childhood, family background, or elsewhere do you think gave you your thirst for adventure?

TRISTAN JONES: I was born at sea of seafaring people. I was raised in a coastal area of Wales, where livelihoods were gained either by seafaring or farming. I don't think I have a "thirst for adventure" any more than anyone else has. My life was, in the main, dictated by my familiarity with the sea. My family, although poor, were well- (mainly self-) educated, and so I became familiar also with the great writers of the past, and with history—as they saw it—at an early age.

I may have been fortunate in that I was brought up by people who had been comparatively untouched by the Industrial Revolution, but that doesn't mean they were restrictive at all. They were nonconformist, agnostic, leftwing Liberals, of a republican bent in a very Royalist country. Old-fashioned as it may be, it seems to me that there are racial traits. One of the Welsh traits is consuming curiosity, the need to see "what's on the other side." (Many of the early American pioneers and explorers, such as Lewis and Clark, were either Welsh or of Welsh descent.) It is a culture where the arts are highly respected, and none more so than poetry. And what is poetry but exploration? What is exploration but poetry in motion?

It may seem banal to mention the importance of ethnic identity now that it is becoming more fashionable in the States, but it is important that a person should be able to relate to the past—for by doing so, by recognizing his or her place in the thrust of humanity from the cave to the stars—he or she can relate to the future. If I were French, for example, I would want to be either a great chef or a great philosopher or whatever else the French do well. Being a Welshman, and not being able to make heads or tails of music, I must either be a good farmer, a poet, or an explorer. Though I might be considered anachronistic in some circles, wandering the oceans in a small sailing boat, I myself feel and hope that perhaps, one day in the distant future, someone will set off for the other side of Alpha Centauri, perhaps sparked by something he or she knows of the old-time navigators.

EW: What do you think makes most people choose lives of security rather than adventure?

TJ: Mostly because they have never bothered to find out what real security is. Also because there is, fortunately, a strong family instinct in Man. Ulysses returned to Penelope, but he couldn't have done it had there not been thousands of people living ordinary lives to support Penelope's existence.

EW: How would you rate the present generation on this score, compared to the generation when you were young, and before?

TJ: My father, who was a master mariner and a cynic, used to say, whenever people brought up differences between epochs or generations: "Ah, yes...and the bloody seas were rougher in them days, too!" Humanity changes very little in several generations. The differences are superficial. Life is physically easier, no doubt, for the rising generation (whatever that means), at least in the industrialized nations. I take some strange comfort from most of those whom I have met and who are aware that this could lead to soft laxity. I suppose the only real difference between the present-day youngster's attitude to "adventure" is that it is more difficult now for them to extricate themselves from the toils of an ever-growing bureaucracy. But all they have to do is open the door and walk out. They can always walk back in. That couldn't happen (or was much more difficult) when I was a youngster. However, it seems to me that the present youngsters are more aware on the "present" level than we were, but less aware on the "past" level. That's not ideal—ask any navigator—it's difficult to know where you're *going* unless you know where you've *come from*.

EW: Do you feel that there has been a decline in adventurousness in recent times?

TJ: Certainly not. When James Cook sailed the Pacific there was only one modern craft there. Now there are thousands upon thousands, and they're all exploring. Just because someone else has been there before you should not make it any less new in your eyes. How many people from Boston, back in 1930, say, had been to India? And how many now? But I'm speaking in only geographical terms. The adventurousness in physics, in medicine, in literature is staggering. One of our problems is that most of us don't fully realize that we're living through the greatest burst of creative energy man has ever known. I wouldn't live at any other time in the past, but I'd give my very soul to be alive this time in the coming century. What adventure I would see!

EW: What is your advice to young people, middle-aged, and old people?

TJ: Young people? Under 25? Hold on to your hats! It's going to be a job supporting the population bulge ahead of you, but stick it out. When population decreases again this world is going to be ten thousand times better for the average human being than it has ever been before. Resist the moves away from the center to the left or right, and hang on! Resist every effort of a growing bureaucracy to depersonalize an ever-growing number of people. They're only fumbling in the dark. Every time a number is allotted to anything ask, "Why?" If you're English-speaking, never use a Latin-derived word when a Celto-Saxon one will serve the purpose. Read Homer, Shakespeare, Lawrence, and Joyce, try to take the bones out of Freud and Hesse, and don't let the bastards grind you down, anywhere, anytime! Don't let anyone ever try to tell you that the bloody crawl from the back of the cave has been for nothing! Middle-aged people? Make do with a bit less. Rome lived well—too well—and Rome paid. Corny as it seems—beware the Ides of March! Old people? I would not be so presumptuous as to advise them. All I can do is be grateful that their leaders didn't make a bigger mess of things than they did and thank my lucky stars that the Edwardians didn't have the atom bomb. That was the real crisis: the years 1900-1915, nincompoops in charge all around. We only just got through (I'm a European, don't forget). Cost us forty million dead in two holocausts, but we scraped through.

EW: What is freedom and what is the relation between money and freedom?

TJ: Freedom is all things to all men. To me it means my own individual and social responsibility to nature, animate and inanimate. Money's a fallacy. I have known, a thousand times, utter freedom when I haven't had a penny to my name. Freedom does not mean the satisfaction of appetite. It means the enjoyment of life within one's limits, not at the expense of others.

EW: What are your plans and what is your dream?

TJ: To head to the nether side of the most distant galaxy. It is my dream that, one day, we will bestride the universe.

EW: What do you think of the woman's movement?

TJ: Charming, especially when they are not aware that I'm watching. I was brought up in a society where, for the past thousand years, women had gone to sea as functioning sailors. There's nothing new in women's participation to the full in society, except among the middle-classes, the bourgeoisie, and they are a mere (but important) fraction of humanity. I do rather suspect, though, that it might be helping the depersonalization of society and creating more prospective consumers-in-their-own-right. The bureaucrats would love it! Rather than that I would see women aim for superiority. *Anything* to stop 1984! I cannot look on a woman as a "person." I respect her to the hilt—as a woman. If some power is to negate woman as woman, what's to stop them, some day, negating woman as "person"? What's to prevent them being declared redundant? The means will be there soon. So women should seek the corridors of power as women, not as "persons."

EW: Who do you admire most in history?

TJ: Homer, Shakespeare, James Cook, Ernest Shackleton, Denizulu, Confucius, Thomas Jefferson, whoever it was that pushed the first log into the water and sat on it. The list is endless.

EW: If you could take only ten books with you on your boat, what would they be (excepting navigational guides)?

TJ: First, the *Odyssey* and Homer's other works; second, the complete works of Shakespeare; and third, the *Oxford Book of English Verse*. Fourth, I would take the definitive edition of Rudyard Kipling. I know he went sour in the end, I know he was an imperialist, a man of his time, but for the way in which he brought out the hearts of everyday people—the soldier, the sailor, the Indian— he is forgiven from the bootnails up. Fifth would be *Ulysses* by James Joyce; sixth, *Remembrance of Things Past* by Marcel Proust (making allowances); seventh, *The Autobiography of a Supertramp* by W. H. Davies; eighth, *Steppenwolf* by Herman Hesse (so I would have toilet paper); ninth, the collected poems and novels of T. F. Powys; and last, *Farewell My Lovely* by Raymond Chandler (the best-structured tale I know).

EW: What is the relation between food and freedom?

TJ: As you will have gathered from my books, my own tendency towards vegetarianism was mainly caused through simply not being able to afford to eat meat. I lived for years on seafood and porridge oats—and natural hop beer and whiskey when I could pay for it, which wasn't often. But that only leads me to realize how fortunate your younger readers are, who can come to this knowledge by learning it. And bloody good luck to them, as the sailors say.

EW: Where does East meet West? Was the West always so materialistic?

TJ: My attitude to the great question of East/West, too, may be a bit simplistic, but anyway I reached it myself. It is this. What the new generation may *think* is Western in fact *isn't*. If we look at the Greeks and the Celts we do not find opulence and an overwhelming love of riches. Quite the reverse. The Greeks despised the Persians because of the latter's love of wealth and power. It seems to me that what is now considered to be Western has been absorbed, over the centuries, from the Middle East via the crusades and Venice, and so forth.

In my country, Wales, a good storyteller, a singer, or a poet, is infinitely more respected than, say, a lawyer or a landowner. And that's the Celtic way, and basically the European way. It is only in the so-called "advanced" cities, with the pant for pelf [struggle for personal gain] in full swing day and night, that I see mentally disturbed people wandering around, that I meet a vast majority of folk who worry themselves sick over *things* and ideas that matter not one whit in the general design of life; the modern hunchback at the bar, the nervous twitch of the knee, the stance a little too upright, and will-the-air-conditioner-break-down and can-I-keep-up-the-payments?

EW: What will be the crucial choice for humanity over the next twenty years?

TJ: To make up its mind to endure, or not to endure, the crisis in resources of fuel and food. We must decide whether to make do with less for the better-off in order to supply a little more to the deprived. But there's a consolation to bear in mind—the world, as a whole, has never been better off. A little example: Up until the mid 1800s the practice of "suttee," the burning of widows, alive, was the general rule in India. Work it out. Say a hundred and fifty a day, 55,000 a year, over a *million* in *every generation* for over a *thousand* years. And now we call doomsday because some megalomaniac persuades seven hundred poor deluded victims to commit suicide? It's always been so, but now we *know* about it. That's the difference, there's the hope. Now we can *know* about it, and try to stop it.

ECOLOGY

Harlan Lundberg

Masanobu Fukuoka

David Brower

Wendell Berry

Wes Jackson

DAVID BROWER

Friend of the Earth
September 1982

David Brower, who has been called the Archdruid of the American environmental movement, has been leading conservation battles for over forty years. As Sierra Club executive director, then as chairman of Friends of the Earth, Brower commanded fights to save California redwoods, keep dams out of Grand Canyon and Dinosaur National Monuments, and protect natural areas across the U.S. His influence and concern ensured continued preservation of wild areas as far apart as primeval forests in Washington State's Olympic National Forest, Cape Cod National Seashore, and the sea islands off the coast of Georgia. International recognition of Brower's effectiveness came in 1978, when he was nominated for the Nobel Peace Prize. Brower's main thrust today is "environmental restoration." He is chairman of the Earth Island Institute in San Francisco, and is currently planning the Congress on Hope for the Earth Conference scheduled for June 1989 in Managua, Nicaragua. He is also writing his autobiography.

Brower was interviewed by freelance writer Ann Fawcett, who observed that he had "an aura of divinity."

EAST WEST: Where do you see the ecology movement going in the next twenty years?

DAVID BROWER: I'm quite optimistic. Shortly, society at large will realize that *they* must be affected by ecological sense. I used to say we need conservation consciousness in what we're doing on this planet. I'm hoping we will acquire a lot more in the future. The organization that I'm trying to get going now, Earth Island Institute, will concentrate on exactly that. Earth Island Institute will try to bring in people from various fields and expose them to the requirements for *natural* law and order. We've been violating those laws rather steadily.

This fall we're planning a conference for New York City on conservation and global security, relating these two topics together. If we can show, by looking ahead, that humans can indeed live more equitably without arms and with greater security, we believe people will then be willing to disarm.

EW: Do you see people becoming more concerned and aware of ecological issues?

DB: Recently, a good many polls have been done—Harris, CBS, *The New York Times*. From these, one of the things we do see and are grateful for is that there seems to be a public out there in the wildlands, the outbacks, the grassroots, whatever you want to call it, that is ahead of the leaders. On the clean air question, there are 80 percent who say don't mess with our clean air standards. They're way ahead of people in the White House. What we're trying to do is find out where these people are. We know they exist and we would like to find them and encourage them to sound off, not just to the poll takers, but to the people who are about to make decisions on their behalf. That requires political activity, which has too long been considered a little less than a nice thing in which to participate. I think we have to consider politics as a good thing to do. A society moves through the device of political interaction and no other way. So I think we have to make politics part of our lives. This includes supporting the people who have the courage to go into political life through working to get them into office. More important than we realize is *thanking* them whenever they do something well once they are there.

I might add, when did I last thank President Reagan for anything? When did I first thank him? I've done neither or anything in between. That's my fault. He came out with a very good statement on the protection of whales. I don't know of any conservation organization that thanked him for it. Ours hasn't yet and we should do it right away. Or how many people thanked President Nixon for helping get the National Environmental Policy Act through, the Clean Air Act? There's no telling what might have happened if he'd been thanked for doing those terribly important things for everybody instead of left there in silence. What would history have been if we had had enough love in us to thank somebody?

EW: Where do you see evolution going? We've already talked about how humans are greedy in terms of energy use, and as a species we're rushing pell-mell into nuclear disaster.

DB: All I can do is answer in the approximate words of Ian McHarg in his book *Design of Nature*. The nuclear explosion exchange has taken place. The earth is covered with grey ash. All life has been extinguished except for a few algae who are summoned to some deep protected spot where they didn't get more radiation than they were able to handle. The algae held a meeting, realizing that evolution had to start all over again, and they came to a unanimous decision—next time no brains.

That's a very poor answer. We have brains; we have the ability and know what has to be done. My latest idea is that it's time for Magna Carta II. At first I thought just a Magna Carta for water was necessary. We're messing up the earth's water resources so badly. We have a bunch of antique laws governing what happens to water. We overuse it, move it to places it shouldn't go; we don't realize that a river is nature's way of moving water somewhere else; we try to send it back where it came from and over the hill. We pollute what we can't dam.

Then I decided we certainly need it for everything else. So I did my instant research and found out that in 1215 King John of England was abusing his barons. They were about to declare war on him, and King John didn't want war. The barons exhorted from him the promise that no free man would be arrested or put into jail, outlawed, exiled, harmed, or his property taken away without the judgment of his peers and the rule of law. That was 1215, and they had to make forty-seven copies of that and send it all around England without Xerox.

There's need for a parallel. The new king, the new abusive monarch, is our own species. There are many things, animate and inanimate, on the earth upon which we humans depend and have been abusing. We put them in jail, take their rights away, exile and destroy them without the judgment of their peers or the rule of natural law.

Our minds have evolved to be capable of moving out of ourselves and mentally placing ourselves elsewhere. Using that ability we're pretty sure that the universe began with a big bang 20 billion years ago. We can visualize what's going on on Jupiter. Mentally we can move to the top of Everest; we can reflect upon what might happen, what has happened. It's an extraordinary capability we have inside our heads. The essential requirement now is to pull *out* of ourselves and imagine what it's like to represent the needs of some country other than our own, maybe two others.

Imagine what it's like to be a tree and what your requirements are. What must the tree know and think? I don't know where a tree's left lobe and right lobe are, but they seem to manage. Or think like a condor or like a child born in the year 2400. We can do that, and we'd better, so we realize that the rights of other creatures who share the earth with us are far senior to us. And, we need to realize the rights of the most important population of all, human beings who haven't been born yet. Their genes are right here, now, in our custody. We can only accommodate their needs by thinking of them now and having that influence or vote. That's the political constituency the environmental movement is most concerned about, but the concern shouldn't be limited to the environmental movement. The whole of humanity should share that conscious concern. Since we're the principal abusers of the rights of nature, we should think pretty hard about that.

EW: What do you recommend that the individual do?

DB: I've given a clue already. I say there are a lot of environmental organizations and they need people, but not many of them pay very well, and F.O.E. probably pays the worst. The other thing I say to people is, "What's your field?" And they will give the field, and I will say, "All right, go right on in that field and find a way to add ecological conscience to it." So I'm back to the Earth Island concept. Or I tell a lawyer, "Join a great big law firm and cheat—in favor of the environment." A lot of lawyers are very busy *fighting* the environment for their big clients. And we'd like their big clients to stop fighting to let their market last longer, like way into the future instead of winding it down in the next five years and be ordered to get a nice black number in the bottom line for the next quarter. Look farther ahead. Some corporations can do it. It'd be nice if they all did.

EW: Do you talk to corporations?

DB: Not very much, but now and then. Our star, Amory Lovins, does that, and one of the ads we want to run someday that won't offend them too much is "When Amory Lovins Talks, E. F. Hutton Listens." They do. It doesn't hurt to have good numbers and good reasoning. The corporate heads are not stupid, but they have had their attentions diverted in other directions. And here's a new direction to go in.

In no small part, owing to Lovins's activity, the investment in nuclear power has ended. The only outfits now willing to invest in nuclear power are government. The marketplace has no use for it.

EW: You really see those investors as recognizing that they are in over their heads and that it's better not to throw good money after bad?

DB: Yes, to have those two reactors at Diablo Canyon remain idle, unless they use some other fuel to heat their water, would be a beautiful turnaround point to show that this civilization had enough sense to change direction. That could be a national monument to national good judgment.

The end somewhere along the line, though, should be related to what Jonathan Schell did in his book, *The Fate of the Earth*. I've done it in my pieces, and I'm just glad to see it get that wide a circulation. Schell said that humanity has been operating under the law of fear. This has produced sovereignty which has brought us to the brink of extinction. This will occur in no time at all unless we change and go by the rule of love. Gandhi taught it; he was coached a bit by Thoreau, so it's not an all-Indian project, but it's something that excites the younger audiences, and I've even found some of the older audiences not finding love that appalling a concept. Love is the extraordinary resource that keeps renewing. We will lose it only if we forget to use it.

WES JACKSON AND WENDELL BERRY

New Standards for the American Farm
August 1985

Wes Jackson and Wendell Berry are two of the most knowledgeable and articulate proponents of sustainable agriculture. Berry is an eloquent speaker, poet, novelist, and essayist, as well as a working Kentucky farmer. Perhaps his most well known book is his essay, The Unsettling of America: Culture and Agriculture. *Berry's newest book is a novel,* Remembering.

Wes Jackson is a prominent environmentalist and educator, a pioneering agricultural researcher and plant geneticist—and a farmer. With his wife Dana he co-directs the Land Institute, an educational and research center near Salina, Kansas. Jackson's latest book, Altars of Unhewn Stone, *is a collection of essays on land issues.*

East West interviewers Thom Leonard and Mark Mayell met with them shortly after the publication of Meeting the Expectations of the Land, *edited by Berry, Jackson, and Bruce Coleman.*

EAST WEST: As you have pointed out in your writing, Wendell, farming is something that comes from a living tradition—the skills of farming are best learned from family and community. Are farmers a "nonrenewable resource," and if so where are we going to get new farmers?

WENDELL BERRY: The soil is a renewable resource as long as we have it. When we don't have it, it's a nonrenewable resource. That's exactly the same for farming people. They're renewable, as long as we have them. Once we've lost them, they're nonrenewable, just like petroleum or coal. What the industrial economy does is work to reduce the organic to the inorganic. It sees life as of no value except as something to be mined. And what this economy does is take the organic world and the inorganic world and treat them as the same. It reduces life to an inert, marketable quality. Inert, expendable, and exhaustible.

EW: Is there a way, at this point, that we can teach people to be farmers? Also, how, even if someone knows how to farm, could she or he get land? What needs to be done to keep people on the farm or get them back there as well as have them farm in a way that's going to work?

WB: I've heard farmers say it took five years to learn a farm. That's a rule of thumb. But they speak of learning a farm the way a musician would speak of learning a piece of music. The significant thing is not numbers, but that it takes a long time. Learning to farm is learning to farm *a farm*. Not learning a bunch of universally applicable rules. That this learning has an economic value both to the farmer and to the whole nation is something that the present economy has no way to acknowledge. And people don't want to talk about this because it isn't entirely quantifiable.

The priority now ought to be helping the farm people who want to farm stay in farming. And to help children from farm families remain in farming. Because they know a little. Some of them don't know as much as their parents and grandparents knew a generation ago when farming was more diversified, but they know some. They're worth saving because of that. The idea of promoting a large scale return of city people to the country is very difficult to contend with. What are you going to do? Turn all those people loose to learn by experience, by trial and error, at the cost of topsoil and a lot of unhappiness to them?

My preference is to see some kind of tendency established again, to make it *possible* for ordinary people to aspire to own land. That would make it possible for the people who are most inclined to farm to do it. The people who know a little something about it could do it. People who have gone to the city and long to go back to the country could do it. But then you've got to restore the country communities. The communities are the best reservoir of the traditions and the knowledge. And newcomers into farming would stand to learn more from the communities than they would ever stand to learn from any deliberate government-sponsored education effort. I think government-sponsored education has its place. But what people who are trying to learn to farm need are families. And if they don't have families who can hand the knowledge on, they need neighbors. So I would put priorities, as I think Wes would, in the remaking of country neighborhoods, on the practice of community.

EW: Is that happening, on a small scale?

WB: No, I don't think it's happening yet, in any noticeable way. I think that before it can happen, the country people have to begin to realize what they have lost in losing their neighborhoods. I don't think that they have yet. The great change in American agriculture occurs when a farmer decides he would rather have his neighbor's field than have the neighbor.

WES JACKSON: This is crucial, for it isn't widely asked how large an area a farmer or a farm family can watch over. That hasn't been settled and, of course, it would be different in different places. And with different families.

I'm just now beginning to get some overall view of the 160 acres that the Land Institute bought. We bought that quarter-section in 1982. So we've had the piece all of '82, '83, and '84, and we're now into the '85 growing season. It requires going around the perimeter of the place. And then going over different parts. Right now we're not winning—in terms of getting that place so that it is non-erodible, so that it is verdant overall, so that it can accommodate its highest and best use. That's going to take a lot of time. There are a lot of mistakes we've already made. This year I'm going to spend a lot of time correcting mistakes that I thought were corrective measures the first year or two. And I was born and raised on a farm. With what I know, 160 acres is too much for me to watch. And 90 acres of that is native prairie under perennial cover that has never been plowed. This eyes-to-acres ratio is a terribly important thing.

EW: Can we presume that the average U.S. farm size of 415 acres is way too high?

WB: I think that's too high in *some* places. You see, the problem is that the situations in which agriculture is done are infinitely varied. Four hundred acres in a broken, many-faceted country is a great deal indeed. It would require more attention than 400 acres in the middle of Illinois, where it's flat, where the topography isn't so complicated. You can't lay down rules. That's the difficulty with people who think there ought to be some way to regulate farming by policing it, by applying some kind of universal soil erosion standard.

People want to try to enforce laws against soil erosion. Well, if you think of the police force it would make you see that you'd have to have a totalitarian government to enforce laws like that. Probably what's necessary is to go at it by paying farmers adequately for their produce to start with, and see if that wouldn't help. People are not going to take care of the land when they're under tremendous economic pressure to abuse it. That's easily understandable. In order to cherish something, you've got to have time. You have to be able to afford to cherish it.

WJ: You have to scale your operation to the slope of the land, how rough the land is, the availability of water, the types of soils. What industrial agriculture does is homogenize landscapes and homogenize people. High energy inputs destroy both biological and cultural diversity. I would almost say that that is a law of ecology; high energy destroys information.

WB: When you talk about "information," you mean the information encoded in plants and species?

WJ: In species diversity, and the high information in the domestic system, both in the domestic species and in the people that are managing it.

WB: And the information in the ambient nature. Ambient and supportive. When you reduce the diversity, you're going to get destruction, soil erosion.

WJ: You see, nature could have set this whole thing up in which there is just a very heavy energy charge on the landscape that kept things sustainable, but nature did not feature a high energy approach to covering a landscape. Nature featured a high *information* approach to covering landscapes. Lots of diversity, as much diversity as can be accommodated. And what we've done in contemporary agriculture, of course, is say that the landscape ought to be as homogenized as possible to accommodate the means of mass production, so that it would deliver as much energy in the form of food as possible. One thing that runs ahead of everything else is that, in spite of all the research that has been done, the efficiency of photosynthesis has not improved. And it's down around 1 or 2 percent. In other words, energy ain't what it's about. And yet, that which characterizes the modern agricultural field is high-energy inputs. Nature denies the opportunity for high-energy capture. There are places in the flow of energy through an ecosystem where energy is efficiently transported or transformed, but at the point of capture by the green molecular traps, efficiency is low.

We have the idea that we should increase production. Well, it just runs absolutely counter to nature. Nature has had a few billion years to increase production to many times the levels of what we have, but it hasn't happened. Maybe partly because energy isn't very pretty. But diversity is.

WB: And nature likes pretty. She seems to approve of elegance, not crudity.

HARLAN LUNDBERG

Growing Organic Rice
August 1978

Lundberg Family Farms, of Richvale, California, has been growing high quality organic brown rice for nearly twenty years and has also developed a popular line of rice products. Lundberg Farms recently won the first annual Bread & Circus Safe Food Award, and was also recognized by the Steering Committee for Sustainable Agriculture by being given its Stewards of Sustainable Agriculture Award.

Leonard Jacobs conducted this interview with Harlan Lundberg, who runs Lundberg Farms with his brothers Homer, Eldon, and Wendell.

EAST WEST: With the difficulties of developing techniques for growing, marketing, and distributing organic rice, why do you do it?

HARLAN LUNDBERG: We're pretty much committed to it. It's a way of life for us. I think we'd be doing it even if we were breaking even, although I think it should maintain a decent living for all of us.

Dad taught us that there's a better way than the chemical way. He believed that there were ways of leaving the soil in better shape than we got it, cultivating techniques like using the vetches. He introduced this to our area, and now it's pretty widely used all around us. He was always telling us boys when we were young to take care of the soil, to leave it better than you got it and be careful about it. He was an ecologist before they really knew anything about ecology.

EW: So the rice is organic not only for the personal health of the people eating it, but also for the planet's health?

HL: Yes. One of these days, after the ground is so poisoned, I think nothing is going to grow on it. I talk to my neighbors, and they're using more chemicals all the time; I can't believe they're not starting to be really frightened. A few of them are.

I have a very dear friend who asked if he could grow forty acres of organic rice for us, and basically it was because of his son, who is very conscious of the ecology. The man isn't, but his son is working on him, so you see a few

exciting things happening. I'm very frightened about this poisoning of our so
It's the basic thing to living as far as I'm concerned. You've got to take care o
it and make sure the micro organisms are fed. One way is working the straw
back into the ground after harvest. These are now burned by the farmers. I
just makes you sick. But we've never burned a field. Dad was against it, we're
against it.

Ideas like that seem like small things, but I think in the long run it's what's
going to make the difference.

MASANOBU FUKUOKA

The Natural Farmer
November 1979

Masanobu Fukuoka is the leading contemporary practitioner of natural agriculture, a traditional form of no-till farming practiced in the ancient world. Without cultivation, fertilizer or prepared compost, weeding or dependence on chemicals, his own farm in Japan has consistently yielded higher and better quality crops than modern chemical or organic farming methods. Fukuoka is the author of The One-Straw Revolution, The Natural Way of Farming, *and most recently* The Road Back to Nature. *Although he lectures and tours farms throughout the world, observing, teaching, and helping people to understand the importance of the natural world, he prefers to stay at home close to his fields.*

East West's Ken Burns conducted this interview during Fukuoka's visit to Amherst, Mass.

EAST WEST: Briefly, what are the principles of natural farming?

MASANOBU FUKUOKA: The first thing you have to do is to realize that the kind of nature that surrounds us now is not true nature. The second thing is to realize that what is growing in nature is not the product of man's activities, it is the product of nature itself. Farmers don't create their products, nature does.

Now, in the U.S.A. you have very thin soil. In the western U.S.A. you have much foxtail grass. In the east you have thin soil that results in a limited variety of trees. In that soil you can only have monoculture agriculture. You have to plow a lot and farm on a large scale. If you do natural agriculture and build up the soil, then on a small piece of land you can raise many different types of crops. You don't need monoculture.

The use of land in the U.S.A. by the present method of agriculture is very inefficient. You could get two to three times more yield by using proper techniques. The reason the yields are so small is that the earth is dying; it has been killed by the modern methods of agriculture. If farmers changed over to more natural methods of agriculture they could very easily increase their yield.

EW: Since American farmers are not going to be able to accept this philosophy or practice totally, what specific thing can they do to improve their farming? What specific thing are they doing now that they could stop doing?

MF: The first thing that could be done is to stop raising cattle. The second involves their thinking, their spiritual outlook. They must realize that it is not the farmer who produces the crop, but nature. If they can grasp that idea, the practice of natural agriculture can proceed easily and directly. If they don't grasp that idea, natural agriculture cannot begin to be accomplished.

I have met various farmers in the U.S.A., and in all cases when I showed my pictures and explained my techniques the farmers were very impressed. What worries me is that they might want to mix scientific agriculture with natural agriculture. That will not work. Before I came to this country I was not sure that rice could be produced by natural agriculture in every area of the U.S.A. But after investigating I became convinced. Some people in the U.S.A. have already expressed an interest. What worries me is that they seem to be more interested in profit than in healing the soil.

The agricultural production of the U.S.A. seems to be very impressive and very great, but this is actually a false greatness because it is based on the use of oil. In effect, your present crops are just a transformation of oil. This is a very weak and fragile form of agriculture. If the oil supplies stopped, production would break down. This is not an agriculture based on nature.

My method of agriculture, which involves no plowing and no use of chemical fertilizers, and which also doesn't involve the use of a single drop of oil, could be practiced anywhere and under any conditions. It is based on the power of nature with a minimum of human interference.

EW: If you don't use any oil for fertilizer or to power machinery, then you need far more people to plant or harvest. That means that more people will have to begin to farm or else our farms will have to decrease in size.

MF: Actually, the amount of work needed for natural agriculture is not so great. In the planting, or in the early stages of farming, all you have to do is spread the seed and put the rice straw on the ground. The main work happens in harvest, when you need many hands to help. I suggest that the entire population should join in as a joyful recognition of the bountifulness of nature.

EW: I think people make a mistake when they consider you just an expert on agriculture. What I was immediately attracted to in your teaching is the universality of its philosophy.

MF: Human wisdom is imitation wisdom. What humanity produces by its own limited knowledge is only an imitation product. The products of modern agriculture, which is based on human knowledge and artifice, are imperfect, imitation products. They are not true, natural plants. In producing and exporting these foods America is helping to destroy the world just as it is doing by exporting tanks and military weapons. Because of its size and production capacity, America can destroy the world through its poor agricultural products. However, by changing to natural agriculture, America can also be a powerful force for the rebirth of the world and of nature. America must choose between the false richness of chemical, scientific agriculture, and natural agriculture.

Scientific agriculture and the destruction of nature that it has occasioned has as its starting point the error of Western philosophy. The Western approach to nature is based on the idea that man exists *separately* from nature, that he is able to know and understand nature, and for that reason man is free to use nature to suit his ends. The Eastern way of thinking is that man is one single creature *within* nature, and that he doesn't have the right to exploit nature. I think that the Western way of life has been determined for us initially by the way of thinking that was set forth by Descartes, the French philosopher, when he said, "I think, therefore I am." In that statement he expressed the assumption that first of all there is I, there is man, and there is a thinking process that is absolute and separate from nature. Man divided himself, his mind or spirit, from things, or the material world. From that separation came all the mistakes of Western philosophy and way of life.

EW: What about our domination and use of the animals?

MF: Of course cows and sheep and other animals are without sin, and they have the right to exist in nature like any other creature. Because of human greed and desire for meat, animals have been domesticated and exploited. In the western U.S., agriculture is based on the raising of cows. Therefore, the environment, the plants that grow there, is an environment suitable for cows. For that reason other types of vegetation die out and the land is becoming a desert. Human greed has made an environment that is suitable only for cows, and this is destroying nature.

Ten thousand years ago in the eastern part of the U.S.A. there was a glacier that devastated the country. Two hundred years ago Europeans came to this country and again devastated nature. The most important factor in returning to a natural state is to begin with the grasses, from the ground up. There must be a wide variety of wild grasses growing. The first step in revivifying nature is to scatter clover seeds and various vegetable seeds. This will begin to replace the weaker lawn varieties and will be the basis for preventing wastage of the soil. On this campus, for example, these varieties of lawn grasses are very weak and artificial. If you were to sow clover and vegetable seeds, you could eventually produce enough food to feed all the students. This would beautify the campus and also make it more functional and productive.

EW: How would you compare your crop yield to that of conventional agriculture?

MF: I am not particularly good at making money, but by now, after thirty years of practicing this method, I am the largest land and forest owner in the village. My methods are very efficient in terms of cost. I manage to sell my products at a much lower price than average. One of the university professors who came to the farm said that because I'm not putting any energy into the land in the form of chemicals or plowing, he had never seen such expert "exploitation" of the land. But the truth is I am only serving the land, and the land gives me what it has left over, its abundance.

SPIRIT

Krishnamurti

Gary Snyder

Ram Dass

Isabel Hickey

Joseph Epes Brown

Joseph Campbell

JOSEPH CAMPBELL

Turning the Wasteland Green
January 1979

Joseph Campbell, who died on October 31, 1987, was the world's foremost authority on mythology, a preeminent scholar, writer, and teacher whose work has had a profound influence on millions. To him, mythology was "the song of the universe, the music of the spheres."

Campbell began his career as an instructor at Sarah Lawrence College, where he taught for almost forty years. "The Power of Myth," the recent six-hour PBS television presentation hosted by television journalist Bill Moyers, recently published in book form, is a great summing up of Campbell's work and stands alongside his two celebrated classics The Hero with a Thousand Faces *and* The Masks of God *and his recent* The Atlas of World Mythology.

East West's then-editor Alex Jack interviewed him during Campbell's ten-day seminar, "The Mysteries of Illumination," at Feathered Pipe Ranch in Montana.

EAST WEST: What is the origin of the differences in myths between East and West? Is there some biological or environmental cause?

JOSEPH CAMPBELL: It must be environment. I wouldn't know how to interpret it otherwise. I divide East and West vertically across Persia. In the western area there have been two main creative zones of high culture. One is the Near East and the other is Europe, and since they're very close to each other there has been constant interaction. The two main creative centers in the East, on the other hand, are North India and China, and each is isolated. So that in each of those areas there have been retained motifs from the early Bronze Age times, when their agriculturally based civilizations were established. In the Western world that whole Bronze Age mythology (of an impersonal power that moves through the plants, stars, the universe, and all of us, of which the gods are just symbolic personifications), has been plowed under. The plowing under has come from two largely barbaric herding and fighting peoples. One was the Indo-European from the northern steppelands, and the other the Semites from the Syro-Arabian desert. These come in with very strong patriarchal mythologies, each very confident of itself, not submitting to the order of nature so much as compelling it. They don't ask the plants to grow. They take from the people who have grown the plants. As a result, this other orientation has become the dominant one in the West, one of aggressive dualism, you might say. "You're different from me, my gods are not your gods." All that sort of thing.

On the other hand, first in the spheres of Greece and Rome and later in Celtic and Germanic Europe, a respect for the uniqueness of the living individual has been increasingly recognized as important, and this seems to me to represent an advance over the archaic social orders that the Orient has preserved. What I see as an ideal interaction of the two would be for the West to learn from the East how to recognize behind its historic Judeo-Christian God the higher mystery of a transcendent power that is immanent in all things, and for the East to learn from the West the value of the individual who incarnates that transcendent mystery in a way unique to himself, or herself, which is to be respected and developed.

EW: You've described the Wasteland as a demythologized world, a world of mechanical existence. What, in your view, causes a culture to lose its mythology, to forget its myths?

JC: One thing that is characteristic of our culture and its loss of mythology is that its mythology is based on a series of texts that have nothing to do with contemporary life. The dates for the shaping of the Old Testament are the last four centuries B.C. It was all put together in the post-Ezra period. Then you have the Christian tradition put together during the next two or three centuries. That was a long time ago, and a very different world from ours. The conditions of life were completely different from those of today's sciences of nature and of human nature; yet we think and speak of our salvation only in terms of that older and now completely alien tradition. Furthermore, we inherit from that tradition the notion that divinity and spirit are not immanent in nature but apart from it. Consider the meditation of Ash Wednesday: "Remember that thou art dust!" God breathed life into the dead clay of which Adam had been formed. In that thought lay the beginning of the demythologizing of our world. All the possibilities for approaching divinity are associated with the temple, the synagogue, and the church. That's where you are to find God. Not in your work and your home, not underfoot, not in your own body. Nature and man (and especially woman) are corrupt, and "fallen." That's a *real* demythologizing. And when you then lose faith in the institutions that are claiming to be the unique resources from which the spiritual life can be acquired (through baptism, circumcision, keeping the Sabbath, and so on), you've lost everything. These are the two stages: First, the demythologizing of life, and then, a loss of confidence in the claims of the institutions that are supposed to have the monopoly on spiritual food.

EW: Has a similar process happened in past high civilizations?

JC: I don't know anything comparable to this anywhere. I think this is uniquely ours. In the first place, the Bible is a Near Eastern work and comes to Europe as from another world. The whole period of the missionizing of Europe was of the destruction of native mythologies: of the Celts, Germans, Greeks, and Romans. This totally alien mythology of totally alien needs and sentiments was imposed by sheer force. It worked as a graft, but with that the integrity of its life was lost. One of the interesting things about the twelfth and thirteenth century Arthurian and Grail traditions is that there was an attempt there to remythologize European life in terms adjusted to Biblical dogma and yet respectful of the individual and the adventurous life of the untrammeled spirit. This was squelched by the Inquisition. With that our spiritual life broke away from the church. I would say that in the sixteenth century there was a divorce that has not occurred in any culture of the world between the authorized religion and the actual spiritual life of the culture. The actual spiritual life of the culture had nothing to do with what the churches were preserving. It came down through men like Leonardo da Vinci, Newton, Goethe, and the great secular leaders of the Western world, who were themselves building a spiritual tradition quite apart from the church.

EW: How do we create new myths?

JC: You don't create myths. Myths come like dreams. You have to wait for them. Meanwhile, the individual can consider his own life and find what the myth is that is actually moving him—or her. We're all living by a myth of some kind whether we know it or not; our value judgments, our interpretations of our relationships to the world outside us, the society, our friends, the cosmos. All of this is implicit in our spontaneous modes of action and reaction: Also in our dream life, which is a sort of personal mythology to which we seldom pay attention. It's a good thing to know what the mythology is that you are living by. It sort of straightens out your life and gives you a confidence in your own authentic experiences. What I'm talking about is that need, and the possibility for the individual to find a new depth and richness in his life by knowing just what it is that is pushing him around.

EW: What do you see as the mythology of the future?

JC: We can no sooner predict the next myth than we can predict tomorrow night's dream. Dreams and myths come from the same source. Mythology is the communal dream, and a dream is a piece of private mythology. There is a totally new world now emerging. No longer are there bounding culture-horizons within which local constellations of mythology can emerge. In early times every mythology we know of developed within a bounded horizon. All those horizons are broken now. Everything is related to everything else. It's a one-world situation. There's no escape from this fact. And yet everyone is pulling back into his or her own small in-group. Those are the movements I see all around me. Whether there can ever be a single mythology for mankind I very much doubt.

JACOB NEEDLEMAN

An Interview with Jacob Needleman
January 1978

Jacob Needleman, noted for his efforts to unify ancient truth and modern science, is professor of philosophy at San Francisco State University. He is the author of many books, such as The New Religions, The Heart of Philosophy, Lost Christianity: A Journey of Rediscovery, The Way of the Physician, *and, most recently, a novel,* The Sorcerers. *Needleman is co-founder and general editor of* Audio Literature, *which distributes a series of "Spiritual Classics on Cassette."*

East West's *Sherman Goldman and Alex Jack conducted this interview.*

EAST WEST: There was an explosion of interest in Oriental religions among a large number of young people, starting about ten years ago and peaking about five years ago. Do you see a decline in that interest?

JACOB NEEDLEMAN: No, it is still going on. I think that ideas of Eastern and what you might call practical, mystical teachings, or psycho-spiritual ideas, are spreading in subtler ways now. It has spread beyond the young people, in some ways that are not so apparent, to the older generation: psychiatrists and educators.

The established religious institutions in the West, Christianity and Judaism, are getting very interested in some of these things, too. I would say that the phenomenon is at least as strong, or more so, than it was five years ago; it is just not quite as colorful. This phenomenon is worrisome to a lot of people, if you include in that the whole spectrum of what you might call the new religions, for example, the Moonies and so forth, but Harvey Cox's [see page 234] book *Turning East* is a sign that this is a legitimate field of inquiry now. When I first got into this field, it was very, very strange for anybody to be interested in this.

EW: What exactly is this movement?

JN: It is a movement of many sides. To me the most interesting side is the appearance in the West of spiritual masters, who for one reason or another have had to come to the West, particularly to America, bringing with them aspects of religious traditions we didn't know were really part of religion: practical methods, experiential disciplines, ideas that are not colored by religious sentimentality, but that are, in their way, as scientific, objective, and sophisticated as anything we have known in Western philosophy. These include not only ideas of great power, but methods to experience these ideas in one's own body.

EW: Why do you think that in the West religion lost that practical aspect?

JN: For many reasons, but overall, I think it happened when the scientific ideas came in. The subject of my book, *The Sense of the Cosmos,* is how science came in originally as a spiritual impulse, and had other kinds of practical applications. The church wrongly fought science. It didn't have to fight science the way it did. By that time, in fact, the representatives of the church who were worried about science had already incorrectly understood their own ideas, their own teachings. To make a long story short, by the time science came in, the contemplative, practical side of religion had already gone on the rocks. And then it was further put aside by the application of scientific ideas to external, practical matters instead of internal, practical questions.

In Western man, if you can use the word "man" these days, gradually the center of gravity shifted more and more to thought, to his head. There was a sense that the head could explain things, could build bridges and so forth, which was very good. But it was assumed that this was the highest development of human nature.

EW: The American Indians seem to stand between the East and the West. As we establish some sort of relationship again with the land, the native soil, do you see some sort of unification happening?

JN: I think the American Indian had an enormously powerful practical spiritual teaching. And therefore, as an ideal, as a possibility, it is one of the many banners in the wind. But I don't think we can make any direct use of that tradition. I think there is a completely different relationship to nature today.

One of the difficulties of the whole religious movement is the difficulty that comes when you take from a whole tradition the parts of it that you like, and leave out the parts that you don't understand or you don't like. This attitude can be very deceptive, and even spiritually dangerous. In effect it can be the equivalent of taking up your own religion, which is one of the meanings of the term "idolatry"—you create your own god.

How do we select something from the American Indian and not the whole thing? I don't think that you can live like the American Indian, and it is only when you live like them that you can experience something that they experience. It is paradoxical: It is the closest thing to us in space, it is right on our soil, and yet in spirit it is very alien, I think, to what we have here now. I don't think our relation to the land can be helped by the American Indian, except to know that there were people who were able to live in intimate relationship with nature.

EW: You mentioned that in the spiritual traditions there are techniques for developing one's intuition. Could you give us some examples?

JN: Socrates, in my mind, is one of the great traditional teachers. From what I gather, to be with Socrates was to be repeatedly shocked into an awareness that "I don't know." This realization, if guided by a master like Socrates, frees one from the head. When one does that, another kind of knowing, another form of attention, sometimes appears. This I find is the basic strategy behind many spiritual techniques and rituals.

What is called humility in the Western tradition is not meant to be "I know how rotten I am," but "I see how much I fall short and how much my mind deceives me, and I need help." And in that state, of seeing one's nothingness and one's need for something greater, a new kind of knowing appears. And that knowing, I think, can penetrate both the body and the mind.

Many rituals, many methods, are based on that strategy, of coming into confrontation with one's all-too-human egoism, painfully being released from it for at least a moment, and then having the appearance in oneself of some greater knowing. Now if the spiritual method is used without this aim, it has the opposite effect, and we are back to consumerism. If you take a ritual or practice, like chanting or Sufi dancing, and don't have this as the aim from your heart, this need that one feels sometimes, then it just replaces the old false knowing with a new false knowing, which is even worse because it is sanctified.

EW: So, if blind faith means turning a practice into a false knowing, a new form of arrogance, what is faith?

JN: I would say, without elaborating on that very much, that faith is a special quality of feeling, which is completely different from what we call *emotion*. Blind faith is the mind following ordinary emotion. That is to say, the mind becomes a slave to egoistic emotion, and that is one of the biggest dangers of human nature. This other extraordinary feeling—one feels it very rarely in one's life—is real discipline, real religion. And to make that feeling more frequent, until eventually it becomes the center of one's life, is called the intelligence of the heart.

In the Russian Orthodox tradition, for example, you have the prayer of the heart, where eventually you have this feeling, which looks from the outside like it is without emotion, but it becomes more and more the center of one's life. And it has many names in Christianity, such as love of God. But when that is taken in an ordinary emotional way, it is just the opposite. It is a mentality which can turn into cruelty.

EW: Where do you think our society will be ten or twenty years from now?

JN: I think we are going to be in a completely new world with the new technologies that are coming. I am organizing a lecture series now in San Francisco about this question, called "The Art of Living in the Cultural Revolution." I think we are about to be hit by an ever-increasing acceleration of technologies. From little waves to big waves. From DNA to little tape recorders, all of these things are changing life in radical ways like the printing press did—but that was only one thing. We have innovations almost every day which are comparable to such an invention. I am not sure how the traditions will meet that fact. I think that externally we are going to be in a completely different world, being able to do things that now seem to be science fiction.

Now we face the question of how to be moral, real, full human beings while all of the external sides of life are changing rapidly. All I can predict is that this is where the drama will be. This is where traditions are going to stand or fall. To survive, they will have to convey their message in such a way that they take that fact into account. They will have to work with this technology and not—whether in subtle or obvious ways—say, "You have got to do away with that," or "The problem of human life is in the technologies." It is not. It's in ourselves.

If at the same time they can recognize just how much effect new technologies are having, then they will be a real help. Those that can't do this are just going to pass away. I think we will see a lot of the things that are very important now pass away; so I won't predict where we will be, but I do predict that this will be the issue. And many of the new religions are not facing that issue. They just don't know about it. Perhaps some of the leaders are not involved enough in the world. They are not at the cutting edge of technological change, and not involved enough to experience all of the forces at work, while at the same time not believing blindly in it, so that they can be free from it.

EW: Could you give an example of the challenge of new technologies?

JN: Well, take genetic engineering. A book came out saying the way to cure breast cancer is to grow women without breasts. That's one of the more dramatic examples. There is something inherently ludicrous and ridiculous about it. At the same time, a lot of people take it very seriously. Now what in yourself do you go to to make this decision? There is nothing in traditional explicit literature, nothing in *Talmud* that asks, "What do you do when somebody tries to change the gene that controls the breast?" So we have to find a teaching that brings us into the source of the intelligence that can face these types of questions.

EW: Where would you say the mentality of genetic engineering comes from?

JN: I think it comes from the scientific mind, the part of us that wants to know everything without necessarily wishing to understand anything. Simply because we can do something, we think we should do it. I don't think it comes from real intelligence at all.

To interpret what DNA is, is as difficult as to interpret what a tree is. We think we have solved something about what a tree is by making or going into the smaller parts of the tree, but the smaller parts are as much like a tree as the whole is.

It is the question of how we can find in ourselves an organ of intelligence that can understand the meaning of nature, whether the little parts of nature or the big part of nature. It doesn't help to go from a big purposeful entity to a little purposeful entity. That is one of the key methods of modern science, analyzing down smaller or finer. Every time they do that, they find that the small one is just like the big one. It has got as much purpose and intricacy and meaning as the big one does. So real intelligence is not more instruments. It is not so much new things to observe that we need, but a new quality of observing, which comes from a better state of consciousness.

HARVEY COX

Lost in Wonderland
May 1978

Professor Harvey Cox of the Harvard Divinity School is the author of a long list of books, to which has recently been added The Silencing of Leonardo Boff: Liberation Theology and the Future of World Christianity *and* Many Mansions: A Christian's Encounters With Other Faiths. *East West interviewer Sherman Goldman said, "Both his study and his home are filled with a mixture of Eastern and Western religious images—a cross next to a mandala, a picture of Buddha facing a Jewish star—yet all these symbols seem unified in his presence with a simple spirit of brotherly love."*

EAST WEST: Your book *Turning East* discusses this question of how the profit mentality can co-opt the spiritual. Could you say a little more about that?

HARVEY COX: I wanted to look at the phenomenon of why people are as interested as they seem to be at this time in our history in movements coming from the Orient. So *Turning East* is about turning; it's not about the movements themselves. I wanted to ask something about the American soul. What I found was both good news and bad news.

The good news is that I think there is a genuine, growing dissatisfaction with the way of life we have elaborated in this society, which is built on competition and success, the accumulation of things and trying to prevent any incursions into one's security by surrounding oneself with shields. I think there is a growing sense that something is wrong with our society. I think a lot of this happens because young people see their allegedly successful parents in middle age now not really being all that fulfilled, humanly speaking. They're beginning to look around for something else.

The other side of this turning movement is a pervasive gluttony, the obsessive need to acquire. Now, since we have almost all the things we want materially, we go to the acquisition of spiritual goodies: Adding up groovy experiences, ecstatic experiences, wonderful teachers, all of that. Some people would argue that at least it's better to engage in spiritual gluttony than in material gluttony, but I'm not so sure. In fact, from a theological point of view, it may be more lethal. At least when you're piling up worldly goods, you can't eat more than a certain portion. With the spiritual world, it's different.

There is a literature in most of the world's great religions, including Christianity and Buddhism, the two that I happen to be most familiar with, which recognizes that spiritual gluttony is the most dangerous kind, and that restraint in one's quest for spiritual fulfillment is absolutely integral to the search. So there are stories of Zen monks who put down the students most severely when they pride themselves on getting close to enlightenment, or the novitiate masters who help the novices to be very careful of their spiritual quest and not to become excessive.

This phenomenon of spiritual gluttony has to do with the fact that we've all been raised in a society where that propensity to gluttony is pervasive, and it fastens on different things. I think this is really very, very unfortunate, because we do live in a very exciting, unprecedented time in world history, in which the great religious traditions are really beginning to come into contact with each other in a way not simply motivated by proselytism. That's never happened before. It's an enormously interesting time, and I'm afraid it's going to be spoiled by the way Americans are so eager to gobble up and misuse the extremely valuable things that come from other cultures.

EW: You say that our modern society encourages gluttony, but what is the origin of gluttony?

HC: Well, I don't know exactly, but I'm intrigued by the fact that gluttony in theological tradition is one of the seven deadly sins, and it comes very close to pride, or arrogance. Pride is the expression of my determination not really to need anyone, not to need God, not to need my fellow human beings. But we are human, and therefore we have some needs that require us to be open to the enormous danger of other people—accepting love from them, exchanging love with them. The effort not to do that is pride. It's then that we need to build a castle of possessions or experiences to shield our fragility from that which we think can destroy us.

EW: What are some of the things historically that have favored a tendency toward gluttony?

HC: I think there are some ways in which societies have been organized that control gluttony or direct it or minimize it, and there are others that really exploit it and make it central. I think our particular, characteristic curse is that we have a society predicated on gluttony, avarice, or greed as its major mode of movement.

EW: Don't we have nicer names for that?

HC: Yes, we call it ambition and so forth.

EW: Could you spell out what you see as the insanity in consumerism from an ethical point of view?

HC: A few years ago I did a study where I had my students bring in tourist literature, looking for the symbolic level. I discovered a curious combination. First is an appeal to get away from everyone: "Get away from it all." There's a picture of you walking along a deserted island beach, and there's nobody there to bother you or ring your telephone. However, on the next page there's a gorgeous creature in a bikini bathing suit, slithering out of the water with all the intimacy, love, and warmth you could imagine—but she won't intrude on you! She'll be there in case you want her, by the pool, but what you have is utter privacy and inaccessibility and, at the same time, utter accessibility of other people to your needs. It's infant gratification.

That's what it's like to be at the breast. But human life is such that, after a little while, you find out that in order to have other people accessible to you, you have to be accessible to them. And there are certain times when you need them that they're not going to be accessible to you; they're doing other things in their lives. We have that inner need, and you can either help people with their maturation process or keep them in infancy. The whole system seems to be designed to keep people in infancy or adolescence—dependent, fearful, insecure, and therefore *grasping*—but that provides the motor to keep the whole system going! Why, if people are congenitally gluttonous and that's the strongest characteristic—why, if there really is an "acquisitive instinct"—why do you have to spend millions of dollars persuading them to go out and buy all this stuff?

I just read about Robert Berger, the forty-one-year-old guy who's head of Seagram's and becoming a legend in the whole business world because he works from 6 a.m. to 11 p.m. every night. He goes to bed at midnight, and he gets up at 4:30. It's really true: People have followed him, and he does that, six or seven days a week. He's the ultimate businessman. Imagine the kind of family life he has, his relationship to his kids! And he has made an enormous success of Seagram's, because he believes in advertising. Just think of the people who read those ads and see those fine, well-dressed people there, drinking Chivas Regal—obviously *they've* got something *you* don't—so the connection is made with this product.

We don't sell things to people anymore because they are going to taste good or clean the floor or wash the dishes. We sell them because they will bring you an illusion of community. But when I visit small, real communities where people are taking care of each other and to some extent learning to listen to each other, they don't seem to need as much of this stuff. And that's not because someone has laid it on them that they shouldn't have it. I think it's because literally they don't need it. They're not interested.

EW: So how do we operate in the world without becoming just like it? Is there some principle we can use in making those decisions?

HC: To be in this world but not of it? That's it. I've begun to notice the way in which some people in religious movements, especially if they're sophisticated people, can sort of be above it all and say, "It's only a game! It's *samsara*; don't take it seriously. Just do what has to be done." There's a sense in which the unreality of the world gives you a license to do things that maybe a repressed Judeo-Christian conscience might have more qualms about. Here I come out for a little guilt: You ought to feel a little guilty about what you're doing.

EW: What is sin?

HC: I don't think it's ignorance. This is where I have one of my philosophical differences with Buddhism, which in other respects I've learned a lot from. Trungpa Rinpoche [see page 246] always talks about the Vajrayana path as one that cleans your glasses. Then you can see what's out there. He's not going to tell you what's out there; he's just helping you clarify your capacity to experience. That's ignorance: the dirty glasses.

I find, however, in many other religious traditions, embedded in the mythology and symbolism, an insight that we as human beings interact and live in a universe that has some kind of flaw. The flaw is *not* just in our perception but also to some extent in the whole thing. We participate in this flaw. We perpetuate it.

Then you have to go into the whole question, which Buddhists are not interested in at all, of where does this come from: What is the source of evil or "sin," and how does one get beyond it? There are no really good answers to this. Especially, there are no good answers if you hold that a belief in God is utterly mythical. But the understanding I have is of God as a participant in the struggle, bearing pain. The doctrine of sin certainly has been the most distorted of all the Christian doctrines—it is almost entirely misunderstood as perpetuating bourgeois moralism and middle class taboos or selling you some movie called "Sin" on Washington Street in downtown Boston.

To me, however, sin is a testimony to the belief that human beings share with the larger cosmic environment some kind of brokenness, which is yearning for restoration or wholeness. St. Paul puts this very beautifully when he says, "The whole creation is groaning in travail waiting for the birth of the sons of God." So it's not just that human beings are ignorant of the way things are, but rather there's some movement that includes brokenness and pain and, in a stronger way, includes healing and salvation. Our relationship to this involves the idea of grace, the energy and strength available to us through history, which we can resist, but we can also allow to flow into ourselves, and we can be healed.

So it isn't just recognizing what's there and then acting on what's there. Even after your glasses are completely clean, there remains the possibility that what you and I are involved in is the recognition of some flaw, a larger flaw of which we are in part perpetrators and in part victims. We're in the middle. We can't understand sin without talking about grace. I think the mystery of grace is real, and where it comes from is a mystery. All of the really impressive saints say, "I didn't do it; it came through me." I think there's something to that; you really have to take that seriously.

EW: What is faith?

HC: For me it's simply openness to grace. It's not believing in a whole list of things. I think that whole idea of faith in a belief system is ridiculous.

EW: The part of your book I enjoyed most was your discussion of the Jewish Sabbath as a pause from activity every seven days. You perceived it as a twenty-four-hour meditation between every six days of work. There you discussed activity and rest as being two fundamental tendencies. Could you elaborate a little more on your point about motion and rest?

HC: My hunch is that the whole understanding of activity and inactivity, or yin and yang, comes from some common historical source and has been developed over centuries and centuries in varying ways. That's why I think my discovery of the similarity between Buddhist sitting meditation and the Jewish Sabbath was not just my putting together two disparate things. It was somehow intuiting a common source in both of these practices. I really believe this, although it goes so far back before the dawn of recorded religious history that it would be hard to document it. For example, the word for what God did on the sabbath is "He caught His breath," breathed like you would if you were working. I think that the various transformations of that ancient insight by the different cultures is not accidental or uninteresting or even unfortunate. I think that's all part of the richness of it. What the Jews did with the idea of meditation is very important. They said it isn't just some people who get to meditate; they said it's everybody, including the cows and chickens. Everybody gets a day off. You don't work your cow on that day or your maidservant or anybody, or even the stranger who's in your house. They democratized it and also gave it a certain ethical significance that meditation doesn't always have in other traditions.

EW: Do you see a connection in general between diet and spirituality?

HC: I think that this has been a neglected field in Christianity. That's another point at which I think Christianity just doesn't have everything. The notion that the quality of what you eat is enormously important for your well-being and the well-being of your neighbor is there in embryo but not developed at all, at least in the mainstream. Where you find the interest in diet is with people on the edge, the Seventh Day Adventists, for example.

One fundamental notion in Christianity is that the actual flesh of a human being is the dwelling place of God, and therefore the temple of God should be honored or perfected, but I think it's a very underdeveloped area. In what is called the mainstream, by those who make the definitions, there has not been very much interest in this subject.

ROBERT BLY

On Gurus, Grounding, and Thinking for Yourself
August 1976

Robert Bly is considered one of the foremost living American poets, with published collections such as The Light Around the Body, *which won a 1968 National Book Award,* Loving a Woman in Two Worlds, Out of the Rolling Ocean, *and many others. His translations of German and Scandinavian poetry have gained wide respect, as have his versions of the works of the Eastern mystic poets Kabir, Mirabai, and Tagore. Bly's analysis of the underlying male/female aspects of myths, legends, and fairy tales was the focus of his interviews in* East West's *August and September 1978 issues. He is currently examining male myths and rituals and working on a book about male emotion and energy while giving lectures and seminars to men's groups and others around the country.*

East West's *Sherman Goldman conducted this wide-ranging interview.*

EAST WEST: What do you think of the current interest in America in spirituality, especially spirituality coming from the East?

ROBERT BLY: It seems to be the destiny of the United States to need the East. But I don't think the project is going very well. Something is missing, and maybe what it is will become clearer if we talk about poetry. The writing of poetry in this country also shows the most amazing growth, and yet that movement is not doing very well either. Poetry pours out in the magazines: banal, flavorless, without ideas—what a writer in *Kayak* called recently "just folks" poetry.

I've come to feel that before all the methodology we have can do the poet any good, an ignored step is necessary—grounding. In the Orient some believe grounding has to do with actually living on the ground where you were born or near it. Tu Fu's poetry is grounded in his family and in the area around the Wei River. William Stafford's poetry became grounded in Kansas. Gary Snyder's [see page 249] in Oregon. After that grounding, electricity can move. The universities are no good for grounding. Very few people in a university are grounded. They deground. A poet can't be grounded by a school, or a way of writing, or a cause like politics or feminism; he or she has to be grounded *first*.

To return to spirituality: We in America believe that the spiritual energy of the East can be absorbed even if we are not grounded. Grounding involves going down. It involves shadow work. My own history is a part of my ground. I can translate Sufi poetry all I want; that doesn't make me a Sufi. My psychic nature can be tampered with only so far. I can't explain it. I feel we have ignored grounding.

That's strange, because the gurus who come over here from India are often well grounded themselves. And then they pour a tremendous amount into the upper brain of an American, and unless the guru really understands Western culture, he is simply going to lift that person further from his ground. The idea of an American taking a Japanese or Sanskrit name is loony, because we are confused enough about who we are without going through that. It isn't that our identity is too strong; it's too weak.

Eastern Yogic disciplines are basically directed at the conscious mind. I like that idea. But the Eastern conscious mind is larger than ours, or is on better terms with the unconscious. When you read Kabir, who was born in 1398, you can feel that up and down are well mixed, the male and female are penetrating each other, Krishna and Radha know each other. That means the conscious and unconscious are fairly well integrated, so that when you speak to one, the other hears. But it's not that way with us. We don't have that union. Between our conscious and unconscious there is a serious chasm and a weak rope bridge. How that chasm widened historically we know, but it is there nevertheless. There's a threshold, a high sill, between the two rooms of the conscious and the unconscious, and the unconscious, "the unknown," is the larger room with us. Jung said something like this: "My experience of it is that when a Westerner undergoes Yogic disciplines, all that happens is that his conscious mind gets more and more stiff." Here's a typical story: A young Tibetan student travels six months on foot to study with a guru he has heard well of at the other end of the country. He gets there, stays with him a few weeks; it isn't right. So he walks on to another teacher he has heard of at the last place. Again this man is not right. He stays a while, gets a donkey to carry his books, walks on. It's hard work traveling in Tibet. It takes him three to four years. At last he finds the right guru for him. To his surprise, he has ended up twenty miles from the place where he was born. He goes to his grandfather: "Why didn't you tell me this man was here?" And the grandfather says, "Listen, you idiot, the point of it was the three years of walking, the physical work you did on the way."

So for us to take a plane to Denver and drive to Boulder and go to Rinpoche's thing is absolutely nothing. It's something, but not much. Nothing comes of it. Nothing can possibly happen. That's a tough thing the Tibetans say, but the world is tough; none of us invented it. The student grounded himself while walking.

EW: How does your idea of "received language" fit in?

RB: In April I attended the annual Jung Conference at Notre Dame. It was a fine conference, but I was struck by the amount of received language in the talks. In kindergarten, we describe creativity as an openness to experience. But I have the idea that creativity begins with a refusal, with the refusal to accept received language. Jung was a good example. He grounded himself very well. How ornery he was! He refused to accept any of the received language offered him by the psychologists just before him.

When you talk about Jung's ideas, for example, it's important never to say the phrase "collective unconscious." That's his phrase. You must make up one for the same experience. Call it "the great lake." If you're an earth type, call it "the granite magma layer." If you're an air type, call it "the beehive of thoughts." Ask your own psyche to rise, slowly eat the phrase, and change it as it wishes. The problem of your own originality will then arise. If instead of "collective unconscious," you say "beehive of thoughts," you'll notice that the concept you've expressed is already different from the concept "the collective unconscious." Then you are responsible for that difference. You'd better be ready to defend it.

If we all did that, we'd see less of the goo that we constantly see in the spiritual magazines. The word *bliss* appears again and again. "Bliss" means absolutely nothing. I have never met an American who felt "bliss." The whole movement is penetrated by catch phrases. "I'm blissed out, man." "I'm experiencing higher consciousness." "I am getting rid of my ego." "The underlying nature of the phenomenal world is process and interconnectedness." *East West* should take a vow to stop publishing this language, even in ads. The political movement of the sixties died because people accepted the language without changing it. The Marxists accepted Marx's language, the students accepted hippie language, the love generation accepted jazz musicians' language. The sixties people—Jerry Rubin is an example—never worked it over, so the underground newspapers were an endless mishmash of received language.

Language is important. Language now is the environment for those who don't go outdoors. If you live in a graduate school, the language spoken there is your environment. If, as in the English department, the language is all received language that the psyche has not absorbed and interpenetrated, then the language is dead. The environment is death.

EW: Would you have anything to say about a possible cause of this tendency to spiritual goo?

RB: The idea of infantilization interests me a great deal. There is a book called *Manchild: A Study of the Infantilization of Man*, written by a woman psychiatrist named Kline and her husband named Jonas. It came out a few years ago, got one review in *The Nation*, and died. I thought it was a wonderful book. The gist of it is that each generation of Westerners after the Industrial Revolution has been more infantile than the one before. Jonas and Kline define an adult as someone who can exist in the physical world without a lot of supportive devices. Many Eskimos in old times were probably adults; they built their houses out of the cold around them. They lived on, with, and next to seals. In some mysterious way, such success matures a human being. Nobody knows why. I like Ivan Illich's [see Society, page 196] self-doing ideas, and the labor of the small farmers. If you walk from Boston to Labrador, you're more mature when you arrive; if you drive, you're more infantile when you arrive than when you left.

The Industrial Revolution brought central heating and the automobile. Not only does maturity fail, but a positive movement toward regression is taking place. Unisex is a part of it, and rock music (which depends on amplifiers—a controlled sound environment), the long adolescence (a controlled educational environment). We all sense it taking place. Infantilization is connected with keeping children indoors. We keep our children in local schools for twelve years, in college another four, and perhaps graduate school another three. That means there are now infants in graduate school. University students are institutionalized children. Visit a Ph.D. program some time and you'll see the truth of it. There's a connection between technology and infantilism. It's sad.

An infant asks his mother to bring him milk. An infant doesn't understand that he could actually go out and milk a cow himself. We treat the Eastern guru as if he were a cow. Chances are that the gurus have been outdoors a lot themselves and are quite adult. Many of them, in my opinion, simply do not realize how infantile Americans brought up in a technological culture are. I am sure they are continually surprised to come back and find that their disciples never revolt.

There's a man I respect a lot whose name is William Irwin Thompson [see Society, page 180]. He points out that in 1851 the English built the Crystal Palace, a building of glass and steel beams that actually enclosed large, living trees. Romanticism means that the psyche is startled—it realizes that trees are in danger from steel beams; the two are enemies. Wordsworth and Herder put themselves on the side of the trees. All the Nazis did was to insert the steel beams and the Romanticism inside twenty-two-year-old Germans, as if technology and nature were not enemies. So the men walk stiffly and love hikes.

We are in a different and more advanced situation now. Today the steel beams are enclosing not only trees, but culture. Technology is now attempting to become a container for *culture*. The government gives grants to poets and artists. Government grants are the clear glass of "The Crystal Palace." Rockefeller's family are meditating. Isn't that all right? It's all right except that meditation is being domesticated, as is poetry.

Let's go back to received language. I have a powerful sense that received language is the new form the steel girders are taking. When someone says, "Man, I'm blissed out," that *is* a steel beam! Imitation happiness creates steel. Language like that creates a crystal palace inside which meditation is dying.

We live in a society without a father. The father is increasingly absent, one way or the other, in the family. That means the sons have no models for maturity. Both the infantile man and the infantile woman want a father. A guru will do, passive spirituality will do, because at least you are receiving. Avoiding despair and suffering will do. So received language wins.

EW: What about the danger of co-optation of creativity by society?

RB: That's the same business, isn't it? The technology of the media reaches out to throw its steel net around any new thing out there that looks fresh. It is a terrific danger.

Universities are becoming part of the media. I feel more and more that the universities degrade poetry by giving degrees in "creative writing." Poetry, finally, is part of the wild side of the personality. There's something healthy about universities and parents saying, "Go ahead and write it, but don't expect any credit for it." I find that healthy. The student then says, "I guess that's right. I can't expect any support for it. Whatever I get from it will have to be my responsibility." Yes, you can get credit now at Bloomington, Indiana, for meditating. There we go! We take a live tree of meditation and a live tree of poetry and enclose each in the technology of the university. We probably have forty universities now giving graduate credit for poetry writing. It's odd how unenthusiastic that poetry coming out of the workshops is. We are only enthusiastic—divine-energy-filled—about what we have committed ourselves to privately. The MFA holders are tame. Then after class they go down in the bars and try to live out their wild life by acting like poets and smashing bars and throwing chairs out the window. And then the wild life leaves them and goes somewhere else. There are certain intensities in university life that are good, and poetry, when intense, helps that. But the way a university takes away the private life of a poet is what I dislike—or the way he or she gives it away.

EW: What do you think we need to do now?

RB: We have to teach each other to respect the principles of thinking: independence from your father, independence from your grandfather, independence from the not-right guru, independence from your mother. I think it is a good time for both men and women to develop the ability to *begin* movements, not follow them; the ability to think new thoughts rather than understand both sides of a question or approve of everything happening.

I don't mean that people should abandon devotion. We have a deep longing in this country to live in devotion and feeling intensities. If people can't do their religious labor, they get ill and remain ill. By thinking, we learn that there is a way to live in devotion and still make distinctions.

RAM DASS

The Return of Richard Alpert
August 1982

Twenty-five years ago Richard Alpert, Ph.D., was fired from Harvard University along with Tim Leary for taking drugs. So began for Alpert an odyssey of self-discovery in which he took the Hindi name Ram Dass ("servant of God") and became guru to a generation of young spiritual seekers. He wrote several books, among them the bestsellers Be Here Now *and* Grist for the Mill, *recorded tapes and albums, and his popularity swelled to celebrity proportions. In 1978* The New York Times *did a cover story on him that attempted to undermine Dass/Alpert's credibility. Although that story seemed to have an effect at the time, it hasn't been long lasting—Alpert continues to travel widely and lecture, carrying his unchanging message of service and compassion to older, more sedate audiences. He is a founder of Seva, an international service organization that combats blindness in India and Nepal, funds reforestation projects in South America and Africa, and has developed health education programs for Native Americans, among other projects. He is currently collaborating with the AIDS Action Committee and Hospice West on a hospice for AIDS patients in Boston and is involved in working with the homeless in New York.*

Ram Dass/Richard Alpert was interviewed by East West *contributing editor Tom Monte.*

EAST WEST: You seem to be a great distance from Ram Dass, the enlightened teacher.

RAM DASS: Your truth is your life. It's not what you're appearing to be. It's not an external image. That's not worth shit, to tell you the truth. That's social fame, public fame. I used to sit up there with thousands of adoring people, and I would sit there and I was starving to death. I mean, I would go back to the motel room and masturbate in pain and agony and loneliness, and there I was being loved by thousands of people. It was absolutely empty. And I look at my friends, I mean people like Carly Simon, people who are famous, who just get burned by that, and they can't go the next step. I don't mean Carly particularly because Carly's working on herself, but I see a lot of people, like the

Grateful Dead and others. It's very hard for them. It's very hard to go beyond that level and go deeper into their own being.

EW: Are you worried about becoming more a metaphor, less a person, to a certain group of people?

RD: I call it the Good Housekeeping Seal of Approval. I used to say I was in "wise person training." I said that's what we're all about now, because we've had enough knowledgeable people, what we need are some wise people. I've been through a number of pop trips already. I mean, with acid and acid junior and yoga. I was the Great American Folk Guru. They all come and they all go. But what really matters is if you're in what the Yiddish call *mensch* training—I mean becoming a person, a human being. If you accomplish that, then you are really something.

EW: How do you feel about having two names, two personas?

RD: Well, that's changing. Because when I became Ram Dass, I really loved Ram Dass a lot. I do love him a whole lot. The name means "serving God," and it's a pretty name. Richard Alpert isn't quite pretty to me. I never felt myself as being the athletic, macho type person. I was never that way. Dick didn't play cello. Richard played cello. I'm beginning to feel more like Dick Alpert, and I feel Ram Dass is so much a part of my being now that I really like the kind of nothing-specialness of Dick Alpert.

You see, I've never learned how to say this properly, but drugs don't bring you to enlightenment but to an "astral analog" of it. It's like the experience of Oneness, but different from Oneness because there is still an experiencer and that which is experienced. It's still dualistic. It doesn't take you, finally, out of dualism. It takes you very high, even to causal planes, but it's not a liberator. And I think that most spiritual people who have had experiences in samadhi states say roughly the same thing. Maharaj ji once said to me, "It's not true samadhi. Your medicine is useful. It will allow you to visit Christ for two hours, but then you've got to leave. It would be better to become Christ. Your medicine won't do that. Love is stronger than your medicine."

EW: Why do you teach?

RD: Every time I try to stop, I wind up doing it again. It's almost like I don't know what else to do. The quieter I get, the more I listen to the harmony of the universe, the more I do what I do. It's more and more like rivers flow and trees grow and Ram Dass teaches. It has that quality to it. It doesn't seem special.

What I'm experiencing up there each evening is that I'm working on myself. I'm working on how conscious I am as I walk out, how much my heart is open, how deep my compassion is, how close to the truth I can approach. That's what I'm doing. I'm slowly getting closer to God through the task of lecturing. I'm not experiencing teaching, because I don't really feel I have anything to say to people that they don't already know. I'm in the role of reminder. I remind them of what they know, but I'm no better than they are because I'm in that role. It doesn't have the *intent* to do service. Like all of us, I am in training to become unconditional love.

CHOGYAM TRUNGPA, RINPOCHE

Spiritual Materialism, A Steppingstone
March 1974 and June 1975

Chogyam Trungpa, Rinpoche (a Tibetan term meaning "precious jewel"), who died in 1987, was born in eastern Tibet and was recognized in infancy as an incarnate lama. He was trained to head a string of monasteries in Tibet, as well as to serve as a major teacher for the Kagyu School of Tibetan Buddhism. Trungpa's arrival in North America in 1970 heralded the beginning of his most lasting contribution, that of one of the foremost popularizers of Buddhism for Westerners, teaching the Buddhist admonition to always realize where you are and what you are doing. For the next seventeen years he traveled and taught extensively, founding many Buddhist organizations, and authored many books including Cutting Through Spiritual Materialism, The Myth of Freedom, *and his most recent* Shambhala: The Secret Path of the Warrior. *In 1986 Trungpa established a new international headquarters for his work in Halifax, Nova Scotia.*

EAST WEST: You have labeled most, if not all forms of spiritual practice, worship, devotion, the desire for the elevation of one's consciousness, as "spiritual materialism." We're wondering what's left, and if it's possible to have spiritual practice without spiritual materialism?

CHOGYAM TRUNGPA, RINPOCHE: The point here is not so much whether or not our path is spiritually materialistic in nature, but the way we follow that path. Are we doing it purely as a form of entertainment, or for discipline? That is the question. If we are doing it as a discipline, and genuinely getting into that discipline properly—not being fascinated by identifying oneself with the teachings—then any practice could be a genuine spiritual path, obviously. The difference is our attitude. For some people any path would become spiritual materialism, even if they were standing right in front of a Christ or Buddha.

EW: Isn't it natural for almost everyone to go through some stage of spiritual materialism during their first flirtation with spiritual practice?

TR: It's absolutely necessary. In order to cut through spiritual materialism you have to know spiritual materialism first. It's a steppingstone, a shaky one but a necessary one.

EW: Is the idea of spiritual materialism one that you developed because you were faced with so much of it in the United States?

TR: No. The teaching has a long tradition, particularly in Tibet during the early 18th century. It developed at a time when Tibetans were trying to turn Buddhism into an ecumenical movement. They became much more concerned with philosophy and rituals than they were with their practice. Spiritual materialism is an historical thing. It is usually a sign of corruption.

EW: You mentioned the importance of discipline. Couldn't self-discipline be looked upon as a strategy to develop the ego even further?

TR: To begin you have to work with your ego; otherwise you have no working basis at all. If the approach is right, then the motives will straighten themselves out.

EW: What is your purpose in trying to bring Tibetan Buddhism to America?

TR: It is not my purpose at all. Yet many individuals have made that demand, asked me to teach it, so I say why not. My purpose is to practice myself. When I was forced to leave my country, I did not have any place to practice. I am grateful to America because it has given me a place. My work is to work on my self.

EW: Why do you think people should practice Buddhism?

TR: It seems to be most fitting. Whether or not people here call themselves Buddhists, there seems to be a cultural context for it. You see it even among scientists with their philosophy of relativity. This is the Buddhist frame of mind. Other than that, many people in America love life very simply and directly. They work on themselves. They are not self-conscious. This is fertile ground for Buddhism.

EW: If Buddhism has arrived in America inherently, what is your function as a teacher?

TR: The function of a teacher is to give encouragement and to integrate that with discipline.

EW: Here is our perennial question: There are many people who feel that the condition of the body has a great deal to do with what the mind is doing. They believe that an unhealthy body, a body that is inactive and not properly taken care of, is going to produce a host of fantasies, projections, strategies, all kinds of things, yet you don't seem to take this into account in either your teachings or practice.

TR: I think that people should develop some sense of intelligence within themselves, else the whole thing becomes a book of rules. The body is an expression of the mind. That is the starting point. Giving people a diet would be like giving them a security blanket.

EW: That to us seems sane, but with some knowledge of your daily practice, [Rinpoche eats meat, drinks large amounts of sake, and generally undertakes no great commitment to bodily discipline] somewhat dualistic.

TR: I don't plan to live for a thousand years. I am not waiting to see the results of my work. I am only an instigator.

EW: What is freedom?

TR: In one sense, freedom is, I suppose, a kind of gyp. When we feel that we have achieved freedom, we have to maintain freedom; we're stuck with freedom, and we are again crippled. Ultimately, freedom does not have to be declared, in the sense that we have no grudge against anything. Freedom does not have to fight for its territory. If there's no center, there's no fringe. Then you're beyond any kind of vulnerability.

EW: How would you advise Americans, practically, to begin the practice of sitting meditation?

TR: We tend to lose a lot of the subtleties that exist in our life, in cooking, or whatever we happen to be doing. I think that sitting meditation basically should not be regarded as a ritual ceremony, but just like your making a cup of tea or whatever. Once that kind of relationship is happening, then sitting meditation becomes real life.

GARY SNYDER

The Original Mind of Gary Snyder
June 1977

Poet Gary Snyder brings to his work the wisdom of his wide range of learning and experience in anthropology; Oriental language, history, and spiritual practice; poetry; ecology; and wilderness living. A part, along with Jack Kerouac, of the San Francisco literary scene of the '50s, Snyder at the time of this interview by East West's *Peter Barry Chowka was a member of the California Arts Council under Governor Jerry Brown. Snyder is a perceptive social critic and advocate of ecological concern, which are reflected in both his poetry and his essays. He has written* Axe Handles, Back Country, Earth House Hold, Regarding Wave, Riprap & Cold Mountain Poems, Turtle Island, *which won the 1975 Pulitzer Prize for poetry, and others. Since 1985 a member of the English Department faculty at the University of California-Davis, Snyder's current work-in-progress is a prose book on "the wild and culture."*

EAST WEST: Did you know when you began sitting in meditation that you liked it and wanted to continue?

GARY SNYDER: I had a pretty fair grasp of what the basic value of meditation is—an intellectual grasp, at least—even then. It wasn't alien to my respect for primitive people and animals, all of whom/which are capable of simply just being for long hours. I saw it in that light as a completely natural act. To the contrary, it's odd that we don't do it more, that we don't, simply like a cat, *be* there for a while, experiencing ourselves as whatever we are, without any extra thing added to that. I approached meditation on that level; I wasn't expecting instant satori to hit me just because I got my legs right. I found it a good way to be. There are other ways to be taught about that state of mind than reading philosophical texts. The underlying tone in good Chinese poetry, or what is glimmering behind the surface in a Chinese Sung Dynasty landscape painting, or what's behind a haiku, is that same message about a way to be, that is not explicable by philosophy. Zen meditation—zazen—is simply, literally, a way to be, and when you get up, you see if you can't be that way even when you're not sitting: Just be, while you're doing other things. I got that much sense of sitting to make me feel that it was right and natural even though it seemed unnatural for a while.

EW: How did you come to choose Rinzai over Soto Zen, or was it a function of the contacts you had made?

GS: It was partly a function of contacts. But if I'd had a choice I would have chosen Rinzai Zen. As William Butler Yeats says, "The fascination of what's difficult has stolen away my natural mind." The challenge of koan study—the warrior's path, almost—and maybe some inner need to do battle (Dharma combat) were what drew me to it. By the time I went to Japan, I had the language capacity to handle the texts enough to be able to do it. Another reason: The koans are a mine of Chinese cultural information. Not only do they deal with fundamental riddles and knots of the psyche and ways of unraveling the Dharma, it's done in the elegant and pithy language of Chinese at its best, in which poetry, a couplet, a line, or even an entire poem, is employed often as part of the koan.

EW: You wrote in *Earth House Hold*: "Zen aims at freedom through practice of discipline," and the hardest discipline is "always following your own desires." Within that context, how is the "original mind" or "no mind" of Zen different from the so-called unenlightened normal consciousness of a non-Buddhist?

GS: Unenlightened consciousness is very complicated—it's not simple. It's already overlaid with many washes of conditioning and opinion, likes and dislikes. In that sense, enlightened, original mind is just simpler, like the old image of the mirror without any dust on it, which in some ways is useful. My own discovery in the Zen monastery in Kyoto was that even with the extraordinary uniformity of behavior, practice, dress, gesture, every movement from dawn till dark, in a Zen monastery everybody was really quite different. In America everybody dresses and looks as though they are all different, but maybe inside they're all really the same. The dialectic of Rinzai Zen practice is that you live a totally ruled life, but when you go into the zazen room, you have absolute freedom. The Roshi wouldn't say this, but if you forced him to, he might say, "You think our life is too rigid? You have complete freedom here. Express yourself. What have you got to show me? Show me your freedom!" This really puts you on the line—"OK, I've got my freedom; what do I want to do with it?" That's part of how koan practice works.

EW: You once mentioned an intuitive feeling that hunting might be the origin of zazen or samadhi.

GS: I understand even more clearly now than when I wrote that, that our earlier ways of self-support, our earlier traditions of life prior to agriculture, required literally thousands of years of great attention and awareness, and long hours of stillness. An anthropologist, William Laughlin, has written a marvelous article on hunting as education for children. His first point is to ask why primitive hunters didn't have better tools than they did. The bow of the American Indians didn't draw more than forty pounds, it looked like a toy. The technology was really very simple—piddling! They did lots of other things extremely well, like building houses forty feet in diameter, raising big totem poles, making very fine boats. Why, then, does there seem to be a weakness in their hunting technology? The answer is simple: They didn't hunt with tools, they hunted with their minds. They did things—learning an animal's behavior—that rendered tools unnecessary. You learn animal behavior by becoming an acute observer—by entering the mind—of animals.

More precisely, certain kinds of hunting are an entering into the movement-consciousness-mind-presence of animals. As the Indians say, "Hunt for the animal that comes to you." I've seen old Indians spearing salmon on the Columbia River, standing on a little plank out over a rushing waterfall. They could stand motionless for twenty to thirty minutes with a spear in their hands and suddenly—they'd have a salmon! That kind of patience!

I am speculating simply on what are the biophysical, evolutionary roots of meditation and of spiritual practice. We know a lot more about it than people think. We know that the practices of fasting and going off into solitude—of stillness—as part of the shaman's training are universal. All of these possibilities undoubtedly have been exploited for tens of thousands of years—have been a part of the way people learned what they are doing.

EW: In a 1975 interview you said, "The danger *and* hope politically is that Western civilization has reached the end of its ecological rope. Right now there is the potential for the growth of a real people's consciousness." In *Turtle Island* you identify the "nub of the problem" as "how to flip over, as in jujitsu, the magnificent growth/energy of modern civilization into a nonacquisitive search for deeper knowledge of self and nature." You hint that "the revolution of consciousness can be won—not by guns but by seizing key images, myths, archetypes...so that life won't seem worth living unless one is on the transforming energy's side." What specific suggestions and encouragement can you offer today so that this "jujitsu flip" can be hastened, practically, by individuals?

GS: It cannot even be begun without the first of the steps on the Eightfold Path, namely Right View. I'll tell you how I came to hold Right View in this regard, in a really useful way. I'm a fairly practical and handy person; I was brought up on a farm where we learned how to figure things out and fix them. During the first year or two that I was at Daitoku-ji Sodo, out back working in the garden, helping put in a little firewood, or firing up the bath, I noticed a number of times little improvements that could be made. Ultimately I ventured to suggest to the head monks some labor- and time-saving techniques. They were tolerant of me, for a while. Finally, one day one of them took me aside and said, "We don't want to do things any better or any faster, because that's not the point—the point is that you live the whole life. If we speed up the work in the garden, you'll just have to spend that much more time sitting in the zendo, and your legs will hurt more." It's all one meditation. The importance is in the right balance, and not how to save time in one place or another. I've turned that insight over and over ever since.

What it comes down to simply is this: If what the Hindus, the Buddhists, the Shoshone, the Hopi, the Christians are suggesting is true, then all of industrial/technological civilization is really on the wrong track, because its drive and energy are purely mechanical and self-serving. The real values are within nature, family, mind, and into liberation. Implicit are the possibilities of a way of living and being which is dialectically harmonious and complexly simple, because that's the Way. Right Practice, then, is doing the details. And how do we make the choices in our national economic policy that take into account *that* kind of cost accounting—that ask, "What is the natural-spiritual price we pay for this particular piece of affluence, comfort, pleasure, or labor saving?"

The only hope for a society ultimately hell-bent on self-destructive growth is not to deny growth as a mode of being, but to translate it to another level, another dimension. The literalness of that other dimension is indeed going to have to be taught to us by some of these other ways. William Penn's father, a good Quaker, never in his life rode in a vehicle until he came to this continent. He wouldn't ride even in a carriage or wagon, saying, "God gave me legs to walk." There are these wonderfully pure, straightforward, simple, Amish, won't-have-anything-to-do-with-the-government, plain-folk schools of spiritual practice that are already in our own background.

The change can be hastened, but there are preconditions to doing that which I recognize more clearly now. Nobody can move from Right View to Right Occupation in a vacuum as a solitary individual with any ease at all. The three treasures are Buddha, Dharma, and Sangha. In a way the one that we pay least attention to and have least understanding of is Sangha—community. What has to be built are community networks—not necessarily communes, or anything fancy. When people, in a very modest way, are able to define a certain unity of being together, a commitment to staying together for a while, they can begin to correct their use of energy and find a way to be mutually employed. And this, of course, brings a commitment to the place, which means right relation to nature.

When we talk about a "norm" or a "dharma," we're talking about the grain of things in the larger picture. Living close to earth, living more simply, living more responsibly, are all quite literally in the grain of things. It's coming back to us one way or another, like it or not—when the excessive energy supplies are gone. I will stress, and keep stressing, these things, because one of the messages I feel I have to convey—not as a preaching but as a demonstration hidden within poetry—is of deeper harmonies and deeper simplicities, which are essentially sanities, even though they appear irrelevant, impossible, behind us, ahead of us, or right now. "Right now" is an illusion, too.

I would take this all the way back down to what it means to get inside your belly and cross your legs and sit—to sit down on the ground of your mind, of your original nature, your place, your people's history. Right Action, then, means sweeping the garden. To quote my teacher Oda Sesso: "In Zen there are only two things: You sit, and you sweep the garden. It doesn't matter how big the garden is." That is not a new discovery; it's what people have been trying to do for a long time. That's why there are such beautiful little farms in the hills of Italy, because people did that.

S. N. GOENKA

Vipassana Yoga: The Path to Enlightenment
December 1982

Vipassana, or "insight" meditation, was developed by Gotama Buddha in India several centuries before the birth of Jesus. Today, thousands of people from diverse religious and cultural backgrounds, including hundreds of Christian priests and nuns, are counted among those who have learned this ancient technique from S. N. Goenka, a native of Burma who teaches in India and the West. Vipassana centers in the U.S. are in Shelburne Falls, Mass., Occidental, Calif., and Seattle, Wash.

EAST WEST: What is it that you're actually teaching? What is the goal?

S. N. GOENKA: I am teaching a way of life, a code of conduct and an art of living. The goal is to learn how to live peacefully and harmoniously, how to live in morality, how to live with control over the mind, and how to live with the spirit of the mind full of good qualities like love, compassion, good will.

EW: How do students learn Vipassana?

SG: They have to join a meditation camp. They have to live with the teacher, cut themselves off from all connections with the outer world—at least for ten days. During this period they must abstain from all immoral activities of the body and the speech. Students train themselves to control their minds with the help of respiration. They start Vipassana by observing the reality pertaining to their own physical and mental structure, and by observing this they come out of their impurities.

EW: You say control their minds with the aid of respiration—are they doing breathing exercises?

SG: It is not a breathing exercise, actually, it is an exercise to develop the faculty of awareness. One starts observing the respiration as it is; not controlled respiration, but natural respiration as it comes in, as it goes out. If it is long, it is long, if it is short, it is short, but natural.

EW: So the student sits and watches the respiration for how long?

SG: For about three days they have to continuously work only on respiration.

EW: And at times they experience discomfort or agitation?

SG: They are free to change their position. This is not a physical exercise; one is not required to sit in a particular posture for a long time. They can sit in any posture that suits them, but, of course, they try to keep the back and the neck straight.

EW: How does this differ from other meditation techniques like the use of mantras?

SG: Vipassana wants you to observe your natural vibrations—vibrations when you become angry, or when you are full of passion, or fear, or hatred—so that you can observe them and come out of them.

EW: And by observing do you control it?

SG: No, controlling is a suppression. So far as Vipassana is concerned there is neither suppression nor giving of free license. Just observe, and you will find that layer after layer of these impurities get eradicated.

EW: Is this approach or technique suitable for all types of people? Are there people who are not capable of learning the technique or sitting for so many hours?

SG: This has been practiced by all sorts of people, and the only difficulty comes when somebody is totally deranged or can't understand what is being taught. Otherwise, a normal, average person can easily practice it.

EW: Many people say to me, "I cannot sit for ten days," or for so many hours.

SG: Someone who has not attended a course may have a vast fear of the heavy sitting program—4:30 a.m. to 9:30 p.m. One gets afraid as to "how can I sit for so long, silently, without doing anything else?" But once one starts working, initially, one or two days, there might be some revolt from the mind, but little by little it becomes so easy.

EW: What are the practical benefits?

SG: Whoever learns the technique of Vipassana meditation tries to apply it to daily life. Every person has some problem in life. There are tensions because of this and that. When tension arises, the mind gets confused and every decision is a wrong decision and one generates negativities that are harmful to oneself and also to others. In the face of difficulties the meditator of Vipassana will remain calm, even for a few moments, and then make a healthy decision, followed by positive action.

EW: Does it interfere with other religious practices?

SG: One thing should be clear—this definitely is not Buddhist religion. At the same time it is definitely the teaching of Buddha. One should understand that Buddha means an enlightened person, a liberated person. Enlightened, liberated persons will never teach a religion, they will teach an art of life which is universal. They will never establish a sect or religion. So there is no such thing as Buddhist religion; it is an art of life. So anybody belonging to any community, to any sect, to any religious group can easily practice it because it is an art.

EW: What do you mean by "enlightened?"

SG: Someone who explores the truth within oneself and explores it to the ultimate end, experiences the reality pertaining to the mind and the body, and then transcends that experience to the ultimate reality beyond mind and matter, is an enlightened person.

EW: Are there other paths that people can take that would lead them to enlightenment or is this the only path?

SG: The technique should be to purify the mind. If there is any path which brings enlightenment without purifying the mind I can't understand it. If there is any technique which purifies the mind, makes the mind free from all the craziness, aversions, ignorance, and illusions then it will certainly enlighten.

EW: Some people feel that physical purification or healing will lead to enlightenment. Is this true, and what is the relationship between mind and body?

SG: Physical health is very essential to develop mental health. You can't practice mental purification properly when the body is unhealthy. So keeping the body healthy is an aid to the purification of the mind. But if somebody feels that if just keeping the body healthy will lead to enlightenment, to me it looks totally wrong because the enlightenment comes from the purity of the mind.

EW: How about diet? How important are diet and eating habits when you are practicing Vipassana?

SG: Any food which agitates the mind, like highly spiced foods, is not healthy. Pure food, simple food, is always good for the health of the body and so also equally good for the mind.

EW: What are the actual steps towards mental purification?

SG: As I said, we start with people coming to the course. They start by taking a vow to abstain from unwholesome activities. They will live the life of morality at least for these ten days, because that is how you can really quiet the mind with the base of purity. Then you start practicing the observation of respiration, which quiets the mind to some extent, and then Vipassana. In Vipassana you start by observing sensations on the body. By remaining equanimous, you are not generating a new defilement, a new impurity, and at the same time layer after layer of old accumulation is eradicated and one feels free from the stock of old defilements.

EW: So Vipassana actually is observing the sensations in the body while remaining equanimous?

SG: Quite. It is observing the body and whatever arises in the body—the sensation. It is observing the mind and whatever arises in the mind. But the mind and whatever arises in the mind also manifest themselves as a sensation on the body, therefore the basic principle is, observe the sensations on the body. Anything that arises in the mind will manifest itself as a sensation on the body; if you observe this sensation you are observing both the mind as well as matter.

EW: So, could anyone just cut themselves off for ten days and observe the sensations on the body, or do they need a teacher?

SG: Because the technique is an operation of the mind—you go to the deeper levels of the mind, and impurities come out on the surface—it is always advisable that the first lesson in the technique should be taken with somebody who is experienced. After ten days it is not necessary that all the time one should depend on a teacher. There is no Gurudom in this technique. Nature is the guru and then you have the path and you can walk upon the path. Initially, when you make the operation, there must be a guide to tell you that something happens. A deep fear complex may come out, a deep passion complex may come out, and one may lose the balance of the mind, so a guide is required to tell them how to work.

EW: What do you mean by an equanimous mind?

SG: This is a very good question, it keeps coming up in many of the courses. People do not understand what the meaning of an equanimous or balanced mind is. Sometimes a misunderstanding arises and they think that by equanimous mind or detached mind they will be leading a life of inaction, that they will live like vegetables, letting anybody come and cut them because they are Vipassana meditators and they are equanimous. Actually it is not so, it is totally different. Vipassana will make the life full of action, but free from reaction. As it is, people are living the life of reaction every moment they keep on reacting. And when you react with negativity, with craving or with aversion, your mind becomes unbalanced, you harm yourself, you harm others. But in a given situation, if somebody remains balanced and equanimous, even for a few moments, and then makes a decision, that decision is always the right decision—whatever action it takes is always positive. So then it becomes a life of positive action; it is not inaction, neither is it reaction.

EW: Can people be involved in social issues and still devote time to doing Vipassana?

SG: "Devoting time to Vipassana" is only when you join a course like this for ten days. Thereafter, it is a part of your life. You may lead a very good life as a social worker, you are serving people, but you will serve people much better if you serve yourself. If you keep your mind pure and full of peace and harmony then you will find that your service is so positive, so effective. But deep inside, if you remain agitated, there is no peace in you and then any service that you give will not be that effective.

EW: You want people to practice two hours a day. How is that possible?

SG: For a new student it seems as though two hours every day is too much because "I am a very busy person." But if one is *strong willed* and continues to work for some time, giving one hour in the morning and one hour in the evening, then very soon one will realize that he or she is not wasting time because their capacity to work will increase many fold. When the mind becomes free from confusion and doubts and hesitation, then, with every problem that comes up in life, the mind is clear—you make a quick decision, you make a right decision, all of your decisions are healthy, therefore all of your actions are healthy, your capacity to work in life, whatever your profession, increases many fold. So therefore, giving two hours to Vipassana every day is not wasting one's time.

EW: What effect does it have on physical illness?

SG: Vipassana is not for curing physical illness, it is to cure the mental illness, to make the mind pure, healthy, strong. This is the aim of Vipassana. But a large number of diseases have as the base the mind; they are psychosomatic. When the mind is purified, naturally these diseases are eradicated easily. Even if it is a purely physical illness, with the practice of Vipassana, when the mind gets more calm, quiet, equanimous, it has an effect on the physical illness also. So curing the physical ailment for us is like a byproduct. The main goal, the main aim, is to purify the mind.

SWAMI SATCHIDANANDA

Three Views of One Truth
December 1973

"The real teaching of a Master or a Guru is his presence and action rather than his words," wrote East West's *Paul Hawken in his introduction to this interview with Swami Satchidananda. Hawken continued, "To sit with the man if for only an hour is an experience which is singular in its impact and strength. I received the most powerful feelings of love and kindness from this man, more than I think I have received from any other person."*

Satchidananda is the author of The Golden Present *and* The Living Gita: Commentaries on the Bhagavad Gita *and is the founder-director of the Integral Yoga Institute in New York City and of Satchidananda Ashram in Buckingham, Va. and in Australia near the Snowy River. Now seventy-three and a U.S. citizen, Satchidananda continues to be extremely active, speaking here and throughout the world.*

Hawken's co-interviewer was J. Richard Turner.

EAST WEST: What is "higher" consciousness?

SATCHIDANANDA: There is only one consciousness. It never goes low or high, for it is the consciousness of self. According to Sanskrit it is called the "atman." What we normally mean as "higher" consciousness or "lower" consciousness is the consciousness of the mind, of the lower self. You can be "conscious" of something or you can be "unconscious" of something—that is all in the realm of the mind. True consciousness is the one that belongs to the self that never varies. It is permanent. True consciousness is reflected on the mind which is more or less acting like a mirror. According to the clarity of the mind, the consciousness reflects brightly or darkly. When it reflects dully you call it lower, and when it reflects brightly you call it higher. What you call "higher" and "lower" is the reflected consciousness. The real consciousness is the atman and it is the original, which is ever permanent, the same, unchanging.

EW: You have devoted many years of your life to helping people to become better reflectors. How did you become interested in the spiritual life?

SS: In the beginning, like any other individual, I was looking for happiness from the outside, through my work, through my possessions, through my friends, and through my name and fame. But later on I found out that all these things have their limits. The person who would admire me will not do it always. He will begin to doubt me. If one tries to gain happiness through the things that one possesses, one will soon find out that they are not really giving happiness. I worked so hard and yet I became so unhappy acquiring these things. The minute I got what I wanted, I seemed to have gotten some happiness, but the very next minute I was worried about how to preserve it. So the fear of losing the happiness comes. There is only a little happiness mixed in with so much unhappiness. This is what we all learn in our lifetime. This is why we say, "Meditate on this constantly." Meditation is not just something where you go and sit and close your eyes. That is all right, but the real meditation is to be twenty-four hours. Whatever you experience, meditate on it. From where does this come? Is it a borrowed one or my own? Is it permanent or temporary? Discriminate every minute your life, your possessions, your friends, your joy, your sorrow. Your sorrow is not permanent and your joy is not permanent. Why worry about this impermanence? Rise above! That is what we call yoga, in a way. To rise above these dualities, the ups and downs, pleasure and pain, profit and loss, praise and censure. Remain balanced, and you will be ever happy there.

EW: Even though the happiness is as unbalanced as the unhappiness, man always seems to pursue one and avoid the other.

SS: Why? Because he seems to be thinking that happiness is something that comes from the outside. That is the trouble. To give a kind of geometrical example, the mind was well balanced. In that balance you feel happiness. You are happy until you see something and you think, "Ah, what a beautiful thing it is, how nice it would be to have it." You saw it, then you built a desire on it, then you want it. You think that if you don't get it you will not be happy. What does it mean? It means you lost your happiness the minute you wanted something. Happiness or peace is always within you. You can always be happy without any of these things. Look at the newborn baby, smiling, without any possessions—it is happy. We are born with that happiness and we are born with peace. That is why, every time something disturbs that peace, you want to regain it. We are born with ease, and when that ease is disturbed, we call it dis-ease. So disease is nothing but disturbed ease. Which then is your original nature? Ease, is it not? That is your birthright and eternal nature. And that is why you don't come across people running to the doctor saying, "Oh, for the past three days I seem to be *peaceful*; something must be wrong." They don't. Why? Because they are living in their own nature.

EW: What makes you happy?

SS: Nothing *makes* me happy. I *am* happiness, and I take care of it.

EW: Everyone should be happy then?

SS: Everyone should be. My simple slogan to people who come and complain about disappointment is this: "Make no appointment and certainly you will have no disappointment." Because after all, what is disappointment but your appointment getting "dissed."

EW: Is that called Guru time?

SS: Call it anyway you like. But you may say then, how can you live without making appointments? You do make appointments, as I made an appointment to come here. But one type of appointment will never bring disappointment. If appointments are made for the benefit of others and not for yourself, then these selfless appointments will not bring disappointment. So the secret is to lead a dedicated life—the selfless life. You have God, you don't need anything else.

EW: This sometimes creates a conflict in people's minds. Many people cannot understand how they can live a detached life and still have a husband, or a wife, and children and a job.

SS: Yes, this really needs a little explanation. Take the case of an eminent surgeon, a very capable man. He can easily operate on any part of the body on any-body. He can take a heart out, clean it, wash it, screw on some nuts and bolts and put it back in. He can take your top off, wash the brain, tighten all the bolts and nuts and put it back. He is an expert. He does it with ease. But ima-gine this doctor if he goes back to his house and his own beloved, beautiful, loving honey, his wife, and she says, "Honey, I seem to have an abcess on my hand. The pain is really terrible. Could you do something?" Seldom will you see a doctor operate on his own wife. He will immediately call one of his own friends and ask him to come over and do it. Why? What has happened to his capacity and his expert surgery? He can do a major operation with ease, yet he cannot do this minor operation. Why? The reason is "my wife." That is what you call attachment. If he is detached from his wife, he would treat her as a companion to his life which God has brought. Both agree to be fellow trav-elers. He has a duty to her, and she has a duty to him, and both have a duty to humanity. They are duty bound, and as a dutiful husband he should treat his fellow passenger. And that is what is called detachment.

EW: You have said that yoga is a scientific system for purifying the body and mind. What is the scientific basis for yoga?

SS: The body and mind are themselves gross and subtle matter. They are like machines, in a way, with the mind like the engine of a car and the body as the body of the car. The main purpose of yoga, or even of any religion, is to keep those two instruments as clean as possible. A clean body and mind will reflect the inner light very well. Imagine that the self, the real you which is the image of God, is a beautiful light. The light is ever burning inside, but unfortunately the chimney that covers the light seems to be coated with dust and other impurities. That chimney is the mind and the body. If they are kept clean, they will allow the light to shed beautifully outside. Others can see the light in you and you can shed your light to others. It is such people that are called "refined," or "holy" people. That is why I say, to keep the body and mind as clean as possible is the goal of religion and it is the goal of yoga. The process of cleaning is nothing but science. Why should a machine get disturbed? Take your own vehicle or motor car. If you put crude oil in the tank it will be clogged. So fuel should be good fuel. If there is too little gas, it will not work and if there is too much gas, it will choke. So take care of your food. The food and liquid you put in is nothing but the fuel to that machine. See that they are pure and clean, that they don't leave too many impurities in the system. A machine should have proper exercise lest it get rusty. So exercises are needed for the body as well as the mind.

EW: Since there are many types of yoga, how would one come to understand which kind of yoga is most suitable?

SS: I agree with all kinds of yoga, even certain practices which you may not call yoga, because my definition of a yogic practice is anything that makes you relax and eliminates your toxins and keeps you clean and pure. You may not even call it a yogic practice. That means the entire life should be a yogic life. The way you talk, the way you walk, the way you associate with people, could all be yogic. Unfortunately, people think that only standing on the head is yoga. I tell people that even before you stand on your head, learn to stand on your feet. That is yoga. Every minute can be yogic. So yoga is not defined by a certain set of practices. Every practice, every action, if done properly without disturbing your physical ease and mental peace, is a yogic act.

EW: Many spiritual leaders today are coming from India to the United States. Some of these say that their way is the only true way and that all other paths are there to test us, to weed us out, and to discriminate among those who recognize the "true" way and those who do not. Some say that they are the only living "Perfect Master" and that the others are false. What would you say to someone who is trying to understand these different men and to assimilate them into a more comprehensible whole?

SS: Personally, I can talk only of myself. I would never say that only the East has something and that is the best way. No! There is no East or West. Truth is everywhere, it is omnipresent, it is full. In a circle, where is the beginning and where is the end? It is endless, so in full truth there is no East or West. There are many sages and saints in the West too. If they say that Eastern thinking is the only way, that is a kind of Eastern egoism. It's all based on egoism. Every religion has the same truth, talks of the same truth.

A real divine teacher will see the divinity in everything and every man. He will never say, "I am the only Divine"; instead he will say you are all divine. My Master always used to address an audience, "You Blessed Divinity." We are all divine. Why only one? or two? Everybody is the image of God. The realized man will always humble himself. He will never claim to be the topmost or the highest. He will say, rather, "I am just trying to learn a little Ahimsa and Sadya." Nonviolence and Truth. If a man like Gandhi could say that, what are we to say? The beauty of wisdom lies in its humility. It's like a wheat crop. When a wheat crop grows up, until it becomes rich, it is very stiff, straight, looking up...egoistic. When it is rich with grains, what happens? It bends down...will not claim any superiority. It will see everybody equally. The man of wisdom will see a wretched animal on the road and the saint as one. A child crawls, a man runs. What is the difference? The man was a child, the child will be a man. Who is inferior and who is superior? There is no superiority to be claimed.

MASAHIRO OKI

Master of Paradoxical Extremes
January 1975

Born in Korea of Japanese parents, Masahiro Oki, who died in late 1985, led a sometimes tempestuous and always influential life. A one-time spy, smuggler, trader, scholar, and master of many martial arts, as well as a teacher of yoga and the healing arts at his dojos in Japan and throughout the world, Oki was a hard task-master yet was revered by his students. He was the author of scores of books on healing, including Meditation Yoga, *and is perhaps best known as the creator of Oki Yoga, or Dynamic Zen, a system of corrective exercises that by adjusting body posture effectively treats many illnesses.*

EAST WEST: How do you define peace?

MASAHIRO OKI: Peace is a state of dynamic balance. In peace we are aware of feeling just in harmony, just right. It is one meaning of satori. Satori is becoming one with God.

EW: Are there stages in that process?

MO: You begin with concentration, centering yourself on the hara. The second step is relaxation, or detachment, not trying. Learning to breathe properly helps that. The third stage is uniting the opposites, subject and object, in a state of true stability. The final stage is oneness. Then both sides of the relationship know each other. For example, how do you hold a baseball bat? What is the correct position for oneness between you and the baseball bat?

EW: Well, I sort of wait for it to connect with my hands.

MO: Very good. The baseball bat tells you how to hold it. Then you are selfless, not thinking. Another example is the art of cooking. When I go into the kitchen, I have no recipe. I say, "Good morning, carrot. How are you? How do you like to be sliced, horizontally, or vertically, in small sections, or large; this way or that way? Ah, I see. Fine, now who would you like for your neighbors? Broccoli? Yes, and onion." And so forth, the carrot teaches you to cook. That is called having respect, or love, or even worship.

    To say "I love you" means "your soul becomes my soul." Satori requires working for that oneness with God. So prayer is not asking for favors or forgiveness; it must be selfless, with detachment, no ego.

EW: How can people apply this to their daily life in general?

MO: The point is that everything has a right to live. Everything wants to exist; respect that. The weaker side in any relationship naturally demands things, because of the need for mutual balance. War, sickness, unhappiness, is imbalance. You can get sick from either over-eating or under-nourishment; excess yin or excess yang. Peace, health, happiness, is balance. The same for justice. In this restaurant, for example, justice in business exists if the owner can make a living and if you also feel that the price is right. Both sides of the picture are satisfied, stable.

Many people don't understand that neither yin nor yang exists by itself. Yin and yang means communication. Communication breaks down in two ways. For example, if I communicate with someone by touching his arm, my hand moves, so it is yang, while his arm is motionless, or yin. If neither of us moves, or if both of us are in motion, no communication can occur. Clear communication takes place between a yin partner and a yang partner.

It's the same thing as dancing. One partner usually leads, and the other follows. Both have the right to exist; the leading depends on the following as the following depends on the leading, and both recognize that. The point of it, the communication, is that transfer of energy taking place between the two. The purpose is not the superiority or the inferiority of one or the other individual, but the flow between them. It goes, for example, in a ballroom stance from the woman's hand on the man's shoulder to his hand on her back. For a different partner, his hand is higher or lower on her back, and the elbows are at different angles. If we don't understand the most suitable position for our partner-beings in life, war occurs.

We must learn the purpose of the dance: not playing roles, such as leader and led, for their own sake, but to understand each other. In this kind of cooperation, the minimum effort gives the maximum result. The basis of peace is not an abstract equality, but cooperation, seeing each other as human beings. We must recognize our wonderful differences, without discrimination or value judgments. Discrimination makes war. For me, the meaning of yin and yang, or macrobiotics, is the power of that respect for everything's nature.

EW: What is freedom?

MO: Perfect freedom is man's freedom to be man, animals' freedom to be animals, and so on, without discrimination. Freedom means manifesting yourself completely, as a human being, as a dog, as a piece of wood, whatever it is.

EW: Why is human history so full of war?

MO: Man does not live a natural life. He has tried to ignore the balance of the universe. White racists, for example, want to manifest their own race selfishly, without respecting the freedom of black people to exist. It's as if the passengers on a ship in the front said, "Everybody come up here where it's very nice!" That ship sinks. For peace, human beings must learn balance as dynamic cooperation and mutual reverence.

EW: What is your general impression of America?

MO: America isn't a country the way that traditional nations are countries. It is a collection of people. The good thing about not being a country with traditions is that you can accept anything new that's necessary. So I like it very much for this freedom it has. Nowhere can you find such diversity. If you want to live without being continually obliged to think for yourself, don't be in America. It's so much freer than Japan was when I grew up, where anyone who didn't follow the traditions was ridiculed as crazy. That tends to cripple people. Americans should be very grateful for the endless possibilities they have to cooperate with each other in all this diversity. It's a lesson for the whole world.

EW: That's the good part. What do you think is the weakness?

MO: Americans still have to learn detachment. Recover beginner's mind. Awaken fully to the opportunities of your freedom. If I live in Japan, I must follow Japanese customs. Even if I feel some of them are foolish, I can do nothing about them. But here you can create whatever you want—if you realize it. Americans don't seem fully free in their minds to that possibility. Yet you have hardly any history, compared to most other countries. Here is the chance to really evolve. Such opportunities, so little of them taken! Awaken to that. I have an image of America as the paradise of freedom. But your education has made you easy-going, self-indulgent.

EW: What steps can a person take against that?

MO: Go to underdeveloped countries and experience for yourself how hard life is. Unveil your pioneering spirit. Just think about the difference in awareness and thankfulness between someone brought up in a poor country and someone brought up in a rich country. The easy-going philosophy comes from America's material resources. There is no end to your desires, because you are bored. A person who has to struggle has no time for all that fooling. No one learns courage from the kind of education you get. You don't see life as an adventure.

EW: What is the cause of this fear Americans have of life?

MO: Money. You think you have to do everything and run endlessly in order to survive. But if you're truly useful in society and honest and open, money will come to you naturally for whatever you really need.

EW: How did America get its attachment to money?

MO: Not understanding happiness. Happiness comes from mental pleasures. Material satisfaction won't do it. I have not seen a happy face in America. We must work, but for a higher purpose. Then you work with detachment.

EW: Many young people in America are now dropping out of the educational system and trying to live with more respect for each other, often in a communal setting. What is your impression of that?

MO: First of all, in terms of the population, "many" is not an accurate word. As far as communities go, I suggest you'll discover that although there are good points in it, and it's an old idea, people need privacy. In general, I feel that what you're talking about is wonderful, but it's only the smallest beginning.

　　Stop pretending that you know the meaning of freedom. A lot of people involved in this movement still are dependent—if not on their parents who have spoiled them, then on each other. That's what's wrong with the way most of these communities actually work. You still have to learn how to live. Ask yourself, what is the aim of life? You have made a start, but you must begin now to study seriously. Without tasting, touching, learning for yourself—for yourself and not depending on others—how can you learn?

Learn to really respect each other. Any being on the earth has the right to survive without being used. This planet is for man, though he has not learned that yet. America has exploited the earth, its mother; you have to learn respect for all beings.

KRISHNAMURTI

I Don't Believe in Anything
July 1983

Jiddu Krishnamurti was born in a small town near Madras, India, and at age four-teen was "discovered" by leaders of the Theosophical Society as the incarnation of Lord Maitreya, a higher entity who had appeared before in the form of Buddha and Jesus. The young Krishnamurti was taken to England and groomed for his role as the new World Teacher. He was never happy with that designation, however, and subsequently broke away from the Theosophists in order to independently devote his life to "setting man absolutely, unconditionally, free" without psychological authority and image-making. The rest of Krishnamurti's life, which ended in February 1986, was devoted to teaching. His talks and discourses have provided the material for many books, and his life was the subject of a biography, Krishnamurti: The Years of Fulfillment, *by Mary Luytens.*

In the introduction to this interview, conducted by East West *publisher Leonard Jacobs, and Catherine Ingram, Jacobs wrote, "His most consistent message has been that there is no path to truth. And his approach to discovering truth is through the dissolu-tion of concepts and images, putting no thought between the observer and the observed. But even this technique is not his technique. Krishnamurti really has no technique."*

EAST WEST: It appears that the Buddha left a technique to practice awareness, and his influence has been very great.

KRISHNAMURTI: He couldn't have left a technique. Buddha couldn't possibly have said, "Seek refuge in me." The systems came after he died. We think because he had attained some illumination, had suffered and gone through starvation, that we must also go through that to achieve what he achieved. And he might say, "Well, that's all childish stuff. It has nothing to do with enlightenment."

Can one person who is illumined—to put it in modern terms, free from all conditioning—affect the consciousness of all the rest of mankind? What do you think, impersonally, objectively, as you look at the world? Two thousand years of Christian propaganda, "Jesus is the savior," and the churches have burned people, tortured people, had hundreds of years of war in Europe.

Christians have been one of the greatest killers in the world. I'm not against nor for—I'm just pointing out that this is the result of two thousand years of "peace on earth." It has no meaning, whether Jesus existed or not. So has all this propaganda, this programming of the brain, after two thousand years of repetition of the Mass day after day, affected man at all? Christ said, "Don't hate your enemy, love your enemy." And everything we do is contrary to that. We don't care. So, what will affect man? What will change man who has been programmed, literally programmed like a computer, to worship Jesus, to worship the Buddha, to worship other gods?

Can the mind free itself from all programs? Is it possible to be totally free of taking in information—what the newspapers say, what the magazines say, what the priests, psychologists, and professors say? Education, television, evangelists—that peculiar breed—are all telling me what to think and, increasingly, what to do. If I have a little quarrel with my wife I go to the specialists—the psychologists, psychotherapists. Dr. Spock or some professor tells me how to raise my children. I'm becoming a slave to these specialists, my mind is conditioned and I'm limited—conditioning implies limitation—I'm in battle with everybody else for the rest of my days. And there's the future of man.

EW: Then what's the point of it all?

JK: Nothing! It has no meaning! What is the point of the Pope going to Poland, or all over South America? Is it a vast entertainment? Sustaining the faith? He says you must sustain faith, which means believe in Christ—which means do what we tell you.

It's all so absurd! So what will you do, with the world pressing you all the time—they won't let you alone. I say, sorry, I won't accept any of it. Whether it's the Buddha, Christ, the Pope, Mr. Reagan telling me what to do...sorry, I won't. This means we have to be extraordinarily capable of standing alone. And nobody wants to do that.

EW: Do you think there is a truth?

JK: Yes, but there is not my truth, your truth. And it has no path. There's no Christian path, Hindu path, Buddhist path, your path, my path. One must be free of all paths to find it. The Hindus have been very clever at this. They said there is the path of knowledge, the path of action, the path through devotion—this suits everybody.

EW: So you say to stand alone we find our truth.

JK: No. The word alone means all one. But people say, "I can't do it alone, so please help me to put my house in order," and invent the guru—not a particular guru but the whole idea of gurus. The world of so-called religion, whether it is the religion of Hindus, Buddhists, Jews, Catholics, the whole structure of religious ceremonies, is put together by thought, is it not? The Mass was invented by man. They may say it came directly from heaven but that seems rather absurd—it's been invented by man. The ancient Egyptians had their ceremonies to shape man. It isn't something new, the worship of symbols and figures. The guru, the mantra, various forms of yoga which have been brought over to this unfortunate country, are all authorities leading you to meditate and everything else.

   We have tried Jesus, we have tried every form of person and idea, theory, system. They have not worked. So it's up to me to put my house in order—I cannot depend on anyone else. If you reject the church, the whole religious structure of the world, any kind of spiritual authority, you are free of it.

EW: Haven't these people and systems been inspiration to some?

JK: What is inspiration? To do something better—you answer it yourself.

EW: Isn't it to add to the potential of each human being?

JK: Yes, but if I am asleep...

EW: Then it is to wake up.

JK: Yes. And all the time I want entertainment to keep me awake. Man wants to be entertained, he wants to escape from himself at any price. This is a fact. The church has done it, and now sports—football, cricket, and so on—is a vast entertainment. I'm bored, I'm harassed, I'm weary, so I come to you and say, "Inspire me. For the moment you stimulate me. You act as a drug for the moment so I depend on you."

EW: You speak of freedom from something—from religion, from politics...

JK: Freedom is in itself without any motive, not from or for, just freedom. For instance, I am not a Hindu—I am free from it. But that's not freedom; I am free from a particular form of prison, but we create other prisons as we go along. The point is, suppose you have understood and have rejected, negated, all this and you want to help me. There is something unethical, if I may use the word, in trying to help me, right? Do you understand? So, then I become an example—that's the worst thing! There have been many examples of all kinds of idiocies: So-called "heroes" who have killed a thousand people in war, and saints who are half demented. Why then do you want help, to follow somebody, look up to somebody, why?

   When there is some kind of disease in me I go to the doctor; if I don't know the direction I seek help from a police officer; the postman is helping when he brings a letter. In the physiological world help is necessary; otherwise we couldn't exist, right? But I'm asking myself, psychologically, inwardly, will anybody help me?

   Man has suffered for millenia. What will help him to end that suffering? He goes on killing, he goes on murdering, he has ambition in everything—which is another form of killing—and what will stop him? Not Gandhi—his nonviolence is really a form of violence. Non-violence is an idea, right? When man is violent and you give him a fact, then fact is violence and non-fact is non-violence. And you are dealing only with non-fact all the time. Why don't we deal with the fact, which is violence? Why do you put that picture of non-violence in front of me? I say deal with what is here.

EW: Do you think we will just keep going on like this—warring among ourselves for all of history?

JK: You're asking the same question in different words—what's the future of man. Unless we radically change, the future is what we are now. It's a serious fact. And nobody wants to change radically. They change a little bit here, a little there. If you want peace, you live peacefully. But nobody wants to live peacefully—neither the Pope, nor the prime minister, nor anybody. So they're keeping up the wars. I've talked to a great many politicians in my life, a great many spiritual leaders, to gurus who come to see me—I don't know why—they never talked about ending conflict, which means finding out the *cause* of conflict. Never. Let's say nationalism is one of the causes. They never talked about it. If the Pope said tonight that the church will excommunicate anybody who joins the army to do organized killing then tomorrow he wouldn't exist. They would throw him out. So he won't say, "Let's talk about peace."

I'm not cynical, I'm just looking at facts. So, what will change man? Apparently nothing from outside—no church, no threats, no wars, nothing from outside. Change implies a great deal of inquiry, a great deal of search. Someone hasn't the time so he says, "Tell me all about it quickly." But one must give one's life to this, not just play around with it. The monks think they have given their life but they have given their life to an idea, to a symbol, to somebody called Christ. The Hindus have their sannyasins, the Buddhists their bhikkus—it's the same phenomena.

EW: It appears that we are at a unique time in history.

JK: Yes, but the crisis is not in the world out there. Rather, it is inside us, in our consciousness. Which means that man has to change.

EW: Do you believe in rebirth?

JK: First of all, I don't believe in anything. Secondly, what is it that is going to be reborn? Say I have been suffering for ten years and I die. Now will I in my next life go on from where I left off? Is there individuality at all? Is there the ego—my ego, your ego, a spiritual essence, the atman? The highest principle?

EW: Perhaps it's just a process.

JK: What is that? It's a process of thought. There is nothing sacred about thought, nor about the things that thought has created in the churches of the world. They worship it but it's not sacred. There is something absolutely sacred but you can't pick it up casually, you can't just believe. Do you understand? Men have searched for this in different ways and never found it, they have given their lives to it. It can't be found in an afternoon conversation or reading a book, or going to some fanciful meditation. If you don't find it what's the point of all this? One has to work on this for years to find out. It isn't just a game that you play. But people haven't the time so they worship the one who has something. Or they kill him. Whether they worship or kill, both are exactly the same.

EW: Isn't there some possibility of transmission between individuals?

JK: Now you are with somebody who is a little peaceful and who doesn't want a thing from you, and you feel quiet. But you have what? You have taken a drug for the time being and the moment you leave here it will all go. It's so obvious.

EW: But if we are climbing some mountain and we've come to see you because it seems that you are a few steps ahead...

JK: I don't believe in climbing. There is no climbing, no "I am this, I have become that." There is only *this*. Change *this*, that's all.

ISABEL HICKEY

A Human Astrology
December 1975

Isabel Hickey, who died in 1980, brought to her practice of astrology the wisdom and understanding of Eastern spirituality and the empiricism of the Western occult tradition. Hickey, who wrote It Is All Right, Astrology: A Cosmic Science, *and* Minerva or Pluto: The Choice is Yours, *was interviewed by* East West's *Sherman Goldman and Meredith James.*

EAST WEST: Does being a Western mystic preclude being a Christian?

ISABEL HICKEY: I found out in my growth and my study, my meditation, that Western mystics are missing a great deal if they don't realize that the Bible has very deep meaning, but that it's an inside job. I, like many others, threw the baby out with the bath water, because I threw it all out and I had to go back and get the baby. For instance, the parables in the Bible. If you meditate on those, you will get tremendous insight. For example, take the disciples out in the boat when the storm was so bad and the Master was asleep in the hold. What was he doing asleep when they were in such trouble? The minute they woke him up, he said, "Peace, be still," and the storm stopped. This is really the story of all the emotional storms we can get into, and the minute we wake that inner self up—or the essential being, call it what you will—and that part says, "Peace, be still," the storms are over.

I think one of the most fascinating things is the Christmas story. It is not understood by most people. Think about it for a minute. What was the very beginning of that story? It was when an angel came and told Mary she was to conceive the Christ. And the way she answered: "Behold the handmaiden of the Lord, be it done unto me according to Thy will." When that Christ principle is conceived in us, the first thing we have got to do, to bring it to birth or expression, is give up our self-will. It was a long time from the conception of that Christ until the Christ child was born. People get very impatient; they are not willing to wait through that darkness, that season of darkness. Yet what was the first thing that had to happen before that baby was born? Every woman who has ever had a baby has had to go through the same thing: The water has to break. Until you break free of being completely taken over by emotions, that Christ child in you can't be born. Doesn't that make sense? Why is the Christ child depicted as being born in a stable when there was no room in the inn? That "no room in the inn" started to play in my consciousness one day. Go into any tavern, any lounge; if you get completely stuck in glamour, there isn't any room for that Christ child. There is no room in the inn. You have to go into the cavern in your own heart. I think it is interesting that only two kinds of people came: The shepherds, who were simple people out on the hill who weren't all fuddled up with a great deal of mind stuff, and those who had gone far beyond the personal, who knew, were wise men.

EW: What is astrology all about?

IH: It is not meant to be primarily a predictive science. It is meant to be for understanding ourselves and also for understanding other people. I've had a number of interviews recently where I was amazed that they thought it was fatalistic. Because it's not—absolutely not. There is nothing in that horoscope, that blueprint, that pattern, that you cannot change if you want to. I've seen this over the years. It's the stories of the cycles and rhythms you are going through, and what you have brought over from past lifetimes to work out. It shows your character. You can read it the day a child is born; you can tell what they have brought over as a blessing and what they have brought over as a challenge that they have to change. But that is only the personality pattern. Back of the personality lies your real self, and you center yourself in that essential thing.

A great while ago an Eastern teacher taught me something, and I have watched it work over the years. We are vibrationally connected to everything that happens to us. There is only one way we can change what we do in this life, and that is by changing our attitude toward it; this changes our consciousness. This is a cosmic law that few people know. By changing your attitude, one of two things has to happen. Either the person or problems will be completely removed without any harm to either person, or that person— supposing it is a person—will change so much that you will be able to live with it very easily. Now, in over thirty years I have never seen that proved wrong in a person who changed their attitude, their consciousness.

It always changes, and I understand much more now than I did when I first heard it, that this world of appearance is not the creative world; this world of appearance is the world of manifestation. We create our conditions inside, either in another lifetime or in this one. If we want to change what is manifesting in the world of appearance, we must change ourselves and our consciousness; that's how we change what happens. I have seen this verified over and over. Never saw it wrong.

There's a secret that, if everybody used it, they would know how to handle any problem. If they changed their attitude, they would start blessing that which they are fighting against. It's always removed without anybody's being hurt, or it changes so that anybody can live with it very easily.

EW: So much that goes on in the world is based on the assumption that opposites are really antagonistic, on a dualistic approach, that views the mind and the body, good and evil, and so on, as being quite separate.

IH: I once had a retreat, and I made up my mind I was going to find out what this business of Communion was all about. If you came from another culture altogether, and you were in a church and you heard either the priest or the minister say, "Drink my blood and eat my body," you would say, "What kind of cannibals are these people?" I knew it had a much deeper meaning than any of us were ever told. I realized that it is paying homage to the body. Bread represents the body. The wine represents the spirit. What good is a body without a spirit in it, or a spirit without a body? They are equal. You can't take the spirit by itself. It has to have a form in which to function. We have to have as much respect for the body as we do for the spirit. Of course, this is a dual universe. On the personality level everything is dual; it can't be otherwise. But take your duality and the third force. That is the triangle—that is why we speak of God as trinity—and the secret is hidden there. The Tarot card, the Lovers: The conscious self (male) looking at the subconscious (female), and the subconscious looking up at the superconscious—there is your triangle. You will never get harmony with two forces. You can get cooperation, but in order to help duality be what it is supposed to be, you have to go to your third force.

A great many people talk about soulmates, and it came to me very strongly: The secret is hidden in the triangle. What everyone is looking for in a love relationship is not what they think it is at all. When they find their own link with their own essential self, that is the real meeting, that is the real unity. I feel that every bit of love we have for anybody, whether it is satisfied or not satisfied, brings us a little nearer that love consciousness we are seeking. There are annuals and perennials in God's garden of love. An annual is no less beautiful because it blooms for a season. There are so many people trying to make a perennial out of an annual or an annual out of a perennial. If they would understand this, they wouldn't get so angry when the annual dies.

EW: Is there really such a thing as evil?

IH: How can we say what's evil and what's good? When we go through a very rough experience, we don't think that's good; but later on we look back and say, "That's the best thing that's happened to me because I learned something." If people were wise, they would not battle evil. They would know that if they grounded themselves in good, nothing could happen to them: "Resist not evil, but overcome evil with good."

EW: Some people talk about the equivalent of a cloud of pollution that is a spiritual or vibrational condition that surrounds the earth.

IH: I do believe that wrong thinking, wrong deeds, wrong emotions can pollute just as truly as matter can pollute. But I also strongly believe that there is more light on earth than there's ever been before.

MUHAMMAD ALI

A Visit with Muhammad Ali
January 1974

Cassius Marcellus Clay, Jr., the boxer who dubbed himself "The Greatest!" won a gold medal in the 1960 Rome Olympics at the age of eighteen. The day after he had captured the world heavyweight crown in 1964 he announced that he had become a Muslim and had changed his name to Muhammad Ali. He incurred the wrath of the American public by refusing induction into the Army to fight in Vietnam, then went on to win the world heavyweight title twice more, making him the first boxer in history ever to seize it three times.

Throughout his long career Ali dazzled his fans as well as his detractors with his fancy footwork and outspoken brashness. "The man who has no imagination stands on the earth—he has no wings, he cannot fly," Ali told East West's *William Dufty and Tom Utne during this interview, in which Ali expounded on Muslim philosophy with characteristic verve.*

Today Ali lives in Los Angeles and contends with neurological problems that have plagued him in recent years.

EAST WEST: We'd like to focus not just on boxing but also on Islam and the influence it's had on your life and your game.

MUHAMMAD ALI: How useless it would be for a whole lot of talk about religion at this late date. This is overdoing it. It ain't necessary. It's getting to be sickening. If you went to every celebrity and movie star and asked him to explain his religion, you wouldn't get it. This is too much, it's just nobody's business what I believe.

EW: Our readers are very much interested in what you have to say about these things.

MA: Tough. You see, Elijah Muhammad is my spiritual leader, and he may get angry if he hears I been giving interviews on my religion. He's a powerful man, Elijah Muhammad. He's REAL religious. He takes wineheads, dope addicts, prostitutes, converts 'em; jailbirds, and makes clean people out of 'em. Once he turns thumbs down on you, you're in trouble. Look at what

272

happened to Malcolm X.

We got Muslim followers all over the world that read this paper; they're over there, and they'll send it in, mail it to him, and I do this without permission I'm in trouble. But you go ahead ask those questions and I'll answer 'em.

EW: You know when I saw you with your jaw wired, on Cavett, I hoped the president had been watching, because it was at the time when, had he followed your example and made a similar statement, he'd still be president today.

MA: You have to admit when you're wrong. You know when you're wrong. We confess our faults; that's in all our prayers, but a lot of people hate to confess their faults. I remember saying that the reason I lost the fight was I didn't take my religion like I should. Didn't eat the proper foods, didn't train like I should, wasn't serious, prayed at the last minute when it was too late. I should have been doing it all the time. I was doing everything I shouldn't do against my religion. I think that's what got me off. It's nothing to be embarrassed about a mistake; everybody makes mistakes. Ain't nobody perfect.

EW: Norman Mailer wrote about you a couple years ago; he said that the flyweight champ will lose on any given night to any of a dozen lightweights; that any light-heavyweight can put the best middleweight in the world out any time they fight—but the heavyweight champion of the world has to live with the knowledge that—he may or may not be, but there is a distant possibility that—he is the toughest man in the world. Now you have this seemingly tremendous burden; you have every reason in the world to have the biggest ego in the world, and yet you don't. How so?

MA: Well, that's a good question. I have every reason in the world to have the biggest ego in the world, and I don't. It reminds me of a story I once heard of a slave named Omar. Goes like this...

Omar was brought to the king to be sold, and the king appreciated something valuable in Omar; so much so, until the king made Omar the watcher over all of his treasures. And those around the king became angry to think of the slave Omar given such a trust overnight. They was always tellin' the king something bad about Omar.

One day one of these envious came to the king. He said, "Sir, the slave Omar, who you made watcher over all your treasures, did you know he goes to your treasure house when he's not supposed to go? Surely, he must be stealing your precious jewels!" The king heard so much against the slave Omar until the king went out and said, "This is true, I seen it with my own eyes." He went to the treasure house and had a hole made in the wall where he could see and hear what Omar did when he came in. One day Omar entered the house, as they said he would. The king was lookin' in and listenin' with two of the onlookers behind, and Omar entered the treasure house. They were watching to see if he would steal anything. Omar opened the chest and he pulled out a bag that he had kept there. And what did he take out of the bag? He took out the same old robe that he wore as a slave. Omar took off the pretty garments that the king had given him, and he put on the old robe, and he looked in the mirror on the wall and spoke out loud to himself. He said, "Omar! Do you remember today, who you were yesterday? You were nothin' but an old slave.

Old slave brought to the king to be sold. But the king appreciated something valuable in you. Perhaps you don't even deserve it. But try your best to be faithful to the king who made you who you are. (So the king saw him.) And do not look down on those who now look up to you, for prosperity is always intoxicating. So keep yourself sober and pray to God that he grants the king a long life." Then Omar took off the robe, put it back in the box, put on his pretty garments and went out the door—and those around the king who said Omar was inside stealin' walked away with their head down in shame. And the king ran to Omar with open arms. He said, "Omar, up to now, you were the watcher over my treasures. But now, you are the treasure of my heart. You, a slave, have taught me, the king, a lesson! You've taught me how I should look up to MY king who could only be God himself. Whom before I was nothin' and whom today I am still."

So this story explains my position. It was not Omar's suggestion and misery as a slave which he had kept with him but the realization that he had come from nothing to an exalted position and he must prove worthy of this position. Right? So I always remember the little house I was raised in Louisville, Kentucky, which cost four thousand dollars. Now I'm building a log cabin here for fourteen thousand. I have a Rolls Royce worth thirty thousand here and one up there worth thirty thousand. This cabin here cost twenty thousand, two bunkhouses cost twenty-four thousand, the gym cost fifty-four thousand. My house in Cherry Hill cost 250 thousand. Got about 600 thousand in the bank, gettin' ready to make two million [for fighting Joe Frazier]. But I always remember how I was brought up. I never look down on those who look up to me. Because the truly great men in history—I wrote something once—it says, "the truly great men in history never wanted to be great nor did they consider themselves great." All they wanted was a chance to be closer to God.

WERNER ERHARD

All I Can Do Is Lie
August 1974

Werner Erhard, born Jack Rosenberg, is the father of "est," a blend of Zen, Transactional Analysis, Transcendental Meditation, and Dale Carnegie. Erhard developed his controversial ("trainees" were cloistered in hours-long closed-door meetings during which they were not allowed to talk, smoke, wear a watch, or go to the bathroom) and very popular self-development course as a response to his own disappointment with existing techniques.

In 1981 Erhard and his colleagues formed Werner Erhard and Associates, based in San Francisco, through which est developed into a new program called The Forum. Both Werner Erhard and Associates and Transformational Technologies, Inc., another Erhard-founded company, are active world-wide in the area of "producing breakthroughs for people and organizations," as their publicity kit puts it.

EAST WEST: What is est?

WERNER ERHARD: est is a sixty-hour experience which opens an additional dimension of living to your awareness. The training is designed to transform the level at which you experience life so that living becomes a process of expanding satisfaction.

Another part of the answer to that question is that there is not an answer. est actually is an experience. But if you go around telling people that, you won't have anything to talk about and you need something to say about it. It is a very individual experience. And because of that, it's something that is created by the individual. In other words, est is not created by me or the trainer or the group that the person goes to train with; it's an experience—like all experiences—which is created by the individual who is experiencing the experience. Now what you and I normally call experience is that stuff that comes in from the outside, but that is part of the experience which I call non-experience. It has its clear counterpart, the other part we don't pay much attention to. Because we do not pay much attention to it, we think the inner part is the outer part, but the way I see it is the other way around: The outer part is an effect of the inner part and the cause of the inner part is the individual self. My notion is that what happens in the training is that the individual is given an opportunity to create original experiences, or to re-create original experiences—experiences which that individual originally created. That individual created himself, and in the training, he gets an opportunity to re-experience that he created himself.

EW: I am interested in the trouble that you have with "spiritual" people. Does it imply that people who have a heavy spiritual background of one sort or another do not come to est?

WE: Oh, no. As a matter of fact, the heart of est is spiritual people, really. You see, I don't know anyone who is not spiritual. I spent thirteen years earning my living in the business jungle. And that is where I learned about spirituality. You see, I think there is not anything but spirituality. So when you try to identify something that is more spiritual than something else, it is a lie. That's all there is, there isn't anything but spirituality, which is just another word for God, because God is everything. When I say I have a problem with spiritual people, I really shouldn't be saying that because I really don't have any problem with them. Being spiritual is just...being spiritual. Of course, I think not being spiritual is also being spiritual.

EW: Somebody into a heavy discipline might come and take est without dropping their discipline and after est continue their discipline. Does this ever happen?

WE: We trained a ghetto chief. Now ghetto chiefism is a very heavy discipline. I mean, it is as heavy as Zen ever thought of being. About half-way through the training, Arthur (the chief) stood up and said, "You know, Werner, I just realized something. You are going to take all my stuff away from me. And if I go back to the ghetto, and I don't have my stuff, I'm liable to get killed. I don't know whether I belong here or not." Anyway, Arthur took the whole training. But that is not the point of the story. The point of the story was, by becoming unattached to his survival mechanism, he became the cause of his behavior instead of the effect of the behavior. He became the cause of his particular kind of discipline, his practice. It's interesting because it is the same thing that has happened to Christians, same thing that has happened to Buddhists.

A lady was training in Hawaii. A devout Buddhist...she got about halfway through the training and left. Could not stand the training. Could never do it. Came back another time and she got through the training to a point where somehow Buddha came, and I told her that Buddha was dogshit. And she started to cry. And I kept pressing that with her until she finally got that Buddha was, in fact, dogshit. And she had a total release from her belief in Buddha. And at the same instant she had the experience of Buddha. She could really tell you about the training. Besides having that incredible experience, she has had all the disciplinary stuff that precedes the experience that then allows you to present the experience to someone else.

EW: What were you doing for thirteen years in the business jungle?

WE: I was doing a thing which today is called "Executive Development and Motiva-tion," and my job was to work with people in such a way that productivity, leadership, and executive ability increased. Someone figured out that I spent 36,000 hours in that thirteen years in one to one and group sessions, which is seven solid years, night and day, if you count it up.

EW: For people who don't know what "executive development and motivation" means, is it a Dale Carnegie type course?

WE: Let's make the pot a little bigger than that. Dale Carnegie, Maxwell Moltz, American Management Association, Industrial Psychology, PACE. Now the one thing that is unusual is that I was also a discipline freak. I did everything that I could find and I found stuff that nobody else found. I subjected myself, I made myself the subject of as many different disciplines as I could find. I either studied them or I practiced them or had people do them to me or I learned to do them to people or whatever.

EW: Various spiritual disciplines?

WE: Spiritual disciplines, psychological disciplines, whatever, philosophical disci-plines, body disciplines. Let me tell you why business is such a beautiful place to do that. If I had been at a university, I would have just dabbled in these things, because they were out of my department. You can't do anything seri-ous outside of your department. Had I been in a religious order or any church or monastery, I definitely could not have done any of this. It would have been heresy. The only place you are really allowed to do things like this is in busi-ness, because business doesn't care what you do as long as it isn't blatantly ille-gal and it produces results. So when I told the boss I was going to use Zen with the sales force, he said, "Great. Don't get any on the walls." So I got a chance to take my experience in Zen and translate it from the usual setting to a new setting.

The other thing was that I had this guru who would not let me get away with any bullshit. And the name of the guru was Physical Universe. Now you and I both know that you have to get beyond testing to get to it. "It" isn't testable, but its effects are testable. Unfortunately, you are so stuck in the effects that you can't ever get to it—you've got to transcend the effects to get to it. Which, of course, I never did because I was so caught up in the effects. But it was an incredible thing, because it really separated the bullshit from the gunsmoke. You see, an incredible amount of what Swami Muktananda presents is tradition, religion, and in there is that essential. A lot of people are blinded by the trappings and the things that were really beautiful about this translation of disciplines into business—you really had to find out what the hell was trappings and drop it fast.

EW: All right, if that did not produce est, what did?

WE: The enlightenment experience that I had. The direct experience of myself. One particular experience. Now, that's a lie actually, because the experience looks like this [makes a linear gesture] and what I am talking about in particu-lar is here [draws a circle in the air] that denies the rest of it.

EW: A very exalted state of consciousness, like samadhi?

WE: Yeah, but I don't think that I would define it quite that way. The state for me was one of total clarity. I suddenly "saw" everything that I had ever done and why it worked or did not work. I saw why all disciplines work and why none of them worked because they all do work and none of them work.

PETER MARIN

est: Who Got What?
December 1975

Peter Marin wrote the cover story for the October 1975 issue of Harper's *on "The New Narcissism," in which he attacked the human potential movement in general for its failure to deal with moral and political consciousness. He is the author of* In Man's Time *and co-author, with Allen Cohen, of* Understanding Drug Use. *He has worked extensively with young people, having taught at the experimental Pacific High School in Palo Alto, Calif., at Hofstra, and at California State in Los Angeles.*

Marin, who was interviewed by East West's *Sherman Goldman, is currently a contributing editor of* Harper's.

EAST WEST: How did you first hear about est, and what was your first impression?

PETER MARIN: I kept running into people in San Francisco who had been through est. Just on the basis of that early contact, it seemed to be one of the most unintelligent and vicious things that I'd come across in a long time.

EW: What led you to write the article in *Harper's*?

PM: Well, I wasn't primarily concerned with est. I had thought of doing the piece a long time before; it was meant to be about the therapeutic movement in general and the fact that it seemed to exclude any kind of serious, intelligent concern with either morality or politics.

EW: Are you referring specifically to what's come out of Esalen?

PM: I meant Esalen, but I meant also what we take for granted as the roots of the "human potential movement": people like Fritz Perls, Maslow, and Rogers— all of whom meant their work, I think, to be an adjunct or an addition to moral and political concerns, but whose work, in the last decade at least, has increasingly taken the *place* of those concerns.

    The essential thing lacking in the human potential movement seemed to be involved in the way the self was defined. It was seen in isolation, in an artificial and almost fictive way. And it's precisely that wrong-headed view of the self that ultimately hardens into something like est.

EW: Many graduates of such courses tend to define truth as a gut feeling. What do you think of that definition of truth? Do you think it's part of that isolated view of the self?

PM: I'd always learned that the interesting thing about truth, and the idea of truth, was that it was the central point around which intelligent and passionate people organized their conversation and their exchanges. The point was not so much who had the truth or what was the truth, as the community formed by the willingness to look for and speculate about the truth. It's precisely that capacity that seems to me not only diminished but almost absolutely destroyed in those persons who've been through est.

EW: When I've questioned them about their isolated view of truth, they all seem to have the stock response, "Everything is relative." Do you find such stock responses arrogant?

PM: It's not only that. It's that the response that is made to any kind of encounter has already been predetermined by the training, so you get a kind of taped robotic response.

EW: You mean the peculiar double-talk they use—the jargon, the strange form of English—or were you referring to other behavioral phenomena?

PM: Well, you find that in Arica people, too, who categorize things in various "levels" and "stages" and have a private language. But the private language is not the problem. It's that the private language reveals a grotesque and already congealed kind of truth that is shared with other people who have also taken est. But the only people who've ever interested me along my own way in the world have been those who have struggled and worked through to their own truths, either through experience or thought, or both. What had made them persons was not what they believed, but the activity and experience of putting together everything that had happened to them and emerging from it as people who were, in themselves, a kind of embodied accumulated truth.

EW: So, do I understand you to mean that instead of struggling continuously towards one's own evolving, these people have settled for an easy answer by accepting pat responses, which they apply in all situations?

PM: Yes, and I would like to say two things about that. First, I think that the pat responses, which may indeed work in certain situations or realms, are taken to be applicable to every situation and realm. Therefore, any question about their applicability in any situation calls the whole belief system into question, which is precisely why it is so inelastic.

Quite simply, the belief is that these too simplistic truths apply without exception to every situation. So, we say that persons are responsible for their own destinies (which is—clearly—largely true) and that what happens to them is largely of their own making (which is also largely true). When one raises the question about its being entirely true and equally applicable to things like starvation or mass victimization, the est people are actually totally unable to respond. Because if they admitted that it was not absolutely true, the whole house of cards would come tumbling down.

EW: So, you think that their truth leaves out the social realm of morality, political awareness, and historical phenomena in which whole communities have been and are exploited and destroyed?

PM: It leaves out both the complexity of individual experience and the complexity of the world's history.

 The second point I'd make is that these truths obviously belong to persons who have come to them through a kind of desperation because nothing else has ever worked for them. In fact, that's what most of them say.

 What I find most frightening about the est people is that they refuse to admit the desperateness of their beliefs. Instead of saying, "We understand that other people can deal with complicated truth and complicated experience, and we can't," and assuming an aspect of humility because of that, they attempt not only to project this view on their own experience but to spread it anywhere they can and to condemn all persons who see things in a more complicated way.

EW: Many people who go to these kinds of courses seem to go because they feel a lack of love in their lives. We heard a theory that it isn't so much a lack of love (although that is an element) as an insensitivity to love.

PM: The people I know best or respect the most are people who have the capacity to love something—which is, to me, different from having received love. In theory, they must have been loved by somebody at some time, but when I look at their lives, I can't find more love around them than I can in anybody else's life. It's as if they had been born with a talent or capacity for loving something other than the self, to be grateful for its existence and to form a relationship with the world that is one of praise, or almost prayer. While they may indeed worry about whether they themselves are receiving the love they need, that isn't primary. Their deep problem is how to live out the love that they feel.

 I have met, God knows, enough people in therapeutic settings now who seem not to be able to love anything but the self. I'm inclined to think that it's a condition that may be endemic among us, but I find myself wanting to say that all persons do indeed have a capacity to love something outside the self. Perhaps the direction of a useful therapy for them would be to help them discover what, outside themselves, they do love, so they could form out of themselves a loving relation to something other than the self.

EW: You mean developing a sense of compassion, for example?

PM: It's not only compassion. One of the things that I've seen in all sorts of sexual therapy is that the most absent feeling is one of genuine desire. So it isn't just compassion. It involves desire. It involves imagination. It involves a kind of tenderness that goes beyond compassion. It involves a kind of receptivity that is the willingness to be actually entered by another person so that, in that process, each person is transformed, since the two of them become together something other than each one was. After an experience like that, it seems to me it's impossible to talk so glibly about the self because, at that point, the self has become other than the self. Almost everybody I know who has lived halfway fully in the world is in themselves a group of persons, having taken into themselves the loved others in their lives. They're the ones who have the most trouble talking comfortably about a self, because they understand that it is, in some ways, a useful fiction.

LYNN ANDREWS

The Beverly Hills Medicine Woman
June 1984

Lynn Andrews is the author of a remarkable series of books, including Medicine Woman, The Flight of the Seventh Moon, Jaguar Woman, Star Woman, *and* Crystal Woman: The Sisters of the Dreamtime, *in which she chronicles her amazing adventures of self-discovery in the world of Native American shaman women. In this interview conducted by Leonard Jacobs, Andrews talks about what she learned from her guides, Agnes Whistling Elk and Ruby Plenty Chiefs, that continues to influence her counseling practice as well as her own personal development.*

EAST WEST: What do Native American societies have to teach us?

LYNN ANDREWS: To understand the energy of the earth—that all things are connected and that all things have soul, all things have spirit. We are truly connected.

EW: In what way?

LA: Agnes has a wonderful way of explaining it. She says we are like pieces of a smashed mirror, and those pieces reflect the light of the Great Spirit. Each person is several pieces of that mirror but they're disconnected. The whole process of going through the teaching of the shields is to fit the pieces of that mirror together like the pieces of a puzzle. Through your dreams and through your visions and experiences, you eventually have macrocosm and microcosm—a shield that you hold up to the world that says, "This is who I am."

EW: What were the first things Agnes taught you?

LA: She taught me that you need to become physically strong to balance out whatever spiritual influence you have, and to balance your male/female energies so that you can be balanced on the earth.

She showed me the importance of being lifted out of your usual existence long enough so that something new can come in to you. The astronauts were shot out of a tin can into the universe and three days later they came back with some crazy, wonderful consciousness experience. Their support systems were taken away completely, what they were used to was taken away. Their maintenance lives were left behind long enough so that something could happen to them, something could reach them.

It was clear to me when I first started working with Agnes and Ruby that their teaching is not borrowed knowledge—they don't just tell you a bunch of things. They simply observe what it is that you need to learn and put you into an experience where you have to change and grow, almost to survive. So that they become, often times, what they want you to know. In other words, Ruby and Agnes work together with me and if Ruby wants me to learn about fear she terrifies me to mirror my fear—make me see it and feel it. So lots of times people say, "In these books they change so. They're like little senile ladies and then suddenly they're warriors." That's the reason they do that. It's enormously effective.

Another thing I learned from Agnes is that a lot of people go into spiritual work without any physical basis—not knowing how to survive in the world, how to take care of themselves, how to support themselves. Agnes often talks about that, building a foundation. If you build the castle, your spiritual life, without any foundation—not knowing how to work, not knowing how to take care of yourself, not knowing how to produce what she calls "an active power" which provides a mirror for yourself so that you begin to see who you are—everything is very unbalanced. It really is the balance of the male and female, balance of the physical and non-physical. I'm sure that's why a lot of kids in the sixties would take a mind-altering drug and be catapulted into the non-physical world and go completely out of their mind. You need a lifeline, like a deep sea diver when he goes down under the ocean.

And I think the other thing, particularly very important for women, is that you need to make an act of power so that you can begin to see who you are. When I went up to Agnes to live with her she was very gruff with me. She threw me out and said, "Do not return until you have written your first book on our work together." I was forced to do that. It was hard for me to make that transition, thrust into the world, organizing things enough to actually write a book. And she would not see me till I was through. In the process of writing that book I learned so much about myself. It was a mirror, a perfect mirror.

We all have similar experiences—very difficult things we must do. And there are teachers everywhere in life. You don't have to go to Canada and work with an Indian medicine woman. A person that you come up against in life as an adversary can perhaps be your greatest teacher.

EW: How does someone take that adversarial confrontation experience and put it into a context that allows for growth rather than repression?

LA: As Agnes says, "You can live like an arrow, or you can live like a target." If you're the target, the prey, you always wait to be hit. If you're the arrow or the spear, you have a direction, you are aimed at something and you are moving. Many people are very vague if you ask them what they really want out of life. I was vague when I first went to Manitoba.

One of the first things Agnes taught me was tracking. She taught me how to hunt a deer—how to take the scat and pull it apart and figure out what the deer eats, and where. You learn how to read prints, to see whether they were made by a buck or doe, and what time of day they were made from the way the impressions are kept in the sand. And you find out where they go to drink and when. Essentially, what you're doing is becoming that deer—so when you hunt it you are that deer. It's the same in the world. When you want something in life, something that you want to become successful at, you must become receptive to it.

EW: How do you define a shaman, for someone who hasn't read your books?

LA: The shamanistic process is a psychology process. If you want to learn medicine, they teach you how to get down to the essence, how to go to the source, to the mystery from which you were born. There's a spiral that you see on almost all petroglyphs and it marks time—the shadows from the solstices fall across this spiral. What it really means, according to what I have learned, is that it is the process of your earth-walk. You were born in the center of the mystery and in your earth-walk you walk in a spiral, further and further from the center. At some point in your adult life you decide you want to get back to the source. Then you begin to walk backwards. You begin the process of unlearning, in a sense. And that stripping-away is the process of shamanism. It's getting back to the source of your power, which you really always have.

But we are filled with addictions, we stand in a swamp, as Agnes says. Addictions are our belief structures, societal conditioning, that keep us very far from our original nature, from our power. To get into power you have to—well, they talk about "shaman's death." Shaman's death is just like in any discipline, where you get to the point where you feel like you're dying, you're losing your ego, you're losing your addictions. It's the same in all disciplines. Shamanism is essentially very similar to Buddhism.

EW: Could you give a description of the two forms of female energy and how they manifest in people's lives?

LA: The understanding of the two forms of energy is present in all so-called primitive societies. To the Native Americans, the earth is female and the spheres of energy around it are female. There is the nurturing mother, the Great Mother type of energy, which is quite different from the ecstatic, Rainbow Mother type of energy. And for each of these positive energies you have a negative side.

For the nurturing mother you have the devouring or Death Mother. For the ecstatic mother, the negative influence is the Teeth Mother or the Stone Mother, which is like a Medusa. She doesn't kill you, she simply paralyzes you. It's terrifying to come face to face with the Teeth Mother—particularly when you've never even acknowledged her existence. It's what you choose not to look at that ruins your life.

The devouring mother, on the other hand, tends to kill you. When a nurturing mother reaches forty and she's raised her children, she suddenly has no one left to nurture. At that point in her life she becomes terrified and feels like there's no reason for living. Then the Death Mother goes after her. It's a very critical time for a nurturing mother type of woman, or man. We call it mid-life crisis. To me, it's really a change in the focus and form of nurturing.

The ecstatic mother is the type of woman or man who is inspirational—the dancer, performer, artist, or writer. They are often on the fringes of society, misunderstood by society, which tends to prefer the nurturing mother type—the raiser of children or the nine to five worker. The ecstatic woman or man challenges society and essentially makes society healthy if that person is allowed to "voice."

EW: Are there different levels of each of those qualities?

LA: Absolutely. It's hard to say, "This person is a nurturing type." But you can feel it. The nurturing type build in their gardens, plant the corn and flowers. An ecstatic person gets their inspiration from learning something new, from accomplishing something creative. Not that a nurturing mother isn't creative—I don't mean that at all—but it really is very different. Put the two together and it's hard for them to understand each other. They can honor each other.

EW: Does the balancing of energies in each of us ultimately mean that these qualities are harmonized?

LA: Not in one person. Each person usually predominately has one or the other mother behind them. The balance of the male and female comes after you understand the kind of basic person you are. A lot of people don't fit into their lives because they've tried to be what somebody else wanted them to be. And first of all you have to help them understand what their energy is. If an ecstatic woman tries to fit into a very traditional nurturing home type of life, she'll go crazy. She won't know why, and will blame it on other things.

It's very interesting. Feminine energy is very different from male energy. I think the Indian people embody female energy. And there's very little place in the world for female energy. We have to make that place. That's the importance of taking one's power. You have to make that place, create it. It does not exist, so you create it.

You have to take power in life. It is not given to you. A lot of people think if you are good then suddenly all will be open to you. And in a sense I think that's true, but to be effective in life one has to have a center of power—one has to be the most marvelous and beautiful person that one can possibly be. And when they want to do something in life, like work for peace, lead a non-violent life, be an example of non-violence, one has to take that power. Agnes was trying to teach me to *take* the marriage basket. Red Dog is not going to go over and give it to you. You have to train, be worthy of it. You have to learn how to make yourself strong. Just wishing for it and being good is not going to make that happen.

EW: What are your male students' biggest problems?

LA: The way I have been taught is that women come into this earth-walk essentially knowing. They understand, even if they can't define what it is they know. Deep inside of them, all women know. Men come into this earth-walk knowing that they don't know and they have to learn. Unconsciously they know that they have to get their power, and learn, from women, or a woman. Men have to be taught how to live; women have an innate sense of how to live—usually.

So men, when they come to me, usually have a problem with their femaleness. They need to know how to heal it. Men are very open. It's just that they have to be presented with the opportunity.

ROLLING THUNDER

Learning from the Earth
December 1983

Rolling Thunder, a Native American of the Cherokee Nation, is a medicine man who believes that humankind is in a critical period of its history, a time of "Earth purification" that may manifest as natural disasters or war. Rolling Thunder is a spiritual teacher as well as a healer of the sick (using Native American techniques and herbs). He spreads his message of concern for the land by traveling and teaching widely and at his home base community of Meta Tantay in Nevada. He has appeared on stage with the Grateful Dead music group and in 1975 toured with The Rolling Thunder Review, which featured Bob Dylan.

East West's Beverly Brough interviewed Rolling Thunder.

EAST WEST: How would you characterize our current age?

ROLLING THUNDER: We are now beginning a time of Earth purifications. It's happened before. Our history is better kept and goes much further back than the white man's. There was a great flood, just like in Biblical history. Out there in the desert, you can see the water marks high on the mountain tops. But we know before that there was a time when the Earth was destroyed by fire, heat, and volcanos.

This next time, it will be by fire and water both. In other words, it could be volcanos, coming from within the Earth, or it could also represent the atomic bomb. The Earth itself will tip, causing climatic changes, according to our teachings. This has happened before too. It looks like there may be an awful lot of destruction.

But the Earth is giving us warning signals. I've seen it—Mother Earth is starting to die. I've seen lakes in northern Sweden, up close to the Arctic Circle—beautiful country, large forests. But the lakes are dead because of the acid rain. The acid rain came over from England and the industrialized countries. I've heard and read a great deal about the acid rain—it's happening now in New England also. You can look at northern Sweden and see what it will be like here soon. Even the trees are dying. Now anything that affects the life of

Mother Earth also affects the people. That shouldn't be too hard to figure out. If it affects one, it affects all.

EW: Do people have the power to affect a positive change so that some of these disasters don't have to happen?

RT: All prophecy is subject to change. By knowing ahead of time what will happen, we can help. We don't set a date by anything, because we like to think the bad things don't have to be. And we do have the power within us, that if enough people think about the good things coming into being, then they will come into being. That's what I'm here for, that's what we're here for, the Indians. We know the laws in this land, and we are here to help. We're here to guide wherever we're wanted and wherever we're invited, and that is all.

EW: How do you respond to suggestions that we can heal the Earth with prayer?

RT: I'm not anti-Christian, but a lot of people who think they are religious waste a lot of time, and meditators too. What do they meditate about? What do they pray about when they go to church on Sunday? Do they pray for Mother Earth? Do they pray for the animals? Do they pray for each other? If what we do in this life doesn't help our neighbors, or other people, then it's empty. It's not good. We're not put here for our own little benefit. We're put here for the benefit of the whole, and Mother Earth too. Too many of these people who claim to be spiritual, religious, or meditators are only interested in their own little selves. They've got too much ego. They should get off their ass and learn how to pray.

Prayer should be twenty-four hours a day. Every thought, every action, every look is a prayer. I go to sleep praying. I wake up in the morning praying. When I take a puff off this pipe the first puff has to be a good thought. A prayer is putting out good energy. It goes clockwise, in a circle, and then it comes back to the person that put it out. It travels in a circle and comes back multiplied by seven. All matter, all energy is composed of a circle. If you put out a bad thought, that travels in a circle too. It goes counter-clockwise and comes back to the starting point. Anyone who wants to get well or feels depressed has to study these teachings and break that pattern. They must realize that what they put out they are going to get back.

EW: Is the Native American philosophy similar to the Eastern religions?

RT: Very much so. Our belief in reincarnation is similar. There are twelve lives, ordinarily, and we are supposed to go to a higher level each life—unless we commit a crime, for instance. Then we might have to start all over again. We might be reborn as a worm or a coyote and have to work our way back up. All ancient religions have basically the same kind of teachings, but I'd say theirs is similar to ours rather than the other way around.

Scientists say that Indians migrated over the Bering Strait from Asia, and there are others who try to say that we are one of the lost tribes of Israel. It's all conjecture, and it's not necessary at all—we know our own history very well. Some of it was written and put away at the time, but we still know it. We were here when the Earth was young. It shook when you walked on it. That's how ancient we are on this land. There were some migrations later, long before Columbus, from Asia, from Africa, from South America and Mexico.

Columbus came much later. Columbus was just a lost honky, and the Indians found him. Not all white people are honkies, just the ignorant ones. At any rate, we don't need the anthropologists digging in our graves. We don't need them kidnapping our children and sending them off to boarding school, or off to foreigners. We don't need the sterilization of our Indian women. We don't need the genocide that's now being practiced in Guatemala, for instance.

EW: How can contemporary society become more connected with the Earth?

RT: We're no different from the plants—we're no better. We're all part of a whole, and everything—a grain of sand, dirt, the birds and the animals—they are all part of us.

If people understood these common teachings, they wouldn't need to pollute the environment. There were other ancient highly technological civilizations that didn't pollute the environment. That is because they were clear thinkers. All the pollution in the world comes from the mind. The minds of modern people are all cluttered up with trash, filth, and greed. There is only so much capacity in the human mind, so if it's all cluttered or even half, with greed, violence, and war, then we don't have the mental capacity to create.

JOSEPH EPES BROWN

Remembering Black Elk
August 1982

"The first peace, which is most important, is that which comes within the souls of men when they realize their relationship, their oneness with the universe and all its powers, and when they realize that at the center of the universe dwells Wakan Tanka, and that this center is really everywhere, it is within each of us. This is the real Peace, and the others are but reflections of this. The second peace is that which is made between nations. But above all, you should understand that there can never be peace between nations until there is first known that true peace which, as I have often said, is within the souls of men."

These words were spoken in the late 1940s by Black Elk, a leader of the Oglala branch of the Teton Sioux. One of only three men to receive the knowledge of the seven sacred rites of the Oglala Sioux, Black Elk felt that he must write down his vision for posterity. In 1931 his book, Black Elk Speaks, *written in collaboration with John Neihardt, was published. Fifteen years later Black Elk completed the writing of his entire vision in a collaboration,* The Sacred Pipe, *with Joseph Epes Brown. Black Elk died in 1950 at the age of ninety-two. Joseph Epes Brown, who was interviewed for* East West *by Beverly Brough, is a professor of religious studies at the University of Montana and is the author of* The Spiritual Legacy of the American Indian.

EAST WEST: The Indians talk about their purpose in life as completing the circle. What did they mean by this?

JOSEPH EPES BROWN: To them, process was always in terms of the circle, whereas for us, process, which we call progress, is in terms of a straight line. This raises a good many questions, because when you come to the end of the line, what is there? A dropping off place? For them, when you come to the end of one life's cycle, a new life continues on again; birth leads into death; death leads into birth. It seems to me that we could learn a bit from this point of view. There is a lot that is implied here, because it is under this dominant concept which we call progress that we hold primitive people as somehow inferior to more recent or more modern peoples.

Black Elk talks about this view in his first book: *You have noticed that everything an Indian does is in a circle, and that is because the Power of the World always works in circles, and everything tries to be round. In the old days when we were a strong and happy people, all our power came to us from the sacred hoop of the nation, and so long as the hoop was unbroken the people flourished. The flowering tree was the living center of the hoop, and the circle of the four quarters nourished it. The East gave peace and light, the South gave warmth, the West gave rain, and the North with its cold and mighty wind gave strength and endurance. This knowledge came to us from the outer world with our religion. Everything the Power of the World does is done in a circle. The sky is round, and I have heard that the Earth is round like a ball, and so are all the stars. The wind, in its greatest power, whirls. Birds make their nest in circles, for theirs is the same religion as ours. The sun comes forth and goes down again in a circle. The moon does the same, and both are round. Even the seasons form a great circle in their changing, and always come back again to where they were. The life of a man is a circle from childhood to childhood, and so it is in everything where power moves. Our tepees were round like the nests of birds, and these were always set in a circle, the nation's hoop, a nest of many nests, where the Great Spirit meant for us to hatch our children.*

EW: I have heard that Black Elk was a Catholic. Did he find any discrepancy between this faith and his own traditional religion?

JB: It is typical of the Plains people that everything that is in their environment, their world of experience—all the animals, all the trees, the grasses, the elements, and so on—all these forms have lessons to teach us. If we could simply look and listen and learn from life's experiences as they are presented to us, we could integrate what is good, and perhaps leave behind what is not useful or not so good. This is a fundamental trait in the lives of the Plains people. Thus when a new kind of religion comes to them, through their past training and openness to take what is good they could see that many of the early "Black Robes," as they called the Catholic priests, were good men who lived lives of sacrifice. They could understand the basic teachings of the Black Robes, because, after all, their own sacred understanding was of a very profound nature.

But they added it into what they already had, so that it was not a conversion as the church understands conversion. It was not for them an absolute either/or decision. There is no way it could be, for after all, they still had their own language—all their own ancient sacred values were born by the language, there is no way that could be thrown away. So Black Elk simply combined the good of Catholicism into the good of his own tradition.

EW: Do you feel that Black Elk's vision has helped bring his people back to their own ways?

JB: Ultimately I see the message of his vision as one of preserving the "seeds of the sacred" at a time when these kinds of things are being eroded away, rejected, and lost. He's an American Indian Noah, establishing a peaceful link between the old cycle and the coming new cycle.

PETER NABOKOV

America's Native Runners
June 1982

Anthropologist Peter Nabokov is associated with the University of California at Berkeley and is the author of several books, including Indian Running, Two Leggings, Native American Testimony, Architecture of Acoma Pueblo, *and most recently,* Native American Architecture, *co-authored with Robert Easton. Nabokov is currently doing field work on "religious association centering around the use of tobacco" at a Crow Indian reservation.*

East West interviewer Beverly Brough spoke with Nabokov about the extraordinary feats of endurance and speed displayed by Native American runners, one of whom reportedly covered nearly 200 miles in less than twenty-four hours.

EAST WEST: Was running a part of their whole spiritual development?

PETER NABOKOV: Yes, in some places. One has to particularize, however; each tribe was different. Among the Yurok Indians (according to an account by anthropologist Thomas Buckley), there is a story of runners running down the hillside on the tops of the manzanita bushes. They reached a state of consciousness which was like effortless gliding. They would establish an extrasensory relationship with the trail, through singing to it, addressing it. They were taught to make room for it, to receive the trail as a being, letting it dictate the run. It was as though the trail was running out behind them and under them by itself.

Another technique was visualization to help the student learn to feel that the actual energies being used are the world's rather than your own. Rather than feeling how your feet hit the ground, emphasis is placed on feeling the ground pushing back up against your feet. Gradually you put more and more trust in the earth, and move into a light trance state when you're no longer interfering in the running. Here the running is just happening: Whether the world is doing it or you are doing it is of no importance. The trainee was taught how to "see" the air rushing by as a sort of rope along which he could pull himself through breathing techniques and hand motions.

EW: What influence do you think Native Americans will play in the future of modern society?

PN: I prefer to stay away from the purpose of the more public forms of influence such as the Hopi prophecies. I feel terribly fortunate in having access to ways of life that make more sense to me in every basic human context and relationship than those that were part of my culture, and a man would be a fool to turn his back on that kind of discovery.

I can't answer questions as far as the larger impact. I'm doing my work about the Indians, and I know lots of people who are, because it's important. And many Native American people are also doing this. I certainly hope that a group that is indigenous to this continent will form a new foundation for a kind of American culture that is human, respectful of the earth, respectful of the heavens, and respectful of the animals. I'm hopeful that a new society will form that learns again from the animals, learns again to preserve that kind of instinctual approach to life that children often exhibit. On the other end of the spectrum this is the attitude that the great prophets and great seers exhibit, a return to a kind of "holy ordinariness."

PHOTOS

PAGE 171

Top row left to right: Liv Ullman, photo courtesy UNICEF; Tristan Jones, photo by Sam Weiss; Jonathan Kozol, Associated Press © 1987, courtesy Crown.
Bottom row left to right: Fritjof Capra, photo © Michiel Wijnbergh; Jeremy Rifkin, photo by Diane Walker/Gamma Liaison; Hazel Henderson, photo courtesy Hazel Henderson.

PAGE 209

Top row left to right: Harlan Lundberg, photo by Peter Milbury; Masanobu Fukuoka, photo by Ronald Kotzsch; David Brower, courtesy Earth Island Institute.
Bottom row left to right: Wendell Berry, © Thomas Victor, courtesy North Point Press; Wes Jackson, © Dana Jackson, courtesy North Point Press.

PAGE 225

Top row left to right: Krishnamurti, photo by Mark Edwards, © The Krishnamurti Foundation; Gary Snyder, photo by Hank Meals; Ram Dass, photo by Peter Simon.
Bottom row left to right: Isabel Hickey, photo courtesy Helen Hickey; Joseph Epes Brown, photo courtesy Joseph Epes Brown; Joseph Campbell, photo courtesy Doubleday.